The Jihadist Preachers of the End Times

EDINBURGH STUDIES IN ISLAMIC APOCALYPTICISM AND ESCHATOLOGY

This series features studies devoted to end-time expectations in Islam and the intellectual, social and political contexts in which they occur and become virulent, from the beginning of Islam until the twenty-first century. Concerning the apocalyptic aspect, the series is dedicated to investigating apocalypticism in Muslim thought and history: notions of the catalytic events ushering in the end of history, mahdism and other forms of (political and non-political) millenarianism. Eschatologically, studies in this series will examine traditions of imagining and reasoning about the hereafter: judgment, salvation, and reward and punishment in paradise and hell.

Series Editors
Professor David Cook (Rice University) and Professor Christian Lange (Utrecht University)

Editorial Advisory Board
Professor Abbas Amanat, Professor Fred Donner, Professor Jean-Pierre Filiu, Professor Yohanan Friedman, Professor Mercedes García-Arenal, Professor Mohammed Khalil, Professor Daniel De Smet and Professor Roberto Tottoli

Titles in the series

'The Book of Tribulations: The Syrian Muslim Apocalyptic Tradition', An Annotated Translation by Nuᶜaym b. Hammad al-Marwazi
Edited and translated by David Cook

Seeing God in Sufi Qurᵓan Commentaries: Crossings between This World and the Otherworld
Pieter Coppens

Eschatology in Classical Islamic Mysticism: From the Ninth to the Twelfth Centuries
Michael Ebstein

The Jihadist Preachers of the End Times: ISIS Apocalyptic Propaganda
Bronislav Ostřanský

The World of Image in Islamic Philosophy: Ibn Sīnā, Suhrawardī, Shahrazūrī, and Beyond
L. W. C. van Lit

An Apocalyptic History of the Early Fatimid Empire
Jamel A. Velji

edinburghuniversitypress.com/series/esiae

The Jihadist Preachers of the End Times

ISIS Apocalyptic Propaganda

Bronislav Ostřanský

EDINBURGH
University Press

To my children:
Maruška and František

Edinburgh University Press is one of the leading university presses in the UK. We publish academic books and journals in our selected subject areas across the humanities and social sciences, combining cutting-edge scholarship with high editorial and production values to produce academic works of lasting importance. For more information visit our website: edinburghuniversitypress.com

Edinburgh University Press Ltd
The Tun – Holyrood Road
12 (2f) Jackson's Entry
Edinburgh EH8 8PJ

Typeset in Cambria by
Servis Filmsetting Ltd, Stockport, Cheshire,
and printed and bound in Great Britain

A CIP record for this book is available from the British Library
ISBN 978 1 4744 3923 7 (hardback)
ISBN 978 1 4744 3925 1 (webready PDF)
ISBN 978 1 4744 3926 8 (epub)

Contents

Preface

Although ISIS has already almost disappeared from the media, its inauspicious fruits will neither vanish soon nor easily. The story of ISIS has been narrated hundreds of times; nevertheless, one of its most prominent aspects has remained the least examined. To be honest, this book has been written in spite of the numerous doubts experienced by its author, mostly concerning the turbulent nature of the subject. Towards the end of 2015, in the period when I was beginning to collect material related to the group's 'apocalyptic agenda', with the eventual idea in mind of writing a study on this subject, ISIS was actually at the height of its power. During the course of writing, the group has undergone a fundamental transformation, shifting from a powerful 'proto-state', occupying a significant part of Iraq and Syria, towards the dangerous, yet incomparably more marginal, underground terrorist network that it is today (May 2018). Being well aware of the standard timeframe of the publication process, I often hesitated as to whether or not to use the present or the past tense.[1]

Regardless of the worldly success or failure of ISIS, some of the

[1] Despite its military failures, ISIS is still active online, spreading its written propaganda (e.g. *al-Naba*ʾ magazine). The following interpretation is based on the sources available before August 2018.

contributions it has made to the arsenal of contemporary Jihadist thought are, even now, undeniable and the remarkable apocalyptic tenor of the group's self-presentation approach belongs among them. Of course, any research into such a hot issue can easily lead us into various degrees of misunderstanding, resulting mostly from a lack of detachment. The whole affair is still too real and grievous. The manifestations of ISIS brutality, more savage than any previous Islamist group, has already provoked substantial debate as to whether or not ISIS is 'authentically Islamic'. On the one hand, ISIS can be seen as an outgrowth of certain trends in Islamic history; on the other, its total extremism can be easily placed beyond the bounds of anything that might be legitimately called Islam, as defined by the historical experience of Muslims all over the world.

Unwilling to enter this broader level of polemics, there is no doubt that apocalypticism as an effective method in how to demonise enemies has become a certain 'hallmark' of these extremists and, as such, it can easily seduce us into unsubstantiated fantasising. Being aware of such a threat, the following interpretation attempts only to summarise and analyse the unquestionable facts relevant to the ISIS 'End-time agenda'.

Of course, the author is fully aware that, in the current state of research, even such a modest intention can itself prove to be a challenging task. His immodest ambition, therefore, is to present this hard-to-classify theme in a way that is intelligible to non-experts, as well as being beneficial to specialists. Indeed, the distinctive apocalyptic message, rooted in traditional Muslim eschatology, is at the very core of ISIS self-presentation and its claim to legitimacy. In the following pages, we will try to find an acceptable answer to the most fundamental question: Why and how did this happen?

Bronislav Ostřanský
Prague, September 2018

Acknowledgements

I would like to thank the many friends and colleagues who, over the years, have shared their thoughts and knowledge with me. My special thanks go to David Cook for his encouragement and kind assistance. I am also grateful to Richard Landes, who provided me with valuable feedback on my original book proposal, as well as for his stimulating suggestions. I am further indebted to Steven Patten and Darren Crown, who helped me to make the language more accessible. This monograph would never have come into existence in the first place without the kind encouragement of Nicola Ramsey, the Head of Editorial and publisher at EUP, and without Sue Dalgleish who performed the painstaking task of copy-editing my original typescript. I am also grateful to Vilém Petrunčík, who drew up the 'apocalyptic map' in Appendix 4.

I owe a particular debt of gratitude to Aaron Zelin for his invaluable website, Jihadology.net, containing a huge set of primary sources relevant to ISIS propaganda, from which many of the materials used in this project were downloaded. The writing of this book was made possible in part by the generosity of my current employer, the Oriental Institute of the Czech Academy of Sciences in Prague. My thanks are due to the Director, Ondřej Beránek, for his encouragement and feedback. And last, but not least, I am really indebted to my family for their endless support. There are really no words that could express my thanks to my wife Zuzana for her sacrifices while I have been working on this book. Needless to say, all the potential mistakes or shortcomings are my responsibility alone.

Note on Names and Transliteration

The form of this monograph has been designed to support its main ambition of being beneficial to experts and, simultaneously, intelligible to the common reader. The applied transliteration of the Arabic proper nouns and terminology follows the standards of IJMES. In an effort to increase accessibility, the basic Arabic terms related to the Muslim apocalypse are explained in a separate vocabulary section (see Appendix 1) as well as in parentheses when they first appear in the text.

As regards the Arabic names of people, I have consistently adhered to the standard way of transliteration, even when they belong to prominent political or cultural figures whose names usually appear in their accepted English spelling (Osama bin Laden, for example). In the second, shortened, usage of particular Arabic names, I have preferred to apply an inconsistent – but hopefully intuitive – convention that identifies characters according to the part of the name under which they have become famous (for instance, Abū Muṣ^{c}ab al-Zarqāwī as al-Zarqāwī, Usāma bin Lādin as Bin Lādin). Concerning the Arabic names of personalities living in the West, I have respected their own choice of transliteration (Hisham Kabbani, for example).

Well-known place names are written in their common form, as listed in the *Oxford Atlas* (e.g. Damascus and Baghdad); meanwhile, less familiar toponyms are transliterated, mostly from the Arabic (e.g. Dābiq and Aᶜmāq). All Qurʾānic citations come from a new translation by M. S. Abdel Haleem.[1] As for the quotations from the crucial Muslim apocalyptic source, *Kitāb al-fitan*, written by Nuᶜaym ibn Ḥammād, an annotated translation of David Cook has been consistently consulted.[2]

The numerous samples of ISIS propaganda, presented in Appendix 3, have been quoted verbatim, including the group's specific usage of religious terms and the applied methods of transliteration from Arabic, even where they do not respect any established rule. Some ordinarily used terms and phrases specific to the ISIS vocabulary, but which might be unclear from the context, have been explained in parentheses.

A separate observation should be directed at the names of our protagonists. The acronyms ISIL or ISIS arose from former official names, i.e. the 'Islamic State in Iraq and the Levant' or the 'Islamic State in Iraq and Syria'. The ISIS/ISIL inconsistency results from different understandings of the terms 'al-Shām' and 'Levant'. The term al-Shām was originally used in the Middle Ages to describe the region between Mesopotamia, Anatolia, the Mediterranean and Sinai, while the term 'Levant' was used by English speakers as a reference to the eastern part of the Mediterranean in general. After 2014, when a caliphate (*khilāfa*) was declared, the group shortened its name to IS (Islamic State), the fact referring to the group's universalistic ambitions, not being bound by any particular region.

With regard to its Arabic designations, the group itself uses 'al-Dawla al-islāmīya', an equivalent to IS, while its opponents, either English-speaking or native speakers of Arabic, mostly prefer 'Daesh' (from 'Dāᶜish'). The latter term has been used as a means of challenging its legitimacy due to the negative connotation of this abbreviation, which, while having no meaning in Arabic, nonetheless sounds

[1] *The Qurʾan*, Oxford: Oxford University Press, 2010.
[2] Nuᶜaym ibn Hammad, *The Book of Tribulations: The Syrian Muslim Apocalyptic Tradition*.

unpleasant.[3] In the Arab world, where the use of acronyms is generally exceptional, Dāᶜish is preferred for its pejorative overtone, which is the reason why Western politicians have also become accustomed to using this term. The reason why the term 'ISIS' has been adopted in this book is based on the simple fact that despite its inaccuracy this acronym has become by far the most widely used one in both journalistic and scholarly circles.

3 The Western approaches to the term 'Daesh' have been full of linguistic misunderstanding. For more details, see https://www.freewordcentre.com/explore/daesh-isis-media-alice-guthrie (last accessed 5 November 2017).

Introduction

Al-Sayfu aṣdaqu inbāʾan min al-kutubi . . . fī ḥaddihi al-ḥaddu bayna al-jiddi wa al-laʿbi. (The sword is more truthful than books. Its edge distinguishes between trueness and fiction.) *Inna al-dhahaba yujrab bi-l-nār, wa inna al-muʾmina yujrab bi-l-balāʾi.* (Gold is tried in the fire, the believer is tried in suffering.)

– Arabic proverbs from the tenth century (from the project *Structure of Culture: Arabic-Islamic Civilization Through the Prism of Corpus Linguistic*)[1]

We offered the Trust to the heavens, the earth, and the mountains, yet they refused to undertake it and were afraid of it; mankind undertook it – they have always been inept and foolish.

– The Qurʾān[2]

The shocking occupation of Mosul and the subsequent declaration of a new caliphate in the summer of 2014 turned the attention of the world's public towards the phenomenon of ISIS, a hybrid organisation with many facets, which, from that time onwards, has become the number one threat and, at the same time, an object of unstoppable exegetical attempts on the part of both scholars and journalists. Although the common media representation of ISIS often suggests a sinister fiend, full of irrational fanaticism, this nightmare image of a spectre from another world, as offered by foreign affairs columnists, is not one that can be justified once we become aware of the group's historical and ideological context, as well as its genuine sources of inspiration.

Besides its enormous levels of cruelty, images of which have been spread around the world, ISIS propaganda has also managed to amaze worldwide audiences with its rhetoric, which contains numerous apocalyptic elements and references. Such a systematic employment of 'End-time' motifs might appear to be pioneering if we are not familiar with the development of the modern Muslim apocalyptic thought and literature (see 'From Dusty Bookshelves to Spiritual Blockbusters' in Chapter 2). Ideas regarding the preordained apocalyptic events that will lead to the End of this earthly existence (*al-dunyā*) took shape in the early period of Islamic civilisation and – after long centuries of mostly 'academic' interest on the part of Muslim scholars (*ᶜulamāʾ*) – contemporary events have revived the persuasiveness of their message. In the case of ISIS, the prominence of its apocalyptic inclinations operates at different levels; nonetheless, it is especially conspicuous in ISIS online proselytisation and social media activities.[3]

Essentially, the utilisation of an 'apocalyptic agenda' is not new to Islam. Although many rulers in the history of the Muslims have come to power precisely as a result of the use of messianic imagery, a much larger number of Mahdī claimants have failed. In any case, the skilful application of apocalyptic proclamations has immense mobilising potential, particularly when placed within the framework of a specific current conflict. The 'satanization of enemies', which can also be found within the Islamic apocalypse, is part of 'a larger pattern of behavior in which people desperately try to make sense of the world and maintain some control over it'.[4] On the other hand, we should emphasise that any apocalyptic call can be authoritatively rejected as being inherently divisive, threatening the very solidarity of the community of believers (*umma*), as evidenced by the many clashes stimulated by millennial sparks that have occurred throughout history.

Albeit that the main intention of this book is to focus on the apocalyptic message spread by ISIS, as well as its context, and to deliberately avoid broader theoretical considerations related to the phenomenon of the apocalypse itself, one more general issue should be mentioned at this point. This relates to the vision of apocalypticism as a mythical and rhetorical solution to the problem of evil in a world created and led by the Divine Will, with apocalyptic discourse resolving this problem of evil by proposing that the final judgement is fast approaching, which will result in the forces of evil receiving their punishment while the forces of good will reap their reward.

The apocalyptic rhetoric, as a specific 'hallmark' of ISIS propaganda, goes beyond the limits of other Salafi jihadist streams,[5] which is one of the main reasons why more 'traditional' jihadists often criticise the ISIS obsession with the millennial message as being thoroughly irrational.[6] In addition, even within 'official' Muslim scholarly circles, the apocalyptic agenda has always been viewed with considerable suspicion. Lately, the boom in modern Muslim apocalyptic literature has led to various 'geopolitical readings' of medieval prophecies and, in doing so, has outlined an approaching period that will be full of violence and absurdity, with everything exceeding normal boundaries. A large number of Muslim thinkers, regardless of their ideological provenance, have reached a consensus that such a gloomy era, one that will usher in the final struggle between good and evil, is at hand.

Undoubtedly, it would be totally misleading to see an apocalyptic aspect in every single word or action belonging to the Salafi jihadists' ideological struggles against their opponents. Nevertheless, as a movement that is comparatively weak, and needs to highlight its own importance, the apocalyptic expressions of these radicals cannot be simply ignored. Moreover, portraying the apocalypse serves as a powerful recruiting tool and, wielded properly, it can also accord the movement with a certain sense of inevitable triumph, closely associated with their chosen designations of *al-ṭāʾifa al-manṣūra* and *al-firqa al-nājiya*, which mean 'the victorious group' and 'the saved sect'.[7]

Essentially, the opinions of scholars mostly highlight an opportunistic aspect within the ISIS End-time ethos, mentioning, for instance, that 'ISIS made from the medieval prophecies an experienced reality, not only a hypothetic goal'[8] or 'ISIS propagandists, through the depiction of their own Caliphate as an idealized society foretold long centuries ago and established as a part of final battle against unbelievers, consistently present themselves as an apocalyptic sect and millennial movement at the same time'.[9] In the case of ISIS apocalyptic rhetoric, there are many questions to be resolved, mainly concerning the anatomy of this propaganda and the genuine nature of its persuasiveness, both issues embodying cross-cultural relevance.

This study humbly attempts, among other things, to suggest an answer to another question of fundamental importance: To what extent does the ISIS reading of the Last Days fall within the traditional patterns of medieval Muslim 'historians of the future' and their modern followers, and what is the group's actual original contribution?

Anchoring the Subject

This monograph fits within the category of religious studies in general and research into Islamic apocalypticism in particular. The latter subject pertains, within the overall context of Islamic studies, to one of the newer branches. Nevertheless, there is a broader academic consensus that reliably affirms the fundamental and increasing importance of the given field. Simply put, a complex understanding of the current 'Muslim world' is inconceivable without a knowledge of Muslim millennialism.

The original geographical demarcation of ISIS within Syria and Iraq has already lost its relevance due to the group's various metastases across the Muslim world, as well as the worldwide dissemination of the ISIS ideology among Muslims. Therefore, we can justly speak about a global phenomenon. As regards temporal delimitation (see Appendix 2), we should not forget that ISIS was not yet born in the summer of 2014 when this group first attracted global media attention. To properly understand its ideology – which also applies to apocalypticism – we must focus on the turn of the millennium, or even a bit earlier when the 'spiritual father' of the group, Abū Muṣᶜab al-Zarqāwī, began to shape his worldview.

As far as the apocalyptic face of ISIS propaganda is concerned, the author is aware of the epistemological limitations pertaining to the current state of research. There are doubts as to whether it is really possible to formulate more than a sketchy outline in a situation where even the most fundamental points remain unclear. We do not know whether the ISIS leaders are actual believers in their own apocalyptic narratives or if they have employed them cynically for propaganda purposes and as an attempt to justify their extreme violence, where the violence 'has been in part a counterbalance to their marginality'.[10] No one actually knows the real extent to which their millennial rhetoric reflects their inner convictions or instead simply expresses an opportunistic ability 'to hijack the main theme of current Muslim discourse'.[11]

Of course, with regard to a phenomenological analysis of the group's propaganda, which seeks to spread a peculiar mixture of brutality and pathos, such questions are largely irrelevant. If nothing else, an extensive discussion of ISIS End-time self-presentations provides us with an opportunity to study the most recent and exceedingly innovative phase of Muslim apocalypticism. What we have been watching live has been the unfolding of a certain 'jihadist apocalyptic transformation'. Certainly, it is too early to make broader judgements related to the impact of this change on Muslim apocalypticism as a whole. Yet, against the ISIS apocalyptic backdrop we should continue to ask whether we are still dealing with an extreme example of the radicalisation of Islam or whether we are rather witnessing the Islamisation of ultimate radicalism.[12]

The Current State of Research

The current state of research devoted to Islamic apocalypticism and millennialism (for the terminology used, see 'Key Apocalytic Terms and Notions' in Chapter 1) reflects an intricate development that has been neatly summarised by David Cook.[13] Beginning with an interest driven by the practical needs of colonial circles in response to the 'slightly different Islam' which led to the Mahdist revolt in the Sudan (1881–98), academic research focusing on the Islamic interpretations of End-time issues has gradually shifted from the older approach, which was exclusively dependent on the so-called canonical sources (the Qurʾān and Sunna), to contemporary achievements, which employ a wider set of resources and rely on more advanced methodological tools.

Thus, this considerable change of perspective has been achieved by the use of non-canonical sources that have enabled scholars to take into consideration previously unknown contexts. Essentially, research into Islamic apocalypticism was, for a long time, limited almost exclusively to ancient Muslim eschatological literature or medieval manifestations of millennialism, while their modern forms remained mostly neglected. In this respect, the pioneering work devoted to modern Sunni apocalyptic literature by David Cook[14] should be mentioned here. Among other fundamental contributions to this field, the insightful works by Richard Landes and Jean-Pierre Filiu deserve special recommendation.[15] The apocalypse in Islam, as part of a body of assorted speculation, has also attracted the attention of many activists and journalists.[16]

From the long list of scholarly books related to the historic manifestations of Islamic millennialism, two particular monographs should be mentioned here as they represent an excellent example of the expert handling of a methodologically challenging task: Hayrettin Yücesoy's *Messianic Beliefs and Imperial Politics in Medieval Islam* and Jamel Velji's *An Apocalyptic History of the Early Fatimid Empire*. Despite their totally different focus, both of them have proved themselves to be inspiring. Furthermore, the latter, suggests stimulating observations on the 'Mahdist paradox' (i.e. how to proclaim the millennial agenda and, at the same time, build a functional state), which is also a recurring theme in the following chapters.

With regard to the phenomenon of ISIS and its precursors, scholarly research is, naturally, quite recent. The complete list of authors whose studies should not be neglected as part of any serious study of ISIS would be notably extensive, but include the following names (in alphabetical order): Abdel Bari Atwan, John M. Berger, Brian Fishman, Fawaz Gerges, Hassan Hassan, Thomas Hegghammer, Brynjar Lia, Charles Lister, William McCants, Jessica Stern, Michael Weiss and Aaron Zelin.

Due to the nature of the subject studied, the dividing line – if one exists – between scholarly and journalistic works based on primary sources is not always clear. In any case, while there has indeed been enormous coverage of the history of ISIS, there has been little scholarship on the subject of how the organisation derives its authority and connects with the Islamic tradition.[17] To sum up, much of the available scholarship devoted to ISIS follows the approaches of area and security studies and, therefore, seeks to present the group in its contemporary context. While some aspects of ISIS have already been thoroughly addressed (the group's media representation, for example), others still await comprehensive research and this is also the case with regard to the group's position on apocalypticism.

In this regard, it is worth mentioning that most studies on ISIS treat apocalypticism on the very margins of their investigations, mostly making only a few general remarks related to their 'apocalyptic beliefs' or their 'eschatological obsession' as being something peculiar to ISIS. The otherwise outstanding work of Fawaz Gerges, *ISIS: A History*, is an obvious example of this approach. In more than three hundred pages, millennialism, as an ideology, appears only once and *Dabiq* only merits three brief mentions.[18] William McCants's *The ISIS Apocalypse* is an exception to the rule since its author devotes a whole and lengthy chapter to the eponymous phenomenon,[19] with the apocalyptic context appearing in many other passages throughout the book.

The reasons behind such a situation are hard to identify. However, one suggestion stands out: those authors specialising in current Middle-Eastern affairs are seldom familiar with millennialism and, vice versa, scholars specialising in religious studies are hardly ever prepared enough to enter the turbulent field of the current apocalyptic movement, raising as this does too many questions and providing very uncertain starting points. As Jean-Pierre Filiu has succinctly summarised,

> this dramatic alteration of the apocalyptic landscape was not taken seriously either by observers of current events in the Middle East or

> by policy makers, for it seemed to have little consequence beyond a popular and superstitious subculture. Nonetheless it created an atmosphere in which a literature explicitly associated with jihad was soon to flourish.[20]

Concerning primary sources, the individual building blocks mostly consist of online presentations by ISIS, particularly the group's propaganda literature.[21] This material can be subdivided into written, audio and video sources. Due to the limited extent of this monograph, it has not been possible to introduce all the manifestations of ISIS apocalypticism in their entirety, in most cases these only being available in cyberspace. Only a very modest taster has been possible. There is no doubt that ISIS deliberately and systematically utilises online social media to activate a sense of the 'apocalyptic times' among its followers;[22] however, a substantial part of their Internet contribution is no longer accessible.

This study is primarily based on an analysis of apocalyptic rhetoric, which has a wide variety of manifestations and includes propaganda texts, sermons, audio or video recordings, informal discussions in cyberspace, as well as diverse references and symbols related to the visual representations of ISIS. Such an approach allows us to achieve a fuller picture of not only how the phenomenon is expressed but also how it has evolved. As regards Internet sources (characteristically ephemeral), a great deal of material has been accessed via Aaron Zelin's website *Jihadology*.[23] This extensive collection of easily endangered data has proven itself to be an invaluable source of inspiration.

The apocalyptic agenda of ISIS, officially recognised even at the highest levels of the military circle (according to General Martin Dempsey, 'this is an organization that has an apocalyptic, end-of-days strategic vision'),[24] raises a number of questions relating mostly to the sincerity of its promoters. On the one hand, the group's official 'showcases', the magazines *Dabiq* and *Rumiyah*, are quite unimaginable without their apocalyptic references, while, on the other hand, there is no single on-line pamphlet devoted solely to the apocalypse among the numerous ISIS publications. This is true of both the so-called 'guidance literature' or its editions of pre-modern Islamic treatises.[25]

Meanwhile, the apocalyptic tenor undoubtedly represents one of the constitutive elements of ISIS self-presentation; the reluctance of the group's propagandists to provide any closer concretisation of their Last Days' expectations also being undeniable. Having learned their lesson from past mistakes (see 'The Apocalyptic March' in Chapter 4), they have become more vigilant.

Structure and Methodology

This book consists of seven chapters. Chapter 1 introduces, in general terms, the phenomenon of Muslim apocalyptic thought and writing, with a focus on its Sunni elements. The historical background, the key terms applied in this book, and also fundamental notions, are all discussed here. One cannot understand contemporary Muslim society without acquiring a thorough grasp of its classical foundations and this equally applies in the case of modern Muslim apocalypticism. Thus, the main intention of this chapter is to make the ensuing interpretation intelligible to those readers who are interested in ISIS but who have only a limited knowledge of Islam.

Chapter 2 focuses on the constitutive elements of modern Islamic apocalypticism, as well as on certain 'trajectories of ideas' that led to its formation. The millennial preoccupation of ISIS did not fall from the sky but followed previous developments in modern Muslim apocalyptic creativity. In fact, 'creativity' is a very appropriate designation since in order to understand current Muslim apocalypticism, a knowledge of the relevant medieval heritage is definitely not all that is required. Together with the development of new Islamist movements, Muslim apocalyptic discourse has undergone a fundamental mutation. It is no longer marginalised as a mere 'spiritual issue' – and this chapter elaborates on how this came about.

Chapter 3 addresses considerations related to what may be metaphorically called 'an apocalyptic topography of Syria and Iraq'. The apocalyptic reading of Middle Eastern geopolitical eventualities provided in the first section is enriched by a broader overview of the visual representation of ISIS, as well as the related symbolism. This chapter simply puts ISIS 'on the map', either in an apocalyptic or symbolic way.

Chapter 4 addresses in detail the role of the millennial agenda within ISIS propaganda. The titles of the individual sections 'The Apocalyptic March', 'From Dābiq' and 'To Rome' symbolically outline the development of ISIS Last Days ambitions as well as its utopian dreams of world domination ('To Rome'), firmly relying on the local apocalyptic traditions ('From Dābiq'). Using primary sources, the interpretation analyses, step by step, the specific segments of the Muslim apocalyptic heritage that have been effectively utilised by ISIS as a tool for the justification and legalisation of the group's military campaign. The main objective of this key chapter is to comprehensibly examine how ISIS propagandists have used chosen apocalyptic pointers, which, from their own viewpoint, have already been fulfilled (referring to the 'apocalyptic past').

Chapter 5 is also devoted to apocalyptic portents. Unlike the preceding chapter, the discussion, which systematically introduces the proclaimed ISIS vision, is focused on the future. The ultimate goal of all millennial Muslim predictions is undoubtedly the victory over evil of the powers of good, as embodied in the redeemer, al-Mahdī, and it is precisely this point that is discussed in a separate section. This chapter also considers the method by which ISIS has been able to promote its End-time dreams ('How to Sell the Apocalypse?').

Chapter 6 provides the reader with a completely different perspective on the apocalyptic narratives of ISIS and depicts how their opponents have sought to locate the group's activities in an apocalyptic context. Such 'apocalyptic responses', as well as their more general patterns, are thoroughly examined here.

The final chapter, Chapter 7, cannot truly be called an epilogue in the correct sense of the word since we are still not in a position to answer some of the key questions. Moreover, until now, nobody has been certain as to the future results of the currently prevailing apocalyptic conviction among Muslims. Yet, despite the above-mentioned limitations to our knowledge, the stormy terrain of the ISIS apocalypse enables us to formulate some particular concluding remarks.

To facilitate study, this book also includes four appendices comprising: (1) a glossary of Muslim apocalyptic vocabulary; (2) a chronological overview of the ISIS phenomenon; (3) an ISIS 'apocalyptic reader'; and (4) an 'apocalyptic map'. In order to make the bibliography more comprehensible, I have not included some of the resources referenced in the text, especially online materials. Full information about these items can be found in the chapter-endnotes.

As regards the popular image of ISIS, common newspaper attributes, such as 'irrational', 'medieval', 'mysterious', 'extreme', regularly appear to refer to the quite exceptional position this group holds in the current world. ISIS is simply different from anything we have seen before. It should be made clear at this juncture that a number of disputable points tackled in the following chapters deserve more extensive explanation in order to be properly contextualised. At the same time, the author has had to resist such a temptation in order to provide an uncluttered interpretation. As one of the major ambitions of this monograph is to be comprehensible to the common reader, the author has endeavoured to provide conciseness and intelligibility. In this respect, the following presentation is necessarily full of compromises.

Methodologically, this book has been designed primarily as an exegetical survey of ISIS propaganda containing apocalyptic elements and rhetoric. In fact, even the limitations associated with the phrase 'apocalyptic elements and rhetoric' are rather problematic since, as we will repeatedly see later on, the very apocalyptic vocabulary does not necessarily refer to End-time issues and, on the contrary, a lot of unquestionable references to the End-time agenda may appear without apparent recourse to apocalyptic terms. Basically, the analysis should not restrict itself merely to 'exegetical casuistry', continuously focused on chosen manifestations of the ISIS apocalyptic ethos, but should attempt to draw a coherent picture of one of today's great Islamic themes. The theoretical interpretations are often interspersed with extensive quotations from ISIS primary sources, thus providing the reader with the specifics of the jihadist approach to apocalyptic rhetoric. Needless to say, a research project devoted to this vast topic cannot always be exhaustive and it was definitely not the author's intention to elaborate here a broader study of current Muslim apocalypticism in general terms.

As far as can be judged from open sources, a preliminary assessment, based on an analysis of ISIS apocalyptic material, brings us to the conviction that the group has deliberately used this agenda to increase its own appeal. Indeed, miscellaneous manifestations of apocalypticism can be found in various aspects of ISIS propaganda. In this regard, it should be stressed that the production of any piece of scholarly work involves a set of choices that inevitably results in an emphasis on certain aspects and the suppression of others. In the case of this monograph, the author's objective was not to deal with ISIS apocalyptic agenda as a peculiar extreme, but to place it in the wider framework of contemporary Islamic thought in order to accurately reflect both its traditional features and its innovative aspects.

Therefore, apocalypticism, as addressed in the following chapters, actually consists of more than simple religious content or rhetoric modus. On this point, I utterly agree with the apt remark made by Jamel Velji:

> I hypothesise that apocalypticism, through its discursive manipulation of temporality, helps to restructure the premises of terrestrial authority through an elision of symbols associated with ultimate good or evil with actors, rituals, or objects on the terrestrial plane.[26]

On the other hand, we should avoid the use of an opposite and extreme approach in order to avoid reading into the apocalyptic perspective more than is actually there. So, the contextualisation of anything that can be contextualised in apocalyptical terms should not be something that is definitely taken for granted. In this regard, watchfulness is clearly necessary.

Essentially, there are a number of appropriate lenses through which the ISIS End-time agenda can be examined. Among them, the concept of 'cosmic war' elaborated by Mark Juergensmeyer, an American sociologist, has proven itself to be particularly inspirational. In Juergensmeyer's own words, 'the idea of cosmic war is compelling to religious activists because it ennobles and exalts those who consider themselves a part of it – especially those who have been desperate about their situations and defiant in resisting them'.[27] Although this cannot explain everything, it may contribute to our understanding of ISIS self-presentation.

Another meaningful framework through which current world affairs can be explored is the history of Islam. Today's earthly conflicts are not understood 'only' as a part of a metaphysical clash between good and evil but also as an outcome of the long historical efforts of pious Muslims seeking a better world. Both perspectives can also be detected in the following chapters.

Of course, the apocalypticism of ISIS, as well as its other manifestations, can basically be studied with a focus on either its social or ideological dimension. This book concentrates chiefly on the latter, textual aspect since the amount we know about the content of ISIS End-time propaganda (its 'spiritual message') is significantly more than what we know about its real social functions and perceptions in relation to the group's supporters (its 'social impact').[28] Fundamentally, both approaches are firmly interconnected and so this study might appear to be incomplete. However, the objective is to become as complete as the current state of research allows, rather than to enter the field of unsubstantiated assumption. This, at least, is how the author of this book views the challenge.

Notes

1. Both cited proverbs come from the project 'Structure of Culture: Arabic-Islamic Civilization Through the Prism of Corpus Linguistics', funded by The Czech Science Foundation. Courtesy of Petr Zemánek (Charles University, Prague).
2. Qur^ᵓān 33:72.
3. Berger, 'The Metronome of Apocalyptic Time', p. 61.
4. Juergensmeyer, *Terror in the Mind of God*, pp. 185–6.
5. For this radical tendency, see Qindīl and ᶜAbd al-Rabbihi, *al-Fikr al-islāmī al-jihādī al-muᶜāṣir*, pp. 355–7.
6. Fromson and Simon, 'ISIS: The Dubious Paradise of Apocalypse Now', p. 28.

7. Cook, 'Abu Mus^{c}ab al-Suri and Abu Mus^{c}ab al-Zarqawi'.
8. Fromson and Simon, 'ISIS', p. 32.
9. Berger, 'The Metronome of Apocalyptic Time', pp. 61–2.
10. Juergensmeyer, *Terror in the Mind of God*, p. 218.
11. McCants, *The ISIS Apocalypse*, p. 29.
12. For specific live stories, vividly illustrating both patterns, see Shandab, *Munāẓara ma^{c}a ^{c}aql dā^{c}ish*, pp. 131–8.
13. Cook, *Studies in Muslim Apocalyptic*, pp. 29–33. For a broader context, see the chapter 'Millennialism as a Field of Study' in Amanat, *Apocalyptic Islam and Iranian Shi^{c}ism*, pp. 31–5.
14. Cook, *Contemporary Muslim Apocalyptic Literature*.
15. Landes, 'Enraged Millennialism'; Filiu, *Apocalypse in Islam*.
16. See, for example, Gorenberg, *The End of Days*; Richardson, *The Islamic Antichrist*.
17. For a thorough overview of the current state of the research devoted to the religious dimension of ISIS, see Mirza, '"The Slave Girl Gives Birth to Her Master"', pp. 3–6.
18. *Dabiq* was a glossy magazine published by ISIS on a regular basis between 2014 and 2016 as the group's main propagandistic tool intended primarily for Western readers. Gerges, *ISIS: A History*, pp. 356, 362.
19. McCants, *The ISIS Apocalypse*, pp. 99–120.
20. Filiu, *Apocalypse in Islam*, p. 103.
21. For the earlier propaganda of ISIS, see, especially, *Majmū^{c} tafrīghāt kalimāt al-qādat bi-Dawlat al-^{c}Irāq al-islāmīya*.
22. Berger, 'The Metronome of Apocalyptic Time', p. 61.
23. Available at http://jihadology.net/ (last accessed 29 September 2017).
24. See, for example, http://www.vocativ.com/tech/internet/cyclops-baby-muslim-antichrist-much/ (last accessed 20 December 2017).
25. Olidort, *Inside the Caliphate's Classroom*, pp. 45–50.
26. Velji, *An Apocalyptic History*, p. 105.
27. Juergensmeyer, *Terror in the Mind of God*, p. 184.
28. See Berger, 'The Metronome of Apocalyptic Time', pp. 61–71. Cf. also Shandab, *Munāẓara ma^{c}a ^{c}aql dā^{c}ish*.

1

The Quest for the Portents of the Hour

Being a reflection of a person's position on social and political matters, prophecies offer information about the speaker's mind with little mediation. Unlike historiography, which usually shies away from openly revealing of biases and prejudices, prophecies offer a one-sided view. They are clearly for or against something.

– Hayrettin Yücesoy[1]

The human soul's desire is to know what will happen in the coming days, be it related to the future of an individual or to the destiny of mankind, as we approach the Hour. The proliferation of soothsayers and fortunetellers in all countries of idolatry is, perhaps, the best proof of that.

– *al-Naba*ʾ[2]

There is of course room for infinite variety: there are countless possible ways of imagining the Millennium and the route to it. Millenarian sects and movements have varied in attitude from the most violent aggressiveness to the mildest pacifism and from the most ethereal spirituality to the most earthbound materialism. And they have also varied greatly in social composition and social function.

– Norman Cohn[3]

The end of this world is a theme that has engaged human imagination since time immemorial. People have always been enchanted by the prospect of dreaming about the future and its associated predictions. All major religions address the issue of apocalyptic and eschatological issues and Islam (which itself probably began as an apocalyptic movement)[4] is no exception. A belief in Doomsday (*yawm al-dīn*) and the Hereafter (*al-ākhira*) belongs among the fundamental articles of the Muslim faith. However, to make the eschatological era possible, this world (*al-dunyā*) must be destroyed and replaced by a perfect realm in which people will find either reward or punishment. In Islam, death has simply ceased to be perceived as the end of life but rather as the conclusion of predetermined time (*al-ajal*), as prescribed to human beings to test them (*fitna*) in preparation for the Hereafter.

Paradise and hell in Islam have manifold functions. In the succinct words of Christian Lange,

> they put words and images to fears of misery and hopes of happiness; they serve to inculcate a catechism of sins and virtues, offering taxonomies of the morally good and bad; they provide allegories for intellectual and spiritual fulfilment and failure; they are structured reflections of earthly utopias and dystopias, as well as blueprints for the creation of various paradises and hells on earth.[5]

As far as contemporary Islamic eschatology is concerned, the majority of Muslim authors actually choose not to discuss the afterlife at all. They are, according to Jane Smith and Yvonne Haddad, 'satisfied with simply affirming the reality of the day of judgement and human accountability without providing any details or interpretative discussion'.[6] Although the collectively shared expectations of Muslims related to the afterlife are, with a gross degree of simplification, rather consensual,[7] they considerably differ in terms of their vision of the 'apocalyptic scenario' that will precede it.

In the following section, the non-consensual sequences of events and tendencies that are predicted as the lead up to the final clash of good and evil that will usher in the extinction of life in this world will be examined. This is important because the ISIS apocalyptic self-presentation is totally inconceivable without any pre-knowledge of classical Muslim fundamentals. The minimum needed for a proper understanding of the group's skilful instrumentalisation of the apocalypse will be provided here since this will help to make sense of the massive outpouring of End-time prophecies that we see today.

If there is one thing we should be aware of before we begin, it is that the ISIS approach to the apocalypse skilfully links a number of very modern features to some of the most traditional elements. Portraying itself, first and foremost, as a 'vanguard driven by eschatological expectations', the group's propaganda systematically highlights its proposals for restoring Islam's glorious past.[8] However, as regards the genuine ISIS attitude towards the Islamic heritage, Younus Mirza has accurately commented: 'The media constantly presents the movement as "medieval" because the group cites classical and medieval traditions. However, although ISIS authors undoubtedly draw on medieval traditions, their interpretations differ from those whose work they have appropriated.'[9] This key point should also be remembered within the apocalyptic context.

From a general perspective, the approach of the End will be foreshadowed by a set of unusual events, ultimately calling mankind to repentance (*tawba*). Neither the Qurʾānic quotations nor the apocalyptic elements in the Sunna allow us to construct a universally accepted Muslim 'road map' that leads us to an understanding of the End. Essentially, its proximity was viewed as being imminent at the very birth of Islam and this is again the case today as we have access to precise data based on sociological research.[10] With the outbreak of the Syrian war, reference to the apocalyptic heritage has clearly become mainstream.[11] In this particular respect, ISIS propaganda is definitely not unique.

The anticipatory millennial zeal of the early Muslims[12] was later replaced by the circumspection of Islamic scholars, who began to deal with apocalyptic portents as if they were merely 'academic' subjects that carried no practical relevance. Nevertheless, there were occasional eruptions of millennial emotions which were either mercilessly suppressed or transformed into an opportunity for 'state-building'.

Key Apocalyptic Terms and Notions

Scholarly literature, and popular discussions on End-time matters in particular, face occasional complications associated with terminology because some terms overlap, are defined differently, are conflated, or even remain undefined. Therefore, in order to avoid misunderstandings related to the terms applied in this monograph, a few initial explanatory remarks are required.

As regards the most frequently used term, 'apocalypticism', this simply refers to a broad spectrum of collectively shared expectations related to the End times, as well as to particular methods associated with their interpretation and exploitation. Both aspects, ideas and their usage, have experienced dramatic developments since the beginning of the new millennium. These changes can be summarised in terms of the decisive shift that has seen an alluring spiritual message with no 'practical' consequences transform itself into to a type of 'ideological weapon'.

In fact, the term 'Muslim apocalypticism' does not refer to any particular ideological platform or branch of knowledge. It is rather a general designation intended to cover the full set of teachings and speculations, as well as their manifestations. These are entirely interconnected by a single common denominator – an inner-awareness of the approaching End. Not all apocalyptic harbingers are in nature necessarily truly catastrophic, albeit that most of them indicate decline and corruption. This is why the Islamic conception resonates with popular usage of the term, where 'apocalypse' has become synonymous with a presupposed catastrophe. The *Oxford Learner's Dictionary* confirms such a perception, explaining the term 'apocalyptic', in the first instance, as 'describing very serious damage and destruction in past or future events'.[13]

What really connects apocalyptists across the 'Muslim world' is definitely not any kind of common narrative or a single account of shared ideas but rather their 'reading of reality', together with similar approaches on how to present their views to the public. Apocalypticism in Islam thus provides an open field where diverse attitudes are able to encounter and compete with each other (see 'From Dusty Bookshelves to Spiritual Blockbusters' in Chapter 2). For instance, the Muslim opponents of ISIS, in their responses to the group's End-time messages, have developed their own reading of the apocalyptic prophecies (see 'Sunni "Apocalypses Light"' in Chapter 6).

The author of this book distinguishes between 'apocalypticism' and 'millennialism', although they are often confused in common usage. The latter term, as understood here, refers to a certain shared conviction about the approaching End. A brief definition has been suggested by Catherine Wessinger: 'Millennialism is an expression of the human hope for the achievement of permanent well-being, in other words, salvation.'[14] The common feature of any form of millennialism is the shared disquieting experience of the proximity of the End. And it is precisely in this respect that millennialism differs, as suggested in this book, from apocalypticism, which can be seen as both an impersonal ('remote') subject of scholarly discourse and an intensely lived ('close') inward spiritual experience.

In such a usage, we can speak about 'apocalyptic excitement' supported by ISIS propaganda as well as about 'apocalyptic chapters' included in medieval treatises. Somewhere, both terms can be used synonymously; however, elsewhere, such a substitution does not fit. Simply put, apocalypticism refers to a doctrine no matter how it is experienced, whereas one of the most distinctive features of millennialism is simply its experience.

Another pair of concepts, 'apocalypticism' and 'eschatology', are not employed synonymously in this book, unlike the way in which they are commonly used. Herein, the former is seen as 'a subset' of the latter. Eschatology is thus referred to as the ultimate destiny of humanity. This difference in the Islamic context has been convincingly expressed by David Cook:

> As will be noted again and again, no victory or defeat is final in the apocalyptic world. Nothing is permanent, even in the messianic future. This, by the way, is the true difference between the apocalyptic future, in which events are still subject to change, and

> the eschatological future, which is not subject to change. This latter future will occur only after the Day of Judgement.[15]

Dealing with terminological subtleties,[16] the distinction between millennialism (originally employed in Christianity) and messianism (originating from Judaism) loses its sense in Islam because the collective belief in the approaching End is intertwined with expectations of the Saviour. In addition, the term 'apocalypse' has its own Christian roots. Of course, the application of the derived terms 'apocalyptic' and 'apocalypticism' to a modality of religiosity outside the Christian framework may stimulate a certain degree of embarrassment, as 'the interdisciplinary study of apocalypticism remains constrained by the concept's continued tethering to its theological and disciplinary origins'.[17] To be consistent, the employment of 'millennialism' or 'chiliasm' within the Islamic framework can also be contested. As Timothy Furnish suggests, 'centennialism' would be a more accurate term, as the traditions associated with the *mujaddid* (renewer), who comes once a century, carry far more resonance within the Muslim context.[18]

As far as the nature of millennialism in Islam is concerned, we can speak about 'catastrophic millennialism' in which, according to the classification proposed by Catherine Wessinger, 'the belief is that transition to the millennial kingdom will be accomplished by a great catastrophe (often caused by a superhuman agent) that destroys the currently evil world so that a collective salvation will be accomplished for the saved'.[19] As regards terminology, a certain level of generalisation must be applied to achieve meaningful communication. To be meticulous, both key terms, apocalypticism and millennialism, should be used herein in their plural forms, which, on the other hand, might seem a little eccentric.

To conclude this section, 'apocalypticism', as used in the following interpretation, is not considered a theological category but, in a much broader sense, as 'a certain mode of authoritative discourse by which actors may construct society throughout the evocation of certain sentiments'.[20] In the case of ISIS, apocalypticism is definitely not only a subject but is also a style.

A number of Arabic terms appear in this book (see Appendix 1). However, only the most fundamental ones, indispensable for further interpretation, have been introduced.[21] Of interest is the fact that ISIS provides its own 'introduction to apocalypse' series, which includes terminological explanations.[22] The most frequent apocalyptic term, in general, is *al-sāʿa* (the Hour), which is how Muslims poetically refer to the End. The Hour also appears in the Qurʾān, particularly in three verses urging Muslims not to attempt to specify its date.[23] Despite this imperative, Islamic scholars have often succumbed to temptation and tried to date it, exploiting various prognostic methods, including numerological speculations.[24]

In Islam, only God knows the time of the Hour; nevertheless, people should be aware of its approach because such an awareness encourages piety, a point that is also stressed in ISIS propaganda.[25] Thus, while any effort to determine the date of the End is discouraged, the very awareness of the temporality of this world is praiseworthy. The Hour, according to majority opinion, is fixed and, as such, cannot be postponed or hastened. On the other hand, considerations about so-called 'hotwiring' of the apocalypse are not so marginal in Islam as it might seem at first glance.[26]

The temporalising of the Muslim apocalypse always had its powerful opponents, mostly among a number of authoritative scholars. By denying the apocalyptic meaning of the particular prophecies, they were often responsible for the relegation of these prophecies to an unspecified future, far distant from this-worldly access.[27] The ambiguous opinions regarding the 'applicability' of apocalyptic portents accompanied Muslims throughout their pre-modern history and later became a starting point for modern Muslim apocalyptic creativity. Here, we must not forget that both the medieval popularity and the contemporary appeal of the End-time speculations actually issue from the same spring, which is the compelling attraction of any apocalyptic reading of the present that offers an easy escape from gloomy reality.

In Arabic, the harbingers of the End are termed *ʿalāmāt* (or *ashrāṭ*) *al-sāʿa*, which means 'the signs of the Hour'. The related traditions generally follow a stereotypical pattern: 'The Hour will not arrive until

X (whatever activity, trait, theological bent, heresy or even person the apocalyptist wishes to condemn) appears.'[28] The signs of the Hour can basically be divided into events and tendencies.

Scholars distinguish between two phases of apocalyptic portents: the lesser (*sughrā*) and the greater (*kubrā*) signs. The lesser signs are mostly moral, religious, social, political, and also include natural events and trends. They are designed to warn humanity that the End is near. The vast majority of them are general and have been present in all known societies: moral decay, crime, natural disasters and wars, for example.[29] The lesser signs are usually 'sufficiently vague to permit non-scholars to connect personal experience to the apocalypse'.[30]

The greater signs include a series of events of ever-increasing severity that will precede the End – mostly the struggle between the forces of good and evil, personified by al-Mahdī (the Saviour), ᶜĪsā (Jesus), al-Dajjāl (the Antichrist) and al-Sufyānī (an ambiguous figure), all of whom are introduced in the following section. The greater signs have been more suited to ISIS narratives than the lesser signs, since the centrality of Syria to the unfolding of the apocalypse gives symbolic meaning to the group's presence there (see 'From the East to Jerusalem' in Chapter 3).[31]

According to the vast majority of modern apocalyptic authors, the lesser signs have already been fulfilled to a large degree, so humanity is inevitably approaching the Hour. All signs can be further classified according to various criteria, for example in terms of their duration and continuity, into (1) events that manifest themselves once and have no continuation, and (2) phenomena that occur, in order to persist, continue or repeatedly return.[32] As regards the exegetical sophistication, due to their very nature, most signs are more or less mysterious.

Another taxonomic approach distinguishes between those signs that have already been fulfilled, those which are currently in the process of being fulfilled, and those which are still awaited. Such a classification, of course, depends on chronology which, in turn, results from interpretation. As regards classification according to a thematic key, Cook suggests the three following 'types':

> 1) Moral decay: Sexual looseness in general is mentioned, with homosexuality, lesbianism and bestiality being singled out. One of the characteristics of the last days is a total lack of shame about public sexual intercourse . . . The result of all this is that belief will disappear, and that God will lift the text of the Qurʾān from the earth and allow evil and ignorant people to lead . . . At the end of time the believer will be insulted for his faith. 2) Physical signs in the society: Paucity of men, trade and interest-taking (which is illegal in Islam) will be common, but people still will not trust each other in the marketplace . . . Murders and crime will increase and there will be civil wars in which the Arabs will be defeated . . . 3) Natural and supernatural disasters: There will be earthquakes, famines, droughts, plagues, so that the earth will not grow anything, or severe rains will fall destroying houses . . . Many of these natural disasters are seen as the direct result of moral laxity.[33]

Finally, a crucial question of any version of apocalypticism remains: which signs are linked to our present and which are still awaiting fulfilment? Muslims have not reached a consensus yet and, therefore, related speculations serve only to feed the millennial fervour of many ideologues.

It is worth remembering that Muslims do not concur even on the number of the signs. Although most apocalyptic versions coincide, more or less, on a particular 'scenario', they differ considerably in relation to how they distribute particular episodes into individual chapters. It is no wonder that the popular Egyptian author, Muḥammad al-Shaʿrāwī, for example, has been able to list three times more signs than his lay apocalyptic colleague, Muḥammad Bayūmī.[34]

The comparative scholarship on apocalypticism confirms the presence of common themes in all religious traditions that have originated in the Middle East.[35] As we will repeatedly observe, the references to universal decline, so easily applicable at all times and in all places, also play a prominent role in the Muslim apocalypse. However, the lists of apocalyptic signs include many exclusively Islamic motifs – two of which should be introduced here.

Basically, any Muslim apocalyptic narrative would be inconceivable without a knowledge of *fitna*. This term – as David Cook aptly points out, is 'the most vexatious word to translate'[36] – originally referred to as 'the process of refining metal to remove the dross'. With such a meaning, *fitna* also appears in Lane's lexicon:

> a burning with fire, the melting of gold and silver in order to separate or distinguish the bad from the good, a trial, affliction, distress, a means whereby the condition of a man may be evinced, in respect of good and of evil, punishment, . . . difference of opinions among the people, seduction, temptation . . .[37]

By extension, *fitna* generally means an earthly test linked to the hereafter, either in the form of a temptation or tribulation. The gradual convergence between the truth and a lie (i.e. *halāl* and *ḥarām*), which is supposedly so typical for the End times, can also be presented as a specific form of *fitna*.[38]

As regards the risk associated with *fitna*, the Qurʾān clearly states: 'For persecution (*fitna*) is more serious than killing.'[39] In Muslim historiography, this term indicates the inner struggle that undermines the unity of the *umma*, in general, and the fratricidal fighting for the leadership of the Muslim empire during the first centuries of *hijra*, in particular. The word used for the upheavals of the Last Days is thus the same word that denotes the early sectarian civil wars.[40] As a feared divisive tendency, *fitna* is seen as the opposite of *jihād*.

In various forms and degrees, *fitan* (the Arabic plural of *fitna*) thus occur throughout all Muslim apocalyptic traditions. As Muslim apocalyptists strongly believe, perfection was achieved at the very beginning of time and was followed by a slow, yet inevitable, decline. This involved the manifestation of a long list of *fitan*, which began with the fratricidal battle of Siffīn (657), together with the appearance of Kharijites (*khawārij*; rebels),[41] events that forever ended the 'golden age' of Islam.

Acknowledging *fitna* to be a divisive feud within the Muslim community leads us to the other pivotal apocalyptic term, the *malḥama* – a fierce battle or massacre, in specific ISIS language 'the bloodiest battle before the Hour'.[42] Within our context, the *malḥama* (plural *malāḥim*) refers primarily to the major conflict between the rightly guided Muslims and unbelievers ('Romans', 'Crusaders'), coupled with an important group of Muslims who have been 'led astray'. In the final phase of the lesser signs, such fighting will usher in the main apocalyptic characters – the Antichrist, the Dajjāl, and the Saviour, the Mahdī – whose coming provides a link between the lesser and the greater signs.

The concepts of *fitan* and *malāḥim* are often merged into a combined notion, *al-fitan wa al-malāḥim*, which is one of the most popular titles of Muslim apocalyptic literature.[43] Regarding the relationship between the terms, in many cases a *malḥama* is a specific type of apocalyptic battle within the genre of *fitan*; however, in other cases the two terms are used rather interchangeably.[44] In ISIS propaganda, the *malḥama* is often discussed, not as a dream, but rather as a tactical step within the group's military plans.[45]

As part of any introductory remarks devoted to Islamic apocalypticism, the discontinuous nature of its sources must be emphasised. This is because the traditional End-time portents are not arranged in the coherent form of 'a roadmap to the future'. As for their original structure, the apocalyptic elements in classical Muslim literature resemble more of a jigsaw puzzle than a fluent narrative. Efforts to transform such a 'building kit' into a chronologically ordered and reader-friendly text are rather a modern phenomenon.

Despite all the exegetical ambiguities that hamper the compilation of a single and universally accepted narrative, an attempt to summarise the key points of any functional Muslim apocalyptic narrative will be undertaken in the following paragraphs (for the modern components, see 'Modern Muslim Apocalyptic Creativity' in Chapter 2).[46] Undoubtably, the chronology of the signs inevitably depends on their exegesis and that is why even the very sequence of the End-time events is a subject of never-ending polemics among apocalyptic authors.

Essentially, the signs of the Hour began to unfold with the very birth of Islam. This is because not only the Prophet's mission but also his death belong among the introductory apocalyptic events, as evidenced by *aḥādīth* related to the so-called 'six events preceding the Hour'.[47] Thereafter, various specific manifestations of societal decay mingled with battles and natural disasters. Numerous inner splits that threatened the unity of the *umma* announced the end of 'the golden age' of Islam, followed by a continuous decline which, at the apocalyptic level, found expression in the appearance of various impostors and those who claimed to be prophets. In apocalyptic perceptions, the heretical tendencies that originated in this turbulent period represent the signs of a general decline.[48]

Over the course of time, a supposed corruption of morals (the colourful depictions of which fill many apocalyptic accounts) followed on from the political and social decay experienced in Muslim countries. Common specific manifestations of this include: the loss of humility, the loss of confidence, the spread of arbitrariness, the loosening of family relationships, the spread of lies and false utterances, greed, greetings reserved only for acquaintances, and last, but not least, hypocrisy in all its conceivable forms.

Muslim religiosity was not immune to this range of sinister impacts and, therefore, similar trends can also be found within Islamic teaching and practice. As apocalyptists often remind us, while the 'Islamic facade' might flourish, the principles will be abandoned. 'The arbitrary treatment of the *Qurʾān*', 'the application of other than God's law' and 'resistance to holy war' are just a few specific examples – if we may borrow here the headings applied by al-Shaʿrāwī.[49] A particularly popular motif among apocalyptic moralists describes a splendid mosque that is full of people, none of whom is a true believer.[50]

Ultimately, the most symptomatic feature of the End times is an increase in brutality and killing, referred to in a series of particular signs. The Prophet's reference to the enigmatic term *harj* (or *haraj*), probably of Abyssinian origin and interpreted by him as 'a lot of killing',[51] supposedly foretold the present situation of the world, that is, full of violence and cruelty. However, this bloody finale foreshadows an even more dramatic scenario, the greater signs of the Hour, essentially a colossal clash between the powers of good and evil that must be fulfilled in order for this temporary world to come to its End, poetically named by Muslims 'the Day on which the Horn is blown'.

The Main Players of the Muslim Apocalypse

Two of the four key players in the Muslim apocalypse may be familiar to the Western reader, since both appear in the Bible. However, the role attributed to Jesus in the End-time narratives of Islam differs fundamentally from the Christian version and the same is true of the Antichrist. The realm of eschatology has thus also become an arena where particular worldly interests interfere and compete with each other. In this respect, Jerusalem may serve as an example, being a site of key importance for all Jewish, Christian and Islamic eschatological visions, and, therefore, the intersection point of various millennial dreams.[52] Comparisons between the Biblical Antichrist and the Muslim Redeemer, and the like, have already attracted the attention of numerous authors,[53] mostly US-based religious fundamentalists. A battle waged in a space fully charged with sacred symbolism is indeed a bestselling theme, whose potential has, so far, only been partially exploited.

The apocalyptic clashes between the powers of good and evil belong to the greater signs of the Hour, among Muslims a terrain of very limited consensus. Nevertheless, the Islamic prophecies foretell a period full of sectarian fighting, when – as aptly expressed by Jean-Pierre Filiu – 'the sword of vengeance will fall upon hypocrites before being turned against infidels'.[54] The following outline focuses on the mainstream Sunni conception, with Shiite Doomsday visions being briefly introduced in Chapter 6.

Basically, most Muslim apocalypses encompass al-Mahdī (the Muslim messianic figure), ᶜĪsā (Jesus), al-Dajjāl (the Antichrist) and al-Sufyānī (a controversial figure, being depicted either as a helper of the Antichrist or as a forerunner of the Mahdī).[55] Needless to say, their identification with living persons is one of the most debated apocalyptic issues.[56] Perhaps the most striking aspect of the Muslim apocalypse is the fact that Muḥammad plays no role in it, as well as the fact that the primary prophetic figure is Jesus.[57] Only he can be found in the Qurʾān, referred to as Ibn Maryam (the son of Mary). He appears in ninety-three verses (*āyāt*), where stress is placed on his role as the messenger of Allāh. Jesus' descent is expected to occur in the midst of wars between the Mahdī and the Dajjāl. Finally, Jesus is expected to kill the Antichrist.[58] Afterwards, wars will cease and, for a limited period, the world will witness peace and justice.

Jesus, considered to be a Muslim, will lead Jews and Christians towards a mass conversion, after which there will remain only one community, that of Islam. Such an anticipated overcoming of past doctrinal differences will, quite symbolically, be concluded by the breaking of a cross and the slaughter of swine, events that are repeatedly mentioned in Muslim sources. According to David Cook, Jesus was the first messianic figure in Islam, and while his role has been minimised during the intervening centuries, it has never been entirely removed.[59]

Jesus' arch enemy is the Dajjāl, which is a shortened version of the name al-Maṣīḥ al-Dajjāl (the false Messiah). Muslim apocalyptists distinguish between a number of 'minor dajjāls' (charlatans and false prophets, often quantified as thirty)[60] and the appearance of the real Dajjāl, the master of evil.[61] As for his nature and description,[62] the medieval traditions are often contradictory and thus modern Muslim apocalyptists even question whether the Dajjāl is a human being or actually an abstract power. In this regard, Cook offers five possibilities:

> (1) The Antichrist is a literal, physical being with a life span similar to that of other human beings . . . (2) The Antichrist is a physical being, but one who has an unnatural life span . . . (3) The Antichrist is not human at all . . . (4) The Antichrist is a malevolent but unseen force . . . (5) One final view . . . that the Antichrist is a Samaritan Jew.[63]

The search for the Antichrist is definitely not just an academic issue, since such effort can result in very practical consequences (see 'The Islamic Armageddon' in Chapter 5). In traditional Shiite eschatology, the Dajjāl has been virtually absent in related writings, though nowadays this figure is gaining more and more prominence in the Shiite apocalypse.[64] In the apocalypticism of ISIS, speculations about the Dajjāl's identity can lead to both 'physical' and figurative interpretations. For example, the latter approach can be seen in the tweet of an ISIS fan after the January 2015 attack on the *Charlie Hebdo* newspaper office in Paris: 'The West is the one-eyed Deceiver.'[65]

The main role in the Muslim apocalypse belongs to the Mahdī, who is an inevitable connector of otherwise incoherent apocalyptic versions. His coming links together both of the fundamental parts of all End-time scenarios, the lesser and the greater signs, into a closed narrative. His name is derived from the Arabic verbal root *h-d-y*, which means to lead in the right way. His appearance, as well as his activities, have been foretold by a great number of *aḥādīth*. Only a small number of conservatives and thinkers (among them such different personalities as Ibn Khaldūn and Rashīd Riḍā)[66] question his very existence because he does not appear in the two most authoritative collections of al-Bukhārī and Muslim.[67]

Although Muslims argue about the exact place of his emergence, they mostly believe that he will come from the East (*Mashriq*). The physical appearance of the Mahdī has also been detailed by many prominent scholars, among them al-Qurṭubī, Ibn Kathīr and al-Suyūtī, all of them mentioning that the Mahdī will arise from the Prophet's offspring. We are informed that his countenance will resemble that of the Prophet. The Mahdī, together with Jesus, are expected to face the barbarian hordes of Gog and Magog (*Yājūj wa Mājūj*).[68] According to most commentators, the Mahdī will appear at the end of a great war culminating in the Muslim conquest of Constantinople, that is, earlier than the appearance of Jesus but later in relation to the Antichrist.

From a Shiite perspective, the Mahdī is identical to their Hidden Imām, referred to as the Master of the Age (*ṣāḥib al-zamān*). Many Muslim scholars, both Shiite and Sunni, even agree that the Mahdī is already living secretly on the earth. For both Sunnis and Shiites, the Mahdī personifies what they are missing in this world: the dominant Sunnis thus expect a humble and very human leader, while the persecuted Shiites long for a triumphant hero. Within modern apocalypticism, the Mahdī constitutes a projection of the powerful, messianic personality that the Muslim apocalyptist feels is most lacking in this world. Although the main task of the Mahdī is to eliminate 'Western tyranny', his principal enemies will be Muslim traitors. What is most remarkable, in our context, is the comparison between the analytical verbosity devoted to most signs leading up to this great finale, and the Mahdī's 'reign of justice', which has attracted much less attention (see 'The Islamic Armageddon', Chapter 5).

Of the four apocalyptic characters, al-Sufyānī is certainly the most enigmatic one. His name refers to Abū Sufyān, who was among the main opponents of the Prophet Muḥammad in Mecca and, at the same time, the ancestor of the Umayyad dynasty (661–750). For Shiites, he is more hated than the Dajjāl; Sunnis are more ambivalent. Albeit most Sunni prophecies about him are negative, a few are positive. As in the ninth century, he is a national hero for some Sunnis today, especially in Syria.[69] On the other hand, many Shiites believe that the Sufyānī's appearance is imminent, but they do not welcome it because of his antagonistic role in the apocalyptic drama. Some of them even believe that what is happening in Syria is the beginning of his emergence, currently in the form of the so-called Free Army, fighting against Shiite Iran's ally, Bashshār al-Asad.[70] In fact, the Sufyānī will be a tyrannical Arab who oppresses the Shiites, so in the past he was often identified with figures such as Saḍḍām Ḥusayn or al-Zarqāwī.[71]

A short survey of Muslim apocalyptic players would also encompass the hordes of Gog and Magog, the enigmatic beast al-Dābba, as well as al-Ḥabashī (an Abyssinian warrior). However, for our purposes, these figures are largely of limited relevance. All of them are actually expected to appear after the demise of the Mahdī, which means in the vaguely described era between the achievement of unity under his rule and the extinction of this world, immediately foreshadowed by a set of catastrophic phenomena both in heaven and on earth. Moreover, the Beast practically disappears from the messianic scene as depicted by present-day Islam[72] and the central place in Muslim End-time visions is accorded to two other figures who are completely absent from the Qurʾān – the Dajjāl and the Mahdī.[73]

Apocalyptic Sources and Historic Manifestations

Current Muslim approaches to apocalyptic literature issue from its contradictory historic development, as well as from the suspiciousness of the traditional *ʿulamāʾ* concerning any material having the potential to ignite a millennial spark. As far as the heterogeneous sources of Muslim apocalyptic imagination are concerned, the words of Abbas Amanat are most apt and can provide us with a helpful introductory note: 'An uneasy marriage of anger, violence, and intolerance with peace and acumen, of naiveté and demagogy with sophistication and creativity, and of folk beliefs with venerable erudition, characterizes the inspirational ramshackle upon which millennial edifices were often built.'[74] Added to this, Cook reminds that apocalypticism is, however, 'more than just another historical source, and deserves to be analysed in the aggregate, noting parallels with other religious traditions at the same time'.[75]

The bulk of Muslim apocalyptic texts include diverse categories of very uneven importance, where the so-called canonical sources (scattered sections from the Sunna, together with a limited number of Qurʾānic references) represent a subcomponent of a very extensive array of material. At a broader heuristic level, Cook distinguishes between historical and metahistorical apocalypses. In the former traditions, 'there exist recognizable historical personalities, and a historical sequence of events that leaves reality at a particular point and moves into the realm of fantasy'.[76] To the contrary, 'metahistorical apocalypses are those that are entirely unconnected with historical events, and are set in the eschatological future'.[77] Basically, historical apocalypses reflect the dramatic events of formative periods of Islamic civilisation, where the martial encounters between Muslims and unbelievers (mostly Byzantines) have become indelibly embedded in the collective memory of the *umma*.

In the following sections, apocalyptic material will be dealt with predominantly in the form of separate prophecies, but we should be aware that the original traditions would have been organised in a completely different manner. Looking into the medieval sources, it is more likely that we will uncover scattered and inconsistent scraps, sketchily drawn items rather than neat narratives, mostly grouped together according to their provenance or prevalent subtopics. Sorting references according to particular signs of the Hour is, in fact, a rather secondary approach.

On the nature of the original Muslim apocalyptic traditions, Cook suggests three fundamental features that should be emphasised:

> (1) The material is in the form of a *hadith* . . . (2) It is placed always in the prophetic future, which is assumed here to be *ex post facto*, but may have some genuine predictive elements. (3) While directed towards the future, it usually makes use of past events with a cyclical view of history in order to interpret this 'future history'.[78]

Muslim apocalyptic texts provide us with much more than descriptions of the religious environment in which they originated. In fact, all apocalyptic revelations not only reveal their creators' ideas in relation to the End-time scenario but also – if not primarily – the genuine imprints of their own past and present. In this respect, some considerations devoted to the Middle Ages also fit well with current conditions, since 'it seems apparent that prophecies offer a unique perspective on the mentalities and overriding concerns . . . and on how the creators and transmitters of prophecies perceived their socio-political realities'.[79]

Refined by reference to the dubious criteria adopted by the medieval guardians of Islamic orthodoxy, the vast heuristic foundation of apocalyptic traditions was gradually reduced to its core essentials, which seemed innocuous enough. However, from time to time, even the harmlessness of this core has proved illusory. Currently, for an important body of Muslims, the apocalyptic elements in the two great anthologies of authentic traditions compiled by Muslim and al-Bukhārī remain the only relevant sources in relation to the End-time agenda.[80]

As we have seen, over time the relevance of particular Qurʾānic motifs (al-Dābba, for example) have been suppressed in favour of figures, motifs and episodes of another provenance. The contemporary 'End-time stage' of Islam is thus occupied by an extremely heterogeneous set of actors. In any case, apocalypticism, as a genre (including its modern forms) contains its own specifics and mysteries:

> The apocalyptic world is a slightly different world than the one in which we live. Nature participates in the action, as it were; thus, we find that stones throw themselves at enemies, both trees and animals frequently speak, and the earth swallows up unbelievers. It is said that during this time that a man's shoes will inform him of what his family (or wife, *ahl*) does when he is not present.[81]

The Qurʾān contains a large number of apocalyptic and eschatological verses, mostly from the earliest period of the Prophet's revelation. As Michael Sells and others have observed, the primary subject of the early Meccan *sūras* was generally the idea of a divine reckoning, and during the time in which many of these *sūras* were revealed, the term *dīn* ('reckoning') was almost synonymous with religion.[82] The End-time agenda, simply referring to the transience of this world, thus played the role of a certain spiritual prologue to the major topic of eschatological reward and punishment in Islam.

The Qurʾānic references alone, however, are insufficient to build an apocalyptic scenario. Moreover, the ambiguities associated with the Qurʾān have given rise to extensive and miscellaneous exegeses – *tafāsīr* (singular *tafsīr*). The long-term process of the Muslim theologians' attempts to cope with apocalyptic issues also incorporated the field of exegesis. Only a part of the extensive apocalyptic legacy has survived the long centuries of mistrust on the part of the official authorities. On the other hand, the End-time ideas from both sources, the Qurʾān and the Sunna, have penetrated into many Islamic works, as well as into secular Arabic folk literature. Finally, since the second half of the twentieth century, Muslim apocalypticism has been considerably enriched by a large amount of Western borrowings, as we will see in Chapter 2 ('Modern Muslim Apocalyptic Creativity').

Any fair, scholarly attempt to correctly analyse the role of apocalypticism throughout the history of Muslims must inevitably encounter an obstacle in the form of the enormous variety of related manifestations across time and space. Any attempt to place such completely different events as, for example, the Abbasid revolution, various medieval Shiite uprisings fuelled by End-time longing, or the insurrection of the Sudanese Mahdi, into a single common folder entitled 'Islamic millennialism', will easily convince us that we are indeed dealing with a complex and ambiguous phenomenon. As a result, any effort to generalise is problematic. The following section has, thus, only one modest goal: to demonstrate this stunning variability – often even inconsistency – by mentioning a few fundamental examples of early millennialism in relation to Islam. Although some millennial episodes in Islam have already become the subject of meticulous research,[83] this field, in all its entirety and complexity, still awaits an appropriate synthesis.

The Shiite apocalypse is intentionally omitted here,[84] even though it is precisely in the apocalyptic field that the difference between the Shiites and the Sunnis reaches its highest peak. Basically, the long list of millennial movements that influenced the early development of the Shiites has convincingly proved the fact that the Shiite offshoots that have survived until today are exactly the same branches that were able to resist the millennial temptation. Conversely, those factions that succumbed to millennial lust were suppressed and have since disappeared.

Nevertheless, End-time obsessions viewed almost exclusively as sources of unrest should not overshadow a more complex picture, one in which millennialism plays a variety of roles that cannot be easily summarised by the common cliché of an apocalyptic threat to an established order. Essentially, millennialism has been a powerful stimulator throughout Islamic history for both toppling existing states and establishing new ones.[85] Perhaps the best example of its 'state-building' role is the rise of the Sawafid dynasty, which developed into a powerful empire. Another millennial surge gave birth to the Bābī uprising, from which the worldwide religion of Bahaism later sprang.

These particular examples, as well as other earlier historic experiences whose legacy was a good deal of strife and bitterness, led mainstream Shia authorities to adopt a circumspect view in relation to millennial rhetoric – which is a claim that can be applied to most of their Sunni counterparts. Furthermore, the millennial agenda was often, if not wholly, associated with political intentions resulting from the turbulence associated with the development of the early Muslim *umma*. The result of this intricate process was that Islamic millennialism became a fundamentally sectarian doctrine, espoused or shunned in line with the overall ideological position of various sects within the Islamic spectrum.[86]

In the Middle Ages, the End-time prophecies were an especially inviting target for all sorts of fabricators. Paradoxically, even ISIS warned its followers that apocalyptic material could be easily abused.[87] In the wars that tore apart the early Muslim community, each side sought to justify its politics by predicting its inevitable victory and the other side's preordained defeat.[88] The early expansion of the Muslim empire was undoubtedly charged by millennial ambitions and apocalyptic rhetoric. The turbulent period of struggle between the two groups that later became known as 'Shiites' and 'Sunnis' brought to the stage a number of apocalyptic arguments that should have supported both adversaries in their dispute.

The justification of worldly ambitions through reference to End-time *aḥādīth* was a strategy adopted by both Umayyāds and their rivals, not only those from Shiite circles. Over the course of time, many prognoses have been fabricated to retrospectively explain the current state of affairs or support the claims of particular players. This is why the current heuristic foundations of modern Muslim apocalyptic authors are, more or less, a product of the early power struggles, where apocalyptic references served as both weapon and battlefield.

A good example of a worldly struggle that was to leave its mark on Islamic apocalypticism is the common identification of the historic Kharijites ('Seceders') as dissenters whose appearance constitutes one of the lesser signs of the Hour (see 'Sunni "Apocalypses Light"' in Chapter 6). In fact, dozens of pages could be filled by descriptions of medieval millennialist manifestations, providing convincing evidence of contradictory Muslim approaches to the End-time agenda. The same official authorities that were suspicious of any anti-regime millennial rhetoric were able to promote other apocalyptic claims in the name of their own masters. As far as the medieval reception of millennialism in Islam is concerned,

> it must be pointed out that in the context of medieval Islam, messianic beliefs belonged primarily not to popular religiosity but to lettered tradition. They were produced, disseminated, written down, and transmitted by the learned elite. In fact, many prophecies complain about the absence of scholars, burning of libraries and books, punishment of scholars, and diminishing knowledge as a portent of declining society. Despite their manifest religious character, messianic beliefs are actually this-worldly and very pragmatic.[89]

The fratricidal wars that fundamentally influenced the collective memory of early Muslims have found their metaphorical reflection in miscellaneous apocalyptic narratives, some of which were favourites in Syria, others in Iraq or Khorasan, and so on. They often contradict each other. Thus, when compared to each other, the current barely clear set of traditions contains narratives originating from often mutually contradictory environments.[90]

Islamic apocalyptic awareness not only reflects inner Muslim struggles but also the wars waged, primarily on the Byzantine border, that were to become an inexhaustible source of inspiration for later authors. As regards the apocalyptic vocabulary of ISIS, the Muslim-Byzantine wars seem to be of utmost importance, a claim which can be substantiated not only by particular *aḥādīth* cited in the magazine *Dabiq* but also by numerous references to the 'apocalyptic topography' of Syria (see 'From the East to Jerusalem' in Chapter 3).

Before we proceed to a review of modern Muslim apocalyptic creativity, the key classical text (whose title repeatedly appears in the following interpretation as an inexhaustible source of inspiration, not just for ISIS propaganda purposes) should be introduced. *Kitāb al-fitan* (*The Book of Tribulations*), considered to be the earliest complete Muslim apocalyptic text to have survived, has considerable value as a primary source that reflects the socio-political conditions in Syria under Abbasid rule. The legacy of its author, Nuᶜaym ibn Ḥammād al-Marwazī (died 843 in jail), vividly illustrates the ambiguity of apocalyptic scholarship in Islam. The vast majority of the supposed Prophet's sayings, recorded by Nuᶜaym, cannot be found in the canonical collections of the Sunna. Currently, Nuᶜaym's book is broadly employed not only by authors of modern apocalyptic best-sellers, but also by jihadists such as Abū Muṣᶜab al-Sūrī.[91] However, this work is often attacked by Muslim scholars as being misleading.[92]

Any account of the medieval Muslim authorities who were also engaged in the elaboration of End-time issues would be enormous and would include some of the most outstanding personalities of all time, such as Muḥyi al-Dīn ibn ᶜArabī, Ibn Khaldūn, al-Qurṭubī and Ibn Kathīr. Clearly, the apocalyptic content, either the subject of scholarly discussion by *ᶜulamāʾ* or misused by ideological adventurers, undisputedly belongs to Islam. However, to properly understand its contemporary manifestations, we must take into consideration various transformations and enrichments that modern Muslim apocalypticism has had to experience.

Notes

1. Yücesoy, *Messianic Beliefs and Imperial Politics in Medieval Islam*, p. 16.
2. See *al-Nabaʾ* 107:8.
3. Cohn, *The Pursuit of the Millennium*, p. 14.
4. Cook, *Contemporary Muslim Apocalyptic Literature*, p. 1.
5. Lange, *Paradise and Hell in Islamic Traditions*, p. 13.
6. Smith and Haddad, *The Islamic Understanding of Death and Resurrection*, p. 100.
7. This applies not only in the case of hell and paradise but also in relation to the 'life in *barzakh*', i.e. the intermezzo of the soul in the grave between death and the Day of Resurrection. For an ISIS interpretation of this issue, see *al-Nabaʾ* 131:9.
8. See Günther, 'Presenting the Glossy Look of Warfare in Cyberspace'.
9. Mirza, '"The Slave Girl Gives Birth to Her Master"', pp. 17–18.
10. Pew Research Center, *The World's Muslims*, pp. 65–6.
11. Nuᶜaym, *The Book of Tribulations*, p. xxxv.
12. Cook, *Studies in Muslim Apocalyptic*, p. 332.
13. See http://www.oxfordlearnersdictionaries.com/definition/english/apocalyptic?q=apocalyptic (last accessed 25 May 2017).

14. Wessinger, *Millennialism, Persecution, and Violence*, p. 6.
15. Cook, *Studies in Muslim Apocalyptic*, p. 36.
16. See Bowie, *The Coming Deliverer*, pp. 1–26.
17. Velji, *An Apocalyptic History*, p. 5.
18. Landes, *Encyclopaedia of Millennialism and Millennial Movements*, p. 187.
19. Wessinger, *Millennialism, Persecution, and Violence*, pp. 8–9.
20. Lincoln, *Discourse and the Construction of Society*, p. 25.
21. For an introduction to Arabic apocalyptic terminology, see, for example, al-Muqaddam, *Fiqh ashrāṭ al-sāᶜa*, pp. 17–21, or al-ᶜArīfī, *Nihāyat al-ᶜālam*, pp. 19–31.
22. See, for example, *al-Nabaᵓ* 107:8; 108:8; 109:8; 110:8; 114:8; 117:8; 120:8–9.
23. Namely the following verses: 7:187 (They ask you about the Hour, 'When will it arrive?' Say, 'My Lord alone has knowledge of it: He alone will reveal when its time will come, a time that is momentous in both the heavens and earth.'), 31:34 (Knowledge of the Hour belongs to God; it is He who sends down the relieving rain and He who knows what is hidden in the womb. No soul knows what it will reap tomorrow, and no soul knows when it will die; it is God who is all knowing and all aware.), and 43:85 (Exalted is He who has control of the heavens and earth and everything between them; He has knowledge of the Hour; you will all be returned to Him).
24. For related Muslim polemics, see Cook, *Contemporary Muslim Apocalyptic Literature*, pp. 84–97. For an illustrative example of the numerological approach in apocalypticism, see ᶜAbd al-Fattāḥ, *Usṭūrat Harmajidūn*, pp. 111–38. For sharp criticism of this method, see al-Muqaddam, *Fiqh ashrāṭ al-sāᶜa*, pp. 208–26.
25. See *al-Nabaᵓ* 110:8.
26. See Hitchcock, *The Apocalypse of Ahmadinejad*, p. 48. For an insightful introduction to Ḥujjatīya, see Amanat, *Apocalyptic Islam*, pp. 222–5.
27. Amanat, *Apocalyptic Islam*, p. 21.
28. Cook, *Studies in Muslim Apocalyptic*, p. 231.
29. Cook, *Contemporary Muslim Apocalyptic Literature*, p. 8.
30. Fromson and Simon, 'ISIS', p. 29.
31. Ibid. p. 29.
32. Abū Mālik, *ᶜAlāmāt al-sāᶜa al-sughrā wa al-kubrā*, p. 8.
33. Cook, *Studies in Muslim Apocalyptic*, pp. 13–14.

34. See Ostřanský, 'The Lesser Signs of the Hour', pp. 1–50.
35. Amanat, *Apocalyptic Islam*, p. 20.
36. Cook, *Studies in Muslim Apocalyptic*, p. 20.
37. Lane, *An Arabic-English Lexicon*, vol. 6, p. 2334.
38. See *al-Naba*ᵓ 130:8.
39. Qurᵓān 2:191.
40. McCants, *The ISIS Apocalypse*, p. 108.
41. For their various historic manifestations, see, for example, al-ᶜArīfī, *Nihāyat al-ᶜālam*, pp. 48–51.
42. *Dabiq* 15:13.
43. For example, Ibn Kathīr's *Kitāb al-fitan wa al-malāḥim*. For an ISIS introduction to this topic, see *al-Naba*ᵓ 109:8.
44. Cook, *Studies in Muslim Apocalyptic*, pp. 22–3.
45. See, for example, *Dabiq* 9:72–3.
46. For a brief outline of Muslim apocalyptic scenarios in English, see McCants, *The ISIS Apocalypse*, pp. 163–71.
47. Cf. *al-Naba*ᵓ 109:8.
48. Cook, *Studies in Muslim Apocalyptic*, p. 253.
49. See al-Shaᶜrāwī, *Ahdāth nihāyat al-ᶜālam*.
50. Cf. al-ᶜArīfī, *Nihāyat al-ᶜālam*, pp. 147–8.
51. For example, Nuᶜaym, *The Book of Tribulations*, p. 12 (no. 54).
52. See, for example, Gorenberg, *The End of Days*.
53. See, for example, Richardson, *The Islamic Antichrist*. The utilisation of the eschatological vocabulary for anti-Islamic objectives seems to be, at least currently, a very productive approach among Islamophobic activists.
54. Filiu, *Apocalypse in Islam*, p. 199.
55. See Smith and Haddad, *The Islamic Understanding of Death and Resurrection*, pp. 67–70.
56. See al-Muqaddam, *Fiqh ashrāṭ al-sāᶜa*, pp. 57–88.
57. Cook, *Jesus' Return in Islam*, p. 180.
58. Cf. Muslim, *Ṣaḥīḥ*, pp. 947–8.
59. Cook, *Jesus' Return in Islam*, p. 181.
60. See, for example, al-ᶜArīfī, *Nihāyat al-ᶜālam*, pp. 52–6.
61. Cf. Muslim, *Ṣaḥīḥ*, pp. 943–6.
62. See, for example, Ayyūb, *al-Masīḥ al-Dajjāl*, pp. 237–48.
63. Cook, *Contemporary Muslim Apocalyptic Literature*, pp. 184–200.

64. Cook, 'Messianism in the Shiite Crescent', p. 95.
65. McCants, *The ISIS Apocalypse*, p. 106.
66. Al-ᶜArīfī, *Nihāyat al-ᶜālam*, pp. 205–6.
67. Landes, *Encyclopedia of Millennialism*, p. 188.
68. See Muslim, *Ṣaḥīḥ*, p. 927.
69. McCants, *The ISIS Apocalypse*, p. 108.
70. Ibid. p. 108.
71. Cook, 'Messianism in the Shiite Crescent', pp. 93–4.
72. For a particular exception, see *Dabiq* 7:66.
73. Filiu, *Apocalypse in Islam*, pp. 197–8.
74. Amanat, *Apocalyptic Islam*, p. 24.
75. Cook, *Studies in Muslim Apocalyptic*, p. 33.
76. Ibid. p. 34.
77. Ibid. p. 92.
78. Ibid. p. 23.
79. Yücesoy, *Messianic Beliefs*, p. 11.
80. Filiu, *Apocalypse in Islam*, pp. 19–20.
81. Cook, *Studies in Muslim Apocalyptic*, p. 15.
82. Sells, *Approaching the Qurʾān*, p. 35.
83. For example, Yücesoy, *Messianic Beliefs*; Velji, *An Apocalyptic History*; Amanat, *Resurrection and Renewal*.
84. For an introduction to Shiite apocalypticism, see especially Amanat, *Apocalyptic Islam* and Sachedina, *Islamic Messianism*. For contemporary Shiite millennialism, see also Filiu, *Apocalypse in Islam*, pp. 141–64, and Cook, 'Messianism in the Shiite Crescent'.
85. Landes, *Encyclopedia of Millennialism*, p. 191.
86. Bashir, *Messianic Hopes and Mystical Visions*, pp. 4–5.
87. See, for example, *al-Nabaʾ* 107:8; 120:8–9; *Dabiq* 11:16, and elsewhere.
88. McCants, *The ISIS Apocalypse*, p. 23.
89. Yücesoy, *Messianic Beliefs*, p. 136.
90. Nuᶜaym, *The Book of Tribulations*, pp. xiv–xxiv. See also Yücesoy, *Messianic Beliefs*, pp. 11–17.
91. Cf. al-Sūrī, *Daᶜwat al-muqāwama al-islāmīya al-ᶜālamīya*, p. 191.
92. See al-Muqaddam, *Fiqh ashrāṭ al-sāᶜa*, pp. 158–62.

2

Muslim Preachers of the Approaching End

If millennial studies has something to offer our current understanding, it is the power of these discourses, the significance of moments when they enter the public sphere with such power, gaining rather than losing momentum when their outrageous, violent hopes become public. Medieval and late antique historians can sail their ships through the iceberg-laden waters of millennial discourse and not know that their ship has sunk. We, today, ignore these phenomena at our own peril.

– Richard Landes[1]

The fifteenth century of Islam was therefore inaugurated by three almost simultaneous shocks: the triumph of the Shiᶜi revolution in Iran, the messianic uprising in Mecca, and the Soviet invasion of Afghanistan. Violence on this scale was enough to rouse the apocalyptic impulse from the lethargic state induced by generations of clerical contempt and, more recently, by the rise of nationalist sentiment; but the impulse did not find expression at once, either in the Sunni world, where for a number of years the Meccan sacrilege silenced millenarian enthusiasm, or in the Shiᶜi world, where the constitutional allegiance to the Hidden Imam in the Islamic Republic of Iran for the most part quieted messianic longings.

– Jean-Pierre Filiu[2]

The main objective of this chapter is to bridge the gap that separates medieval Muslim apocalypticism from the 'End-time agenda' of ISIS. The process could metaphorically be referred to as 'packaging the apocalypse for the mass market' – a designation which is definitely not as much of an exaggeration as it might seem at first glance. Although ISIS propagandists often stress their alleged 'Islamicity', we cannot avoid the exceedingly innovative phenomenon that is modern Muslim apocalyptic creativity, which is actually full of Western borrowings, in order for the ISIS End-time messages to be properly contextualised.

The apocalyptic rhetoric of ISIS should be assessed with a knowledge of the transformations that Muslim approaches to the End times have undergone since the middle of the last century. From this point forwards, the subject – traditionally considered to be 'too academic' or 'remote' and mostly based on stereotypical 'jigsaw puzzles', with the *aḥādīth* related to the individual signs of the Hour – started to be notably enriched by many new elements borrowed from non-Islamic sources, thus becoming extremely attractive.

Certainly, the issue of modernity within Islamic approaches to the apocalypse can easily lead us to paradigmatic considerations about the traditionalism or modernity associated with current Islamist organisations. This point is also of crucial importance for today's polemics about ISIS. Regardless of the cautious and conservative-looking attitudes expressed in the group's propaganda linked to the final-days' agenda, a lot of its favourite tools instead belong to the modern Muslim 'apocalyptic ammunition'. In other words, while the content pretends to be medieval, its utilisation and the ways of argumentation pertain to the age of the Internet.[3]

The staggering speed with which modern Muslim apocalypticism has developed can hardly be overestimated. It is roughly only a decade since the first publication of Jean-Pierre Filiu's book *Apocalypse dans l'islam* and some of his conclusions need to be reconsidered. The chapter 'An Apocalyptic Tale in Search of an Author'[4] starts with the following sentence: 'So far, only a few elements of messianic symbolism seem to have been used – and then only intermittently – as instruments of recruitment to the cause of jihad.' The very fact that the set of apocalyptic motives systematically exploited in propaganda of a jihadist organisation is the subject of the following interpretation serves to illustrate how fast time flies in this 'arena'.

From Dusty Bookshelves to Spiritual Blockbusters

On its road to modernity, the medieval Muslim apocalyptic heritage had to pass through a double sieve: on the one hand, the canons of the medieval exegetes, and on the other, the numerous experiences of millennialist insurrection. An apocalyptic impulse has actually played an important role in many turbulent events throughout Muslim history. Thus, it is no wonder that the prevailing attitudes of both the Sunni and Shiite authorities are to remain suspicious of apocalyptism.

While searching for an appropriate explanation of the undoubted success of modern Muslim apocalypticism, we should definitely avoid two extreme approaches: the degradation of the extensive apocalyptic writings to the role of mere 'folk subculture', and an exaggeration of their real political relevance. Both approaches run the risk of leading us up a blind alley of misunderstanding. Nevertheless, so far, the former type of underestimation has been significantly more widespread compared to the latter temptation to overestimate.

As far as the modern development of Muslim apocalyptic discourse is concerned, we should be aware that the common features connecting both contemporary and medieval apocalyptists in Islam still outnumber those that divide them. Primarily, both apply similar 'building elements' in order to achieve completely different goals. And the profits associated with bestseller sales are just one of them.

Certainly, the methods used to attract the reader are numerous and the attempt to present an apocalyptic narrative that provides a fascinating story with a happy ending, one which makes earthly suffering more bearable, is nothing new. Regardless of their ideological provenance, apocalyptists are usually able to stimulate ambivalence among their readers, since they write not only to console and encourage by the promise of a happy ending but, simultaneously and primarily, to warn and frighten by the inclusion of gloomy outcomes. They have mostly been moralists, accusing their own societies of being thoroughly corrupt and thus heading toward inevitable annihilation.

The mentioned approaches are common to apocalyptic authors throughout history. However, the twentieth century brought about new, and formerly unknown, challenges. The Muslim perception of End-time issues experienced a remarkable transformation in this time, the key milestone being the catastrophic defeat of the Arab armies at the hands of Israel in 1967, followed by the so-called 'Islamic awakening' (*al-ṣaḥwa al-islāmīya*), aptly referred to by the French scholar Gilles Kepel as the 'revenge of God'.[5] One of the most remarkable features of this period was that an increasing number of lay people became involved in various 'Islamic activities', including political activism and charitable works. Neither was apocalyptic speculation exempt from this phenomenon.

A recapitulation of the intricate development of modern Muslim apocalyptic thought and literature lies beyond the scope of this study. What is presented is the minimum information necessary for an understanding of its further interpretation. Essentially, until the second half of the twentieth century, Muslim apocalyptic literature was almost exclusively the domain of traditional *ᶜulamāᵓ*. According to Cook's suggested chronological classification of modern Arab apocalyptic literature, the first group of conservative authors, who mostly emanated from this scholarly milieu, were not writing in order to start a wave of expectation; they were writing in order to dampen down, and hopefully destroy, such speculation that was already present in society. Their real contribution to the apocalyptic agenda was thus 'designed for religious leaders to use like a bucket of cold water on the excited masses'.[6]

To the contrary, the following so-called radical school was to enrich Muslim apocalyptic thinking by incorporating a number of new topics and tendencies. This group, in Cook's words, 'has also assimilated into its scenario anti-Semitic conspiracy theories – which are very popular in many parts of the Middle East – as well as using Christian interpretations of the Bible or playing off of them'.[7] Such radicals were often accused by their conservative competitors of lacking religious education, as well as relying on non-Islamic borrowings. They were blamed for being engaged in peddling misinterpretations and – above all – for focusing too much on responding to the needs of their readers. Whatever the case, radicals succeeded where conservatives had failed. They successfully transformed the acclaimed, even though boring, subject of theological discourse into the content of bestsellers. This new sort of Muslim apocalyptic writing represented an unforgettable innovation in both its form and content, whose essence has been aptly summarised by Richard Landes:

> First, it discarded the conventional mold of Islamic apocalyptic writing, which limited the writer's creativity to the selection and ordering of previous apocalyptic passages (mostly hadiths). Second, far more than earlier literature (but perhaps not earlier preaching), these books and pamphlets elaborated extensively on various apocalyptic themes including detailed accounts of the war between the Dajjal (antichrist) and the Mahdi, of Islam's victories, and even discussion of what would come after Islam's world conquest and what a Muslim millennium would look like.[8]

A reader-friendly synthesis of both approaches, conservative and radical, has been achieved by the establishment of the so-called neo-conservative school, founded as a result of the harsh criticism focused on the non-Islamic innovations promoted by radicals. Its authors 'have abandoned a boring writing style, brought the Islamic sources back into the discourse, and assumed the rest of the radical approach that they could not prove from their own material'.[9]

To understand current Muslim views on End-time matters, it would be helpful to provide a brief historical outline at this point. The revival of interest in the apocalypse from the beginning of the 1970s, the period which saw the rise of the 'revenge of God' movement, was further encouraged by the events of 1979, roughly corresponding to the year 1400 in the Islamic calendar. The Islamic revolution in Iran, the Soviet occupation of Afghanistan and, above all, the dramatic uprising at the Great Mosque in Mecca,[10] were all events that supported an apocalyptic reading of history.

In a simplified way, 1979 can thus be tagged as the first shift in a series of decisive events. From this point forward, apocalyptic literature ceased to be regarded as theoretical yet entertaining speculations, which had no relationship to 'real life'. In those days, a large number of Muslim apocalyptic pamphlets became bestsellers, capable of attracting millions of readers. However, until the beginning of the new millennium, they were still considered to be easily believable fiction, which had no inward impact on the lives of their readers.

The second decisive shift occurred two decades later. The dramatic events following September 11 brought about a completely different perception of the Muslim apocalypse.[11] The geopolitical reading of medieval prophecies has since then become a mainstream activity among a significant section of Muslims, an assertion supported by sociological research.[12] 'The millenarian surge that gathered impetus following the American invasion of Iraq', as Jean-Pierre Filiu has noted, 'is as puzzling as it is incontestable'.[13] The results of such a transformation are still appreciable, not only at bookshop check-outs but, primarily, in the minds of millions of Muslims. It was perhaps only a matter of time before some gifted person, having plenty of imagination and radical views, would recognise the enormous potential of an apocalyptic interpretation of current affairs. The stage was ready for such an interconnection of power, ambition and eschatological motivation.

As ISIS became a new and quite innovative phase of jihadism, the group's propagandists did not hesitate to connect dreams of the caliphate with unceasing references to the millennial dimensions of their struggle for dominance, a task which was facilitated by the End-time preoccupation of their spiritual gurus (see 'The Jihadist Fuse and the Millenial Charge', later this chapter). Moreover, in many countries, above all Egypt and, to a lesser degree, Jordan, that had made peace with Israel, apocalyptic writings served a certain compensatory function.[14]

Just as the first decisive shift endowed modern Muslim apocalyptic literature with popularity and commercial success, the second, following September 11, actually brought about the inner adoption of apocalyptic beliefs by an important section of the Muslim community. However, this was not the case for most religious leaders and world authorities. The invasion of Afghanistan and Iraq by US-led coalition forces, which foreshadowed a period full of turbulence, has now transformed what could be called a lukewarm interest in the apocalypse into a firm conviction. This corresponds with the global religious climate of the post-September 11 world – 'intensely polarized, with growing terrorist attacks, evangelical calls for eliminating the evil of Islamic radicalisms, and fear of nuclear confrontation'.[15]

Apocalypticism has thus finally ceased to be perceived as a remote yet attractive topic and has become an inseparable part of Muslim religiosity. In the words of Richard Landes, 'the public sphere in the Muslim world saw a dramatic rise in discourse that, while not necessarily explicitly eschatological – predicting or dating the end, proclaiming a Mahdi – articulated the most troubling forms of cataclysmic apocalyptic rhetoric and action'.[16]

To fully understand the role of Muslim apocalypticism we must firstly distinguish between the spiritual level of folk religiosity and the institutional level of various organisations, mostly referred to as 'messianic' or 'Mahdist'. In both, the underestimation and overestimation of their influence are equally dangerous. Unlike during the Middle Ages, the current millennial sensitivity of Muslims is, to some extent, measurable. An extensive piece of sociological research, undertaken in 2012 by the Pew Research Center, asked Muslims in twenty-three countries whether they expected the Mahdī to return in their lifetime. Its findings show that

> in most countries surveyed in the Middle East and North Africa, South Asia and Southeast Asia, half or more Muslims believe they will live to see the return of the Mahdi. This expectation is most widespread in Afghanistan (83%), Iraq (72%), Tunisia (67%) and Malaysia (62%). It is least common in Bangladesh (29%) and Indonesia (23%). Outside of these three regions, belief that the return of the Mahdi is imminent is much less prevalent. Across Central Asia, no more than about four-in-ten Muslims surveyed in

> any country think they will live to see the Mahdi return; the exception is Turkey, where about two-thirds (68%) expect to witness his return ... In some countries with sizable Sunni and Shia populations, views on the Mahdi's return differ by sect. In Iraq, for example, Shias are more likely than Sunnis to expect the Mahdi to return in their lifetime, by an 88% to 55% margin ...[17]

While, in the past, Sunni Muslims often denounced a belief in the Mahdī as a doctrinal specific associated with Shiites, the current boom in Sunni apocalypticism has, to the contrary, further nourished an increase in Shiite millennial sensitivity to the degree that today's Iran is 'rife with messianic aspirations; even more, arguably, than at anytime in recent Shiᶜi history'.[18]

The increasing extent of millennial belief corresponds with the growing variety of movements all around the Muslim world that are either slightly influenced or fully driven by the Mahdist ethos. In his book, Timothy Furnish enumerates a long list of allegedly Mahdist organisations or movements (millennial circles from Iran; several groups in Iraq claiming to be preparing the way for the Mahdī;[19] a number of self-styled mahdīs all over the Muslim world, and so on),[20] claiming that Mahdism is 'a very real concern in the majority Sunni branch of Islam'.[21] In some particular cases, for example Ḥamās and Ḥizbullāh, their eschatological rhetoric goes hand in hand with strong anti-Semitism and anti-Zionism, as well as with a justification of violence.[22]

Moreover, the End-time ethos has already affected not only Salafists (see 'The Jihadist Fuse and the Millenial Charge', this chapter), but also their spiritual counterparts from the Sufi environment. The importance of the Muslim apocalyptic discourse in the public sphere has been aptly expressed by Richard Landes: 'Although it has not set the entire population of over a billion Muslims afire, it burns ardently in significant areas, and continues to start new conflagrations, as well as to revive older ones.'[23]

Finally, the third – and so far, the last – decisive shift in End-time beliefs has been caused by the ISIS apocalyptic ethos. The group's propaganda has successfully transformed what was formerly a potentially powerful but, on the part of official structures, quite overlooked agenda into a peculiar part of its 'state ideology' (see 'The Apocalyptic March' in Chapter 4). Yet, we still remain unclear about the central issue, that is, whether the instrumentalisation of the apocalypse by ISIS will reinforce or weaken the attraction of End-time issues among other Muslims.

Modern Muslim Apocalyptic Creativity

Modern Muslim apocalyptic creativity stems from the above-discussed medieval sources. Furthermore, it has been profusely enriched (or distorted, depending on one's point of view) by a colourful set of non-Islamic elements, as well as the delusional imagination of a particular set of authors, who often self-confidently describe their approach as a 'read and supervise' description of the facts.[24] The trajectory of ideas, in this respect, seems crooked and unclear. Furthermore, the approaches adopted by individual authors, due to their generational background and ideological preferences, differ not only in how they have decided to interpret their End-time visions but also in relation to the extent they have been willing to employ foreign innovations in their Last-days 'screenplays'. In accordance with their responses to both of these fundamental questions, they have managed to assemble miscellaneous compositions, basic building blocks of which are the subject of this section.

When speaking about modern Muslim apocalyptic literature in a book on ISIS, we should stress, right at the beginning, that this kind of writing is itself definitely not helpful to the radicals since it mostly promotes a sense of fatalism by depicting preordained events. Regardless of how sophistically fabricated these narratives are, they have the ability to attract the attention of readers, but without ever becoming an incentive to action, since they present the future as a firmly fixed matter. The most useful form of apocalyptic text for radicals, according to David Cook, is one

> in which fighting is portrayed as an open-ended process that will continue until either victory or martyrdom are obtained. Probably

the most useful tradition conveying this message is the following: 'A group (*ta'ifa*) of my community will continue, fighting for the truth, victorious over those who oppose them, until the last of them face the Dajjal . . .' Needless to say, this tradition is featured frequently in jihadist journals from Iraq.[25]

Basically, modern Muslim apocalyptic authors – derisively referred to by their critics as *ᶜābithūn* (frivolous people, transgressors, and so on)[26] – have attempted to support their visionary constructions not only by reference to Islamic texts, but have also drawn on non-Islamic, sometimes even Christian, sources of inspiration. Even if they have not incorporated such segments directly into their narratives, they have used this material in parallel with 'Islamic interpretations'. In this respect, everything that supports the adopted vision is welcome, starting with the Biblical exegesis and including the various hi-tech references to modern mysteries (UFOs and the Bermuda Triangle, for example), occasionally even presenting these as the fulfilment of Muslim prophecies. The non-Islamic segments include material elements (cars, electronic devices), spiritual influences (the anti-Jewish conspiracy) and, predominantly, generally known phenomena (modern means of transportation and communication).

The creativity exhibited by modern apocalyptists has facilitated a revival of interest in a topic, which, until recently, was considered to be 'inedible' by the common reader.

Modern Muslim apocalyptic imagination is not the product of a passive society. On the contrary, related books and brochures seek to address and mobilise all believers, regardless of their education and piety, in order that they might transform themselves before the arrival of the Hour. Apocalyptic authors, many of whom were laymen, definitely cannot be accused of a detachment from reality, since their innovative ways of interpretation have unambiguously proven to be a viable and acceptable way of thinking.

The apocalyptists, whether conservatives or modernists, have gladly seized on any opportunity to moralise. In analysing various referenced examples of moral decay that will be witnessed before the

Hour (sexual transgressions are among the most preferred issues),[27] apocalyptic authors have emphasised that these are not merely portents of the approaching End but they should be, above all, a powerful stimulus for the spiritual improvement of mankind. The apocalypse has been depicted as a challenge to the existing order and, thus, its crucial theme is the need to fight in all conceivable ways, armed or spiritual, against tyrants or one's own vices.

Readers of modern Muslim apocalyptic brochures, so often ridiculed by religious authorities as unworthy of deeper attention, are attracted by dreams of an empire of justice, but are simultaneously frightened by never-ending visions of various enemies. Such literature has the capacity to address the masses, since its effortlessly comprehensible narratives denounce all the well-known ills of society. Apocalyptic belief, furthermore, is able to establish conviction in relation to the meaningfulness of suffering. This point is of crucial importance because misery is projected to exceed all boundaries before the Hour, a time when everything will experience extremes. The accumulation of evil will precede the Islamic happy ending, which remarkably is not as clearly elaborated as the entire process through which it shall be achieved. Simply put, in apocalyptic terms, the journey is definitely more important than the destination.

As we have seen, the role of Muslim apocalyptic literature should neither be underestimated nor overvalued. Although the medieval apocalyptists were 'the historians of the future', their texts never instigated millennialist uprisings, no matter how attractive such an idea might have been.[28] Apocalyptic narratives have more often served to justify and explain existing tensions, an assertion that also applies to modern creativity, since uptil now they have not been the cause of any significant social disturbance.[29]

Within current Islamic discourse, apocalypticism has become a battlefield where modernists, often lacking any religious education, have been able to face up to the Muslim scholars. As regards the actual distribution of apocalyptic writings, there are significant differences between individual Muslim countries. While in Egypt apocalyptic literature has enjoyed great popularity and official authorities have generally not interfered with its publication, the Saudi-Arabian regime continues to carefully regulate such publications.

Nowadays, as already stated, an important section of Muslim society really does believe that they are living in the Last Days. However, nobody is certain as to the future manifestation of such apocalyptic convictions. In fact, we do not even know whether this tide of millennialist sensitivity is just a temporal reaction to the current Middle Eastern chaos or is rather the beginning of a long-term tendency. In any case, the staggering boom in folk apocalyptic brochures seems to be over, at least in the case of Egypt, which is the largest Arab book market.[30]

The process of establishing meaning in relation to modern Muslim apocalypticism would be impossible if we restricted ourselves solely to the religious aspect of this phenomenon. For a better understanding, we also need to consider the marketing context. The flamboyant cover-pages of apocalyptic brochures themselves suggest a radical shift from the style adopted by traditional Islamic treatises. Their appearance reflects the hasty nature of their writing and, in particular, Arab apocalyptic authors rarely care about formal matters at all.[31] Such authors use modern means of mass communication to propagate their message and all their innovations and improvisations actually have a single goal: to interpret the current traumas facing Islam as signs of the coming End.[32] The factual thematic composition of their works clearly reflects such an objective.

Our starting point for a brief survey of non-Islamic elements in modern Muslim apocalyptic writing, which is generally full of anti-American and anti-Semitic rhetoric,[33] focuses on Christian borrowings. Within traditional Muslim discourse, employing Christian sources to support Islamic argumentation is inconceivable since – as the *ᶜulamāᵓ* often emphasise – the revelation of the Qurᵓān has eradicated the relevance of the Biblical message. Muslims have traditionally been discouraged from studying, or even reading, the Bible. Despite this, the utilisation of Biblical motifs in Muslim apocalyptic exegesis can be found in countless examples. In particular, the apocalyptists favour the books of 'Revelation', 'Daniel' and 'Ezekiel'. However,

Christian borrowings have been fully rejected by those apocalyptists who loudly emphasise their 'Islamicity', for example, in the case of ISIS.

The anti-Semitic conspiracy constitutes one of the main sources of enrichment where modern Muslim apocalypse writing has diverged from its medieval patterns. The currently proclaimed hatred of the Jews mainly results from geopolitical and conspiracy sources, whereas the Islamic references (the struggle between the Prophet Muḥammad and the Jews, for example) are of secondary importance. The *Protocols of the Elders of Zion* have found warm acceptance among many Muslim authors of apocalyptic and conspiracy literature[34] who are deeply frustrated about Israel's very existence. Nonetheless, until the end of the last century, the strong anti-Semitic ethos of apocalyptic pamphlets seemed like a foreign import of limited significance. It is useful to note that the merciless anti-Jewish attacks have been further intertwined with other apocalyptic tools, for instance with numerological speculations related to the expected duration of the state of Israel.[35]

At the beginning of the new millennium, as Richard Landes has argued, 'the most delirious and apocalyptic of these memes – blood libels, *Protocols*, child-murder – gained an intensity and originality that both revived indigenous Islamic strains and fused with the worst of European strains'.[36] David Cook, in his attempt to analyse the assimilation of the anti-Semitic conspiracy into the Muslim apocalypse, distinguishes three phases, starting with (1) the takeover of the classic European anti-Semitic conspiracy theory, continuing with (2) the conspiracy theories related to Israel and culminating with (3) the conspiracy resulting from the frustration Muslims feel about their inability to deal with this state.[37]

From such frustration, Muslims have also absorbed a distorted view of the United Nations, which is often perceived as the means by which the Antichrist and Jews are able to exercise their control over the world. Currently, the vast majority of modern Arab Muslim apocalyptists are obsessed with Israel.[38] A convincing interpretation of this fact has been put forward by Landes:

> People can live unhappily but quietly, with disgrace as long as no one reminds them. Most Muslims in most places in the world could ignore their (comparative) failures and live local lives as before. The success of Zionism, however, greatly intensified modernity's humiliation, especially for the Arabs . . . To the articulators of the Islamic apocalyptic anti-modern discourse, Israel's very existence, indeed modernity, threatens the destruction of Islam as a community of belief . . . Only by wiping out this enemy, can Islam survive – in other words, the apocalyptic paranoid position: *exterminate or be exterminated*.[39]

This anti-Semitic ethos is also symptomatic of ISIS apocalypticism, where the supposed unveiling of Jewish plots often mingles with anti-Shiite conspiracy theories (see 'To Rome' in Chapter 4).

The third category of Western inspiration pertains to modern science and technology. The contemporary Muslim apocalypse is hardly imaginable without speculations on how to interpret the mysterious medieval references in relation to modern technological achievements. As regards the ambivalence in the apocalyptists' approaches to the West, although they may hate the West, there is no question that they are impressed with the success of modern technological societies.[40] In any case, references to various hi-tech devices as the fulfilment of prophecies remains one of the most typical properties of apocalyptic creativity.

The rapid development and subsequent sustained popularity of modern Muslim apocalyptic works have also been encouraged by their authors' efforts to associate medieval indications with current events. This process of actualisation constitutes the fourth essential feature that should be mentioned here. This method is definitely not new since analogous examples can be found throughout history. Currently, such an updated reading of classical texts has once more gained great popularity, not only among Muslims. If the previous element is hardly utilisable in ISIS propaganda, the 'apocalyptic reading of current geopolitics' represents one of its most productive features.

From a general perspective, the competitive search for new material among modern Muslim apocalyptic authors reflects not only their fascination with mysteries and hi-tech issues but also their inner conviction that such borrowings do not in any way violate the proclaimed Islamic nature of their publications. Such an approach further reinforces the impact their interpretations have among readers who would otherwise not be interested in religious affairs.

The success of modern Muslim apocalyptic literature can be explained in various ways. First of all, the timeless human love of riddles and enigmas should be emphasised, with the Muslim Endtime prophecies offering a deep well of mysteries. From another point of view, the Last-days narratives have become a compensatory tool, having the ability to heal some of the common frustrations that beset today's Muslims. This point has been elaborated by Muḥammad al-Muqaddam, an Egyptian scholar, who argues that the global maltreatment of Muslims, including Islamophobic attitudes in the West, together with the disintegration of the *umma* and the decline of its scholarship has further strengthened the popularity of apocalyptic speculations.[41] The strong belief that all current miseries are no more than a part of a wider Divine plan which has a happy ending has the power to console millions of Muslims.

The new millennium, however, has introduced a new sort of apocalyptist onto the stage – the jihadist. And the ground-breaking achievements of ISIS are part of this disturbing development.

The Jihadist Fuse and the Millennial Charge?

To understand ISIS ideology without a knowledge of Salafism is not possible.[42] The term Salafism can be confusing since it has a plethora of interpretations.[43] Salafists are usually defined as Muslims who claim to follow *al-salaf al-ṣāliḥ* ('the venerable forefathers') as closely and in as many spheres of life as possible. According to Joas Wagemakers, Salafism can be seen as 'a grounded utopian movement, focusing on the "ideal place" or "utopia" of the first generation of Islam, while simultaneously being grounded in the very real places Salafists live in and the actual people they meet'.[44]

An important feature of Salafi self-presentation is their exclusivity. They often call themselves *al-firqa al-nājīya* ('the saved sect') or *al-ṭāʾifa al-manṣūra* ('the victorious group'),[45] claiming to be the group that has remained steadfast in its quest for a 'pristine' version of Islam to become triumphant.[46] Salafism, to whose classics ISIS overtly claims allegiance,[47] contains a number of manifestations, with Salafi jihadists representing the most extreme.[48]

In the specific case of ISIS – who are wittily described by the *Financial Times* as 'Wahhabis on steroids'[49] – Salafi jihadism was further 'enriched' by an acceptance of takfirism (*takfīr* refers to the act of declaring another Muslim to be a non-believer, *kāfir*), interconnected, moreover, with anti-system approaches, including the group's resistance to traditional Islamic authorities, as well as certain kind of anti-intellectualism.[50]

The specifics of the ISIS worldview are such that Brian Fishman has even suggested labelling it simply as 'Zarqawiism'. As the driving force behind ISIS, he questions whether Zarqawiism can be considered as an ideology, while offering another definition: 'Zarqawiism is a dystopian cultural movement wrapped around a core set of ideological principles.'[51] On its symptomatic features, he has remarked that

> Zarqawiism is perhaps best understood more as a hyper-violent, anti-establishment ethos than a formal ideology, but it is ultimately distinguished by two core ideas: (1) An extremely narrow vision of what it means to be a 'true Muslim,' such that the vast majority of the world's Muslims are considered apostates deserving death . . . (2) A dramatic redistribution of ideological and political authority from a rarified class of religious scholars to frontline jihadis, who by committing to violence for their faith are considered better Muslims.[52]

The main point to be made here is that both takfirism and apocalypticism can complement each other since both are headed in the same direction – to building a bipolar world where everybody is either a devoted follower or a hated enemy. As Salafi jihadists strongly believe, *jihād* may also be launched in the Muslim world against so-called 'apostate leaders' for their alleged unwillingness to apply the *sharīʿa* in its entirety.[53] We should not forget that this type of *jihād* can also be waged by 'apocalyptic means'.

Such Salafi jihadists have taken what they regard as a weak distorted substitute and have replaced it with a more vibrant and coarse form of religion, which they imagine to be a genuine one. Compared to other Muslims, they are considerably less receptive to various innovations. However, while technical achievements that facilitate the dissemination of their message, such as the Internet, have been welcomed, other Western 'novelties' that have an impact on most Muslims (the concept of free elections, for example) have always been viewed with suspicion. And apocalyptic speculations, based on unstable Islamic pillars and significantly influenced by non-Islamic elements, have been regarded by them as being untrustworthy. Salafists have thus long remained immune to apocalyptic temptations.

The title of this section has been borrowed from Jean-Pierre Filiu's book *L'Apocalypse dans l'Islam*, where he summarises the development of modern apocalypticism as follows:

> Up until now, the jihadist fuse has not been brought into contact with an explosive millenarian charge. No inevitability pushes humanity in the direction of catastrophe, even if the popular fascination with disaster may seem somehow to favour a sudden leap into mass horror. And yet, coming after the gold of Euphrates, widely interpreted in the wake of the American invasion of Iraq as a sign of the Hour, a fire of Hijaz may be all that is needed to set in motion a new cycle of eschatological tension, inaugurating an age of widespread fear and expectation that the end of the world is at hand. If an inflammatory and incandescent event of this sort were to occur, the chance that global jihad might undergo an apocalyptic mutation would give grounds for genuine apprehension.[54]

This book, first published in 2008, outlines an eventuality that has in the meantime become, more or less, realised. In recent times, the above-mentioned 'apocalyptic mutation' seems to have become a reality. The substantial penetration of the 'End-time agenda' into the Salafi jihadist environment has been unambiguously confirmed, even by those authors who are otherwise not interested in this aspect of the ISIS phenomenon, for example, Fawaz Gerges.

> The world according to ISIS is frozen in time and space, incorporating the rules and laws of seventh-century Arabia into the twenty-first century. Baghdadi and his associates depict themselves as battling the 'antichrist' and paving the way for the ultimate triumph of the 'Mahdi' and Islam . . . This millenarian thinking is at the heart of ISIS's caliphate ideology and the global jihadist movement in general.[55]

On the other hand, despite the traditional distrust of Salafists with regard to End-time speculations, further cemented by the Saudi experience with Juhaymān al-ᶜUtaybī's spectacular millennial uprising,[56] as David Cook argues, it is not difficult to also understand the reasons why they might be attracted by apocalyptic prophecies: 'Because they constitute a fairly small minority within the overall Muslim community – but define themselves as a fighting vanguard – their fixation upon the future is necessary.'[57] Moreover, Islamists, in general terms, have become accustomed to placing current earthly conflicts and political problems into a broader transcendental context that emphasises the metaphysical clash between good and evil.

As part of his irreconcilable resistance towards the Saudi regime – identified by him as the tyrannical monarchy (*mulk jabrī*) foretold by an apocalyptic *ḥadīth* – al-ᶜUtaybī outlined a millennialist vision of the Prophetic caliphate, which was inspired, arguably, by Ḥamūd al-Tuwayjirī's book entitled *Itḥāf al-jamāᶜa bi-mā jāʾa fī al-fitan wa al-malāḥim wa ashrāṭ al-sāᶜa* (*Donation to the community of what appears in the apocalyptic tribulations, battles and the signs of the Hour*). In his millennialist intoxication, al-ᶜUtaybī interpreted, in his short treatise entitled *al-Khilāfa allatī ᶜalā minhaj al-nubūwa wa al-mulk al-jabrī* (*Caliphate Based on the Methods of Prophethood and Tyrannical Kingship*),[58] various tensions within Saudia Arabian society as portents of the End and finally, in 1978, he even declared his companion Muḥammad al-Qaḥtānī to be the Mahdī.[59] It should be noted that al-ᶜUtaybī's ideas also had an influence on Abū Muḥammad al-Maqdisī (b. 1959),[60] the mentor of al-Zarqāwī.

It is not easy to capture the essence of this Salafi 'apocalyptic changeover' since a preoccupation with End-time issues within a framework of Islamic radicalism is a quite recent phenomenon. Basically, the road to apocalyptic jihadism has gradually been paved by a number of authors,[61] drawing mostly from the inexhaustible sources of strong anti-American rhetoric and various conspiracies, often driven by an irrevocable anti-Jewish ethos, and, above all, from the political unrest following the US-led invasion of Iraq. The latter event totally changed the perception of the apocalypse all over the Muslim world.

The key role in introducing the apocalypse into the Saudi-Arabian environment was played by Shaykh Safar al-Ḥawālī (b. 1950), a major figure within the local Islamist political and religious dissent group known as al-Ṣaḥwa (Awakening). He is closely associated with globalist Islamic radicals and his charisma, erudition and radicalism were to inspire a whole generation of jihadists.

Al-Ḥawālī's influential contribution to the Muslim apocalyptic discourse is incorporated in his hate-filled pamphlet *Yawm al-ghaḍab* (*The Day of Wrath*).[62] In accordance with its name, it furiously attacks so-called Christian Zionism, considered by the author to be the most dangerous of all powers threatening the *umma*. His reckless attacks have also been reflected in the 'End-time backdrop' because, in al-Ḥawālī's opinion, the Hour is near but it will arrive only once the opponents of Islam have disappeared in the battle of Armageddon. With regard to the nature of the 'eschatological ammunition' he uses against the aforementioned archenemies of Muslims, Jean-Pierre Filiu writes:

> Notwithstanding his obligation to cite the Qurʾan and the prophetic traditions, Hawali's primary interest is in turning the Christian apocalypses back against the American partisans of Israel . . . Not content merely to identify the five kingdoms that appeared in a dream to Nebuchadnezzar, Hawali proceeds to denote the signs of the apocalypse, whose key he delivers 'as a gift to the Jews and the Christians': New Jerusalem is Mecca; the Paraclete is the prophet

> Muhammad . . .; the messiah is Jesus . . .; the Antichrist is the false messiah; the Beast is Zionism . . .; the false prophets are Paul and his popes; the 'small horn, or the abomination of desolation, is the state of Israel'; the New Babylon is Western culture in general, and American culture in particular; and finally, the new Roman Empire corresponds to the United States.[63]

The apocalyptic path so skilfully articulated by Sheikh al-Ḥawālī did not remain without challenge for long. For Salafis, a hitherto unattractive agenda thus began to attract more and more attention. A number of possible reasons for such a sudden revival have been suggested by Richard Landes:

> The Muslim apocalyptic millennial response to modernity is not the only response in the Arab world. But it is at once an exciting, comprehensive, and effective response . . . certainly the most exciting and comprehensive, and possibly the most effective response to the four humiliations of modernity – Western superiority, Israel's existence, women's liberation, and globalization.[64]

From a Salafist perspective, the apocalypse has simply ceased to be a taboo subject, a fact which is exemplified by reference to the texts of a number of specific authors, including one of the most popular preachers, Muḥammad al-ᶜArīfī. He attempted to weaken the dangerous millennialist tendencies encouraged by al-ᶜUtaybī's explosive ideas by providing an 'academic' explication of the 'End-time agenda'. His book, based on the *aḥādīth* and meeting the strict standards established by Nāṣir al-Dīn al-Albānī, contains, in addition to a standard enumeration and interpretation of the apocalyptic signs, a set of instructions on how to properly deal with this delicate material in accordance with Islamic law (*fiqh*).[65] Essentially, al-ᶜArīfī's approach has a lot in common with the otherwise completely different interpretation of Islam provided by Sheikh al-Shaᶜrāwī, since both of them were seeking to bring scholarly calm to a potentially combustible situation.

Of course, apocalyptic vocabulary does not necessarily determine apocalyptic content, a truism that equally applies to the process referred to as the 'satanization of enemies', a concept examined in detail by Mark Juergensmeyer.[66] It would be misguided to jump to such a simplistic conclusion and attribute all anti-Crusader rhetoric, so characteristic of Muslim radicals, to a 'clash of civilizations' agenda in its genuinely millennial meaning. The strong anti-Western ethos pronounced by Bin Lādin, for instance, did not lead him automatically into adopting an apocalyptic worldview. It is certainly a seductive idea, but there is no evidence for such a claim. Of the plethora of seized al-Qāᶜida documents, only one letter ventures onto millennial terrain.[67]

But that is not to say that al-Qāᶜida's leaders were not interested in the apocalypse at all. As Aaron Zelin succinctly notes, 'obviously they believed it, but they just weren't trying to pursue it, so to speak'.[68] Yet, this situation fundamentally changed around the turn of the millennium and especially after September 11, when the above-mentioned second decisive shift totally transformed the view of Muslims to a substantially apocalyptic perspective. Together with this Islamic paradigm shift, apocalyptic global jihad also emerged quite suddenly from the outermost margins and found itself at the centre of both Arab and Muslim thinking.[69] The newly found self-confidence of jihadists, further reinforced by their command of new technologies, has manifested itself through various announcements about their intentions to dominate the world.[70]

The language and form of these jihadist proclamations, however, diverge considerably from traditional patterns. The cardinal constitutive elements of this newly transformed apocalyptic discourse have been summarised by Richard Landes:

> Conspirational genocidal anti-Semitism . . .; Suicide terrorism . . .; Global jihad . . .; Culture of death: The apocalyptic trope so characteristic of active cataclysmic scenarios, the *embrace of death and killing as salvific*, has a long history in Islam as well as a prominent role in the apocalyptic revival that first breaks the surface in 1979.[71]

The 'spiritual cocktail' depicted above should also include another distinctive ingredient – violence. The very fact that the Muslim

End-time narratives are full of blood is undeniable, but what underpins the possible link between 'lived apocalypticism' and the extreme violence exercised by its followers is a complex issue that lies beyond the scope of this study.[72]

In any case, ISIS not only projects a message grounded in apocalypticism but uses its millennialist ethos as a justification for cruelty. Not only does the claim that ISIS is fulfilling prophecy serve to legitimise the group's authority, but the idea that a terrible reckoning is coming inspires loyalty among its supporters, infusing their communications with a sense of urgency that facilitates the transgression of all boundaries, including violence.[73] Furthermore, recurrent threat, as Abdel Bari Atwan aptly reminds us, supports 'a mindset where the desire for martyrdom is normalised and death is sought and celebrated'.[74]

While speaking about violence, the ruthless 'othering' of Muslims[75] who do not accept the ISIS interpretation of Islam can also lead to the justification of any violent measures against 'others' (see 'Symbolism and Imagery of the Apocalyse' in Chapter 3). From the group's perspective, most Muslims are not seen as 'brothers in faith' but rather as 'legitimate targets'. Faced with the impending final apocalyptic struggle, the division between sinners and the saved becomes an all-encompassing concern. A perfect example would be the ISIS propaganda article 'The Extinction of Grayzone'[76] (see 'From Dābiq' in Chapter 4), which points to such an apocalyptic bipolarity, taken to its extreme. Put simply, there is no in-between.

Apocalyptic Messengers and Forerunners

Once the door into the apocalyptic sphere had been slightly opened, it did not take long for this topic to thrill Muslim radicals and militants all over the world.[77] In fact, as late as the end of 2001, major radical Muslim thinkers such as Abū Muṣᶜab al-Sūrī were still busy ridiculing the use of apocalyptic prophecies at a popular level. Even now, many leaders of global jihadism have chosen not to employ clear-cut apocalyptic visions, probably fearing their dangerously divisive nature.[78]

Roughly a decade later, the chaos unleashed by the Arab Spring and the subsequent violence has prompted many Arab Muslims to wonder whether the End of the world was indeed nigh.[79] Even the Arab Spring itself was sometimes seen through an apocalyptic lens.[80] Furthermore, al-Qāᶜida, previously so cautious about millennialism, has undergone a certain 'apocalyptic mutation'. Apocalypticism, from a jihadist perspective, is still far removed from the systematic drafting of treatises. Rather, it represents a not very well organised set of quotations from the End-time *aḥādīth*, various millennial comments devoted to the current state of the *umma*, fragmentary remarks related to the expected social and political development, scattered references to an 'apocalyptic reading' of particular Middle-Eastern problems and, above all, the pervasive ethos of a belief that current misery is no more than a part of a far-reaching plan which will have a happy ending. However, the apocalyptic speeches about the struggle between good and evil (or belief and disbelief) do not in themselves necessarily prove their protagonists' apocalyptic beliefs – this point should be emphasised again and again.

The specific examples of the two Abū Muṣᶜabs (al-Sūrī and al-Zarqāwī), introduced below as key representatives of two totally different and yet complementary ways of thinking, convincingly illustrate this fundamental transition within the Muslim perception of End-time issues. Both of them are actually central figures in the continuing development of the jihadist apocalypse, while the genuine relationship between them has been aptly expressed by the title of David Cook's study *Abu Musᶜab al-Suri and Abu Musᶜab al-Zarqawi: The Apocalyptic Theorist and the Apocalyptic Practitioner*.[81]

As will become increasingly clear, the key to understanding the ways in which ISIS apocalyptic rhetoric has been deployed rests on the discussion of how to effectively control the passionate millennial ethos resulting from any End-time discourse. In other words, how – if at all – is it possible to systematically exploit the apocalyptic agenda from a medium-term or long-term perspective in order to increase the appeal of an organisation (movement, sect) and to be able, at the same time, to suppress its unwanted 'millennial by-products'?

This is by no means a new question. An analogous challenge has occasionally emerged throughout the history of the Muslims, with the beginnings of the Safavid Dynasty and the early Fatimid Empire being just two better-known examples. As well as modern day ISIS, a number of medieval actors attempted to solve the same dilemma: how to harness the utopian dimension of apocalypticism but at the same time distance oneself from the imminence of its realisation.[82] Simply stated, ISIS, in this respect, is not alone.

> ISIS most clearly resembles the Fatimid precursor in the conspicuous conjunction of two elements in its rhetoric and propaganda: an immanent or already realized millenarianism and an unambivalent embrace of violence against other Muslims . . . As with the militant Shiᶜi groups of early and medieval Islam, so too with ISIS: notions of a saved minority and a sinning majority; an absolute distinction between the upright and the errant, the damned and the saved, with no room for 'grayzone' in between; and an imminent judgment that will destroy the moderates and their false leaders, ushering in a new era – all of these themes, alongside an embrace of truly spectacular violence, the fostering of a state of ultrafitnah, a war of all against all in the Muslim community – all of these serve to support the creation of a new state, grounded in arguments based on the traditional sources of Qurʾān and *ḥadīth* read through a conspicuously sectarian lens, in the service of a new, militant, perfectionist order that eagerly anticipates the coming of the apocalypse.[83]

In the ISIS context, the decisive shift from the stress being placed on the imminent coming of the Mahdī, supported by the group's former chief ideologist Abū Ayyūb al-Miṣrī, towards the 'tamed apocalypse' of the official group's propaganda since 2014 will be discussed later (see 'The Apocalyptic March' in Chapter 4). In this section, the spiritual foundations of the later 'apocalyptic edifice' contained in the works of both Abū Muṣᶜabs will be introduced. Accurately speaking, they are inspirers rather than ideologists in the true sense of the word. For this reason, the broader title of 'messengers and forerunners', paving the road to the proto-state of ISIS, has been deliberately used.

Before we discuss the Abū Muṣᶜabs, one additional name in particular should be introduced in order to act as a complementary factor – Abū Bakr al-Nājī, an Islamist strategist whose real identity is the subject of dispute.[84] Clearly, al-Nājī is not one of those Muslim authors enamoured of End-time visions; however, his teaching in practice leads, in a sense, to 'apocalypse applied'. In his extremely influential treatise *Idārat al-tawaḥḥush: Akhṭar marḥala satamurru bi-hā al-umma* (*The Management of Savagery: The Most Critical Stage through Which the Umma Will Pass*),[85] al-Nājī's chief preoccupation is with the 'near enemy', that is, secular, and thus supposedly renegade, Muslim rulers.[86] This fits perfectly within the Muslim apocalyptic context, since the fighting between the righteous Muslim vanguard and those Muslims who have been 'led astray' constitutes a basic element of any End-time scenario in Islam.

His significant manual, also containing a set of recommendations on how to improve the media image of jihadists, had a decisive impact on ISIS propaganda,[87] which is actually another reason why his name appears in this section. In addition to narratives about their invincibility and intransigence, jihadists were advised to present themselves as a source of mercy and freedom. In fact, al-Nājī's strategic advice, as well as the specific stress he placed on the polarisation of society,[88] resonate perfectly with the black-and-white contours of the ISIS message, where no degree of grey is possible. However, his core legacy that will be repeatedly discussed below is that total polarising society through brutal violence is actually valuable to mobilise a reticent Muslim population.[89]

The 'apocalyptic theorist' Abū Muṣᶜab al-Sūrī was born in Syria in 1958 as Muṣṭafā Sitt Mariam Naṣṣār.[90] At a very young age, he joined the Muslim Brotherhood and, after the Ḥamā massacre in 1982, he moved to France and Spain, where he married and acquired Spanish citizenship. In 1987 he joined the Arab *mujāhidīn* in Afghanistan, adopting a *nom de guerre* which referenced the emissary of Prophet Muḥammad, Muṣᶜab ibn ᶜUmayr.[91] In Afghanistan, where he founded the al-Ghurabāᵓ training camp, he became a severe critic of both Usāma bin Lādin and Ayman al-Zawāhirī. The collapse of the Taliban in 2001 forced him into a nomadic life in Iraq, Iran and Pakistan, the latter being the place of his arrest in 2005.

The life and works of al-Sūrī have been examined by Brynjar Lia in his meticulously researched biography *Architect of Global Jihad: The Life of Al Qaeda Strategist Abu Musᶜab al-Suri*. However, the apocalyptic dimension of his legacy has largely remained unexplored. Starting with his appearance, this man is simply the antithesis of the common stereotype of a fanatical and backward Islamic terrorist – and the same applies to his thinking, which differs considerably from the common jihadist pattern. He has defined the goal of jihadists as liberating the Muslim world from foreign domination or domestic non-Islamic governments.

> During his twenty-five-year career as a global jihadi militant, al-Suri has used his training as an historian to collect, record, summarize and analyse his jihadi experiences. In doing so, he discarded traditional jihadi rhetoric about God's promised victory in favour of brutal honesty, putting hard-nosed realism before religious wish-fulfilment and pragmatic long-term strategies before utopianism.[92]

Not long before he was arrested, al-Sūrī composed a massive two-volume, 1,600-page, compendium entitled *Daᶜwat al-muqāwama al-islāmīya al-ᶜālamīya* (*The Call to Global Islamic Resistance*),[93] which can be regarded as a jihadist encyclopaedia. It has no equivalent among the writings of Muslim militants, including references to End-time questions. In an attempt to grasp the author's apocalyptic message, Jean-Pierre Filiu has remarked: 'In his increasingly frantic attempt to formulate a message that would appeal to the greatest possible number of Muslim believers, Abu Musab al-Suri wound up succumbing to millenarian temptation – and plunging into the apocalyptic abyss.'[94] *The Call* is, in its entirety, imbedded with an apocalyptic ethos, with the portents of the Hour addressed as a separate subject in the final chapter, *Jawla maᶜa mukhtārāt min al-aḥādīth al-malāḥim wa al-fitan wa aḥdāth ākhir al-zamān wa ashrāṭ al-sāᶜa* (*The Excursion with Excerpts from the Traditions about Fierce Battles, Tribulations, Events of the End Time and Portents of the Hour*).[95]

The complete work begins with a broader, apocalyptically laden, sketch of the current joyless state of Muslim countries, and contains an analysis of various forms of decline, either in religious or political terms, suitably preceded by considerations devoted to the phenomenon of the 'strangers' (*ghurabāʾ*),[96] whose End-time connotations are undeniable (see 'From Dābiq' in Chapter 4). Thus, the very beginning of *The Call* noticeably corresponds with its very end (for illustrative excerpts from both sections, see Appendix 3). In his compilation of apocalyptic *aḥādīth*, including not only the 'sound' traditions but also the 'weak' ones, al-Sūrī decided to exclude those heralding events that occurred between the death of the Prophet and the present time, thus concentrating on events that have yet to take place.[97]

The first explicitly apocalyptic issue discussed by al-Sūrī is the general decline that will take place at the End of time. He immediately follows this with a chapter on the decline of scholars before the Hour, seeking to address 'the loneliness of the righteous at the End of time'.[98] Only at this point does he begin to enumerate the expected signs of the Hour, starting with 'the discovery in the bed of the Euphrates of a mountain of gold over which people will fight'[99] (see 'They Plot but Allah Also Plots' in Chapter 5). It is no wonder that this apocalyptic prophecy has become a favourite topic among both ISIS supporters and their opponents because it can be actually put into any apocalyptic screenplay, referring to the increase in violence prior the End, thus reflecting a general tendency of Last-day dynamics.

Of the eight categories into which al-Sūrī divides his apocalyptic material, all can be found, either overtly or covertly, in ISIS End-time propaganda: (1) the corrupt circumstances associated with the Final days and the suffering that will be experienced by believers; (2) the decline of the *ʿulamāʾ* before the End; (3) the loneliness of the righteous before the Hour; (4) the signs of the Hour; (5) the Mahdī and his signs, the black banners, al-Sufyānī and al-Qaḥṭānī; (6) wars with Byzantines; (7) the appearance of the Antichrist and the descent of Jesus; and finally (8) the appearance of Gog and Magog. Some of these chapters are more developed and significant, while others remain rather marginal. The corruption of the *ʿulamāʾ*, seen as being subservient to corrupt rulers, clearly pertains to major issues addressed by Salafi jihadists in particular. In addition, the narratives relating to the wars with Byzantines are often utilised as a simile for the current clashes 'between the East and the West'.

The chosen apocalyptic *aḥādīth* are mostly devoted to the final struggles that will foreshadow the coming of the Mahdī. The End-time motifs explored by al-Sūrī, which mostly rely on the authority of Nuᶜaym ibn Ḥammād,[100] encompass all the main episodes and actors: the Byzantines, who are identified as the Western powers, appear in a number of heroic narratives about 'the greatest of all battles' (*al-malḥama al-kubrā*), as well as Jesus and the Antichrist, whose struggle also includes the infamous homicidal *ḥadīth* about trees and stones denouncing the Jews who are hiding behind them.[101] The more or less traditional apocalyptic combat fresco is located in Palestine, culminating with the section that focuses on the Mahdī and his two forerunners, al-Sufyānī[102] and al-Qaḥtānī,[103] as well as the descent of Jesus and his battle with the Antichrist. Concluding remarks on Gog and Magog are also presented.[104]

During his turbulent career, al-Sūrī underwent several changes of attitude towards the apocalypse. At the time of writing his *Daᶜwa*, he neither de-emphasised nor overemphasised the role of the apocalyptic prophecies. According to David Cook, it is clear that 'he actually believes them, and that more than most Salafis he was willing to accord importance even to the comparatively weak traditions with the argument that they give hope to the Muslims'.[105] It is likely that al-Sūrī, being aware of the increasing acceptance of millennial beliefs among Muslims, included such an extensive discourse on End-time matters in part to increase his book's appeal. In any case, his attempt to compile an apocalyptic overview is not particularly novel. Al-Sūrī quite mechanically adds apocalyptic brick to brick in order to cover a subject about whose relevance he was strongly convinced, while totally refraining (for him, very uncharacteristically) from reflecting his own opinions.

The term 'architect', as Brynjar Lia has noted, 'is an appropriate one for al-Suri. Through his writings he has designed a comprehensive framework for future jihad.'[106] On this point, he has succeeded. As far as his 'End-time seedlings' are concerned, Filiu's evaluation of the possible impact of al-Sūrī's apocalypticism a decade later indeed proves to be prescient: 'Whatever may have become of Abu Musab al-Suri, his belated embrace of apocalyptic prophecy can be expected to shape the course of terrorism in unforeseeable ways.'[107]

The second Abū Muṣᶜab, al-Zarqāwī, born in 1966 as Aḥmad Faḍīl al-Nazzāl al-Khalayla, was a prominent Jordanian terrorist, who was responsible for a number of atrocities, including beheadings, and this is why he became known as the 'sheikh of the slaughterers'. In fact, the extremely violent and ruthless military approach espoused by al-Zarqāwī in Iraq marks a turning point in the history of global jihad.[108] Despite the fact that he was killed in 2006, al-Zarqāwī is generally considered to be the 'spiritual father' of ISIS and, thus, the impact of his thought and practice on the group's later development can hardly be overestimated. His life has been examined in a great number of books and chapters,[109] so in the following section only the points relevant to our apocalyptic focus are discussed.

Basically, al-Zarqāwī represented the antithesis of Usāma bin Lādin in that their origins, careers, education and worldviews were totally different.[110] Their mutual relations were also rather problematic[111] – which also applies to the preoccupation with the End time, since we have no knowledge of Bin Lādin's closer interest in these matters.[112] Other jihadist leaders were also largely reluctant to cite apocalyptic prophecies.[113] Their occasional usage of 'anti-Crusader vocabulary' was in keeping with the common jihadist rhetoric used against the West and had, unlike in the case of al-Zarqāwī, no obvious millennial overtones. Such a discourse was usually aimed at the corrupt Muslim rulers and religious leadership, without precisely stating 'who their messianic candidate is or how specifically such a candidate will bring this transformation about'.[114]

Neither was the nature of al-Zarqāwī's affection for the apocalypse (as well as its very accuracy) unambiguous. What is certain is the fact that his violent sectarianism aligned conceptually with al-Nājī's *The Management of Savagery*, but it was far from universally accepted among jihadists.[115] According to Brian Fishman, 'combining the religious absolutism of Abu Muhammad al-Maqdisi with the raw violence of Abu Abdallah al-Muhajir and the street-savvy anti-elitism of Zarqawi himself, Zarqawism is insular, irrevocably violent, and deeply resilient. Zarqawism is revolutionary, but it is not new.'[116]

In fact, the potential for locating al-Zarqāwī's genocidal anti-Shia ideology into an apocalyptic framework (see, for instance, the anti-Shiite attacks published by the *Dabiq* magazine)[117] does not question its very personal sources: his inherent hatred combined with and amplified by Iraqi geopolitics. In Fawaz Gerges' words, al-Zarqāwī 'was a sectarian psychopath who harboured a genocidal worldview against the Shias' and, as such, he 'belonged to a new wave of Salafi-jihadists who are obsessed with identity policy and the struggle to purify Islam and Islamic lands of apostasy. The Shias top their list of real and imagined enemies.'[118]

Concerning his long-term vision, from the very beginning al-Zarqāwī's strategic goal was to trigger a total Sunni-Shiite war and to mobilise and co-opt Sunni opinion.[119] So, al-Zarqāwī's warlike dreams about the extermination of Shiites – retrospectively associated in his speech with Ibn al-ᶜAlqamī, a perfidious Shiite vizier supposedly responsible for the Mongol conquest of Baghdad in 1258[120] – could easily be utilised in a millennial way. At the same time, it is extremely unlikely that his sectarianism had a real apocalyptic motivational impact.

Although at the time of writing his 'selected speeches' the Americans were an occupying power in Iraq, al-Zarqāwī saw the Shiites as the greater threat. As Cole Bunzel has correctly summarised, while 'the Crusader forces will disappear from sight tomorrow or the day after', the Shiites will remain 'the proximate, dangerous enemy of the Sunnis. The danger from the Shiᶜa . . . is greater and their damage worse and more destructive to the Islamic nation than the Americans.' The supposed Shiite historical hatred against Sunnis cannot be overcome with goodwill, according to al-Zarqāwī. The only solution is a battlefield victory.[121]

Besides the Shiites, al-Zarqāwī's biographers often recall his other obsession: the glorious career of Nūr al-Dīn Zengī, a twelfth-century Syrian ruler based in Mosul and famous for his ruthlessness in turning back the Crusaders.[122] In this respect, al-Zarqāwī became increasingly convinced of the key role that the region of Iraq would play in future events. According to William McCants,

> there have recently been found writings from Al-Qaeda members, including Sayf al-Adl, discussing Zarqawi's appeal for Iraq and how it came about In one letter, Sayf al-Adl mentions that Zarqawi's plan for the future Islamic world may have developed from his sudden interest in the medieval Caliph [sic!] Nur al-Din Zengi. Sayf writes, '[Zarqawi] was always asking for any book about Nur al-Din . . . I believe that what he read about Nur al-Din and his launch from Mosul in Iraq played a big role in influencing . . . his [own] decision to go to Iraq after the fall of the Islamic emirate in Afghanistan.'[123]

Whatever, there is no doubt that al-Zarqāwī's statements were suffused with apocalyptic rhetoric.[124] An example can be found in his letter to the *mujāhidīn* inside al-Fallūja.[125] He was even dreaming about 'the return of the caliphate on earth'.[126] While there is no proof that he adopted apocalyptic views from his former mentor, Abū Muḥammad al-Maqdīsī, while in jail,[127] the time al-Zarqāwī spent living in the midst of a multitude of other jihadists was undoubtedly a transformative time for him. What appears to be certain is that al-Zarqāwī was influenced by the belief that Iraq would play a decisive role in a new campaign against the present-day crusaders and that such a belief was the real motivation behind his strategy.

His voluminous collection of speeches, hardly to be expected of a man often regarded as an uneducated fanatic, clearly reflects such a conviction. His writings clearly reveal that, more than any other contemporary jihadist leader, he made use of apocalyptic imagery and, essentially, tried to create an apocalyptic scenario in Iraq.[128] Furthermore, in his 'Arabs versus Persians' motifs, he benefited from the residuum of official anti-Iranian propaganda formerly developed under Ṣaḍḍām Ḥusayn's regime.

Regarding the spectrum of his apocalyptic rhetoric, according to

David Cook, al-Zarqāwī used three main paradigms in order to communicate his struggle: (1) positioning himself in an apocalyptic struggle against the Persians or Shiites (reminiscent of the initial conflict between Muslim Arabs and Zoroastrian Persians), (2) referencing the historical situation of the conflict between the Byzantines and the Muslims (reflected in the A^{c}māq apocalyptic cycle) as a parallel to current clashes (the Byzantines are mainly identified with the United States), and (3) positioning himself as a type of the Prophet Muḥammad in his battles, citing all of the major battles as exemplars of what he is accomplishing in Iraq.[129]

The best-known of al-Zarqāwī's apocalyptic words, stirring up the millennial sensitivities of Muslims all around the world, have become a motto of the magazine *Dabiq*. The sinister remark has, in fact, foreshadowed rhetoric which its author had not anticipated: 'The spark has been lit here in Iraq, and its heat will continue to intensify – by Allah's permission – until it burns the crusader armies in Dābiq.' This famous statement (in the original Arabic *Wa hā hīya al-sharāra qad inqadaḥat fī al-^{c}Irāq wa sayata^{c}āẓamu uwārīhā – bi-dhni-llāh – ḥattā tuḥriqu juyūsh al-ṣalīb fī Dābiq*) can be found in his speech entitled 'Ayna ahl al-murū$^{\circ}$āt?' ('Where are the people of knightly virtue?').[130] To illustrate al-Zarqāwī's way of expression, a brief translation from the corresponding passage has been included in Appendix 3.

For a few short years Iraq was on the verge of the very outcome that al-Zarqāwī had predicted – that is, total war between the Sunnis and Shiites. This point, together with the presence of the American forces in Iraq, may have provided suitable ground for initial apocalyptic speculations to sprout. Although al-Zarqāwī's earlier statements were specifically focused on jihad, he later began to rely more and more upon apocalyptic rhetoric, especially during the double siege of Falluja in 2004.

Perhaps it is the case that al-Zarqāwī was able, at that time, to foresee a civil war spreading outside Iraq and gradually engulfing the entire Middle East. In any case, his immense ambitions manifest themselves in many of the passages from his collected speeches, for example in the address eloquently entitled 'Riyāḥ al-naṣr' ('Winds of Triumph'): 'We wage jihad here while our eyes are on Jerusalem, and we fight here while our goal is Rome, thinking good of Allah, that He may make us the keys of the prophetic, good news and the divine decrees.'[131]

The main point to be made here is that until the beginning of the Iraq war, apocalypticism was rather an unpopular topic among the vast majority of modern-day Sunnis, who looked down on the Shiites precisely because they were so obsessed with the Mahdī's return.[132] During this period, apocalyptic beliefs were by no means mainstream and, therefore, the End-time preoccupation of both Abū Muṣᶜabs was actually, at least in al-Qāᶜida circles, an exception.

In his concluding evaluation, David Cook has characterised al-Zarqāwī as 'an apocalyptic fighter who sought to take the most violent apocalyptic-jihad traditions and turn them into reality in Iraq', whose 'language is suffused with both Qurᵓanic and *hadith* citation that are apocalyptic in tone and content'.[133] Moreover, he supplied 'the framework for a landscape of warfare enabling him to portray the conflict as an absolute life or death scenario'.[134]

Despite the obvious differences between al-Zarqāwī and al-Sūrī, both undoubtedly shared something important – a conviction that jihadists should reorient their fight toward the Fertile Crescent, which is where many prophecies locate the final battles.[135] Both of them, according to Cook, 'place themselves very carefully within the flow of Muslim history, and see apocalyptic predictions as the logical outcome of that history, and furthermore one that mandates victory.'[136] Finally, both of them also avoided the issue of the Mahdī and did not attempt to date the End. Their focus was on 'the close connections between apocalyptic predictions and jihad and benefit from the additional authority those traditions grant them'.[137]

Regardless of the persistent ambiguities relating to al-Zarqāwī's thought, there is clear evidence of an early apocalyptic ethos that existed and motivated the trajectory of the precursors of ISIS (i.e. AQI and ISI). His transformation of the Iraq war into an apocalyptic Internet-based spectacle has become paradigmatic.[138] The apocalypticism of ISIS thus has its own 'spiritual genealogy'.

Notes

1. Landes, 'Enraged Millennialism', p. 466. [My thanks to the author for supplying me with this study.]
2. Filiu, *Apocalypse in Islam*, p. 79.
3. See Atwan, *Islamic State*, pp. 9–25.
4. Filiu, *Apocalypse in Islam*, pp. 192–3.
5. See the very title of his famous monograph: Kepel, *The Revenge of God: The Resurgence of Islam, Christianity, and Judaism in the Modern World.*
6. Cook, *Contemporary Muslim Apocalyptic Literature*, p. 15.
7. Ibid. p. 15.
8. Landes, 'Enraged Millennialism', p. 421.
9. Cook, *Contemporary Muslim Apocalyptic Literature*, p. 18.
10. For the explicit apocalyptic legacy of its leader, see Rifᶜat, *Rasāʾil Juhaymān al-ᶜUtaybī*, pp. 183–223.
11. See Landes, 'Enraged Millennialism', pp. 445–66.
12. See Pew Research Center, *The World's Muslims.*
13. Filiu, *Apocalypse in Islam*, p. 139.
14. Ibid. pp. 102–3.
15. Amanat, *Apocalyptic Islam*, p. 19.
16. Landes, 'Enraged Millennialism', p. 461.
17. Pew Research Center, *The World's Muslims*, pp. 65–6.
18. Amanat, *Apocalyptic Islam*, p. 221.
19. For a nuanced view on Shiite millennialism in Iraq, see Cook, 'Messianism in the Shiite Crescent', pp. 97–9. Cf. Cook, 'Iraq as the Focus for Apocalyptic Scenarios'.
20. Furnish, *Ten Years' Captivation with the Mahdi's Camps*, pp. 210–12.
21. Ibid. p. 210.
22. For the specific case of Ḥamās, see Juergensmeyer, *Terror in the Mind of God*, pp. 69–78.
23. Landes, 'Enraged Millennialism', p. 465.
24. Al-Muqaddam, *Fiqh ashrāṭ al-sāᶜa*, p. 81.
25. Cook, 'Iraq as the Focus for Apocalyptic Scenarios'.
26. See, for example, al-Muqaddam, *Fiqh ashrāṭ al-sāᶜa*, p. 47.
27. See Kabbani, *The Approach of Armageddon?*, pp. 123–9.
28. Cook, *Studies in Muslim Apocalyptic*, p. 325.

29. Filiu, *Apocalypse in Islam*, p. 193.
30. Based on the author's personal observations during the last of his numerous stays in Egypt in March 2018.
31. Cook, *Contemporary Muslim Apocalyptic Literature*, p. 4.
32. Landes, 'Enraged Millennialism', p. 422.
33. Solberg, *The Mahdi Wears Armani*, p. 168. For broader and more inspirational considerations about 'America as enemy', see Juergensmeyer, *Terror in the Mind of God*, pp. 178–82.
34. See, for example, ᶜAbd al-Ḥakīm, *Laᶜbatu al-mutanawwirīn*, pp. 43–9.
35. See ᶜAbd al-Fattāḥ, *Usṭūrat Harmajidūn*, pp. 109–38.
36. Landes, 'Enraged Millennialism', p. 462. See also Landes, 'Jihad, Apocalypse, and Anti-Semitism.'
37. See Cook, *Contemporary Muslim Apocalyptic Literature*, pp. 18–35.
38. Ibid. p. 21.
39. Landes, 'Enraged Millennialism', pp. 437–9.
40. Cook, *Contemporary Muslim Apocalyptic Literature*, p. 71.
41. Al-Muqaddam, *Fiqh ashrāṭ al-sāᶜa*, pp. 47–51.
42. For an excellent introduction to this subject, see Wagemakers, *Salafism in Jordan*, pp. 27–59.
43. Beránek and Ťupek, *The Temptation of Graves in Salafi Islam*, p. 8.
44. Wagemakers, *Salafism in Jordan*, p. 28.
45. For both notions, see Qindīl and ᶜAbd al-Rabbihi, *al-Fikr al-islāmī al-jihādī al-muᶜāṣir*, pp. 362 and 364.
46. Wagemakers, *Salafism in Jordan*, p. 40.
47. See, for example, an advertisement by ISIS for Ibn ᶜAbd al-Wahhāb's treatise 'Kashf al-shubuhāt' ('The Clarification of Doubts') published in *al-Nabaʾ* 22:11.
48. For an excellent overview of jihadist thought, see Qindīl and ᶜAbd al-Rabbihi, *al-Fikr al-islāmī al-jihādī al-muᶜāṣir*.
49. Atwan, *Islamic State*, p. 195.
50. Cf. Fārūq, *Dāᶜish*, pp. 351–62.
51. Fishman, *The Master Plan*, p. x.
52. Ibid. pp. 60–1.
53. Wagemakers, *Salafism in Jordan*, p. 57.
54. Filiu, *Apocalypse in Islam*, p. 193.
55. Gerges, *ISIS*, p. 26.
56. For his millennial message, see Hegghammer (ed.), *Jihad in Saudi*

Arabia, p. 24. For his ideology, see Beránek and Ťupek, *The Temptation of Graves*, pp. 150–6.

57. Cook, 'Abu Mus^{c}ab al-Suri and Abu Mus^{c}ab al-Zarqawi'.
58. Rif^{c}at, *Rasāʾil Juhaymān al-^{c}Utaybī*, pp. 64–5. For apocalyptic topics, the most important chapter is 'al-Fitan wa akhbār al-Mahdī wa nuzūl ^{c}Īsā ^{c}alayhi salām wa ashrāṭ al-sā^{c}a' ('Tribulations, News about al-Mahdī and the Descent of Jesus, Peace be upon Him, and Portents of the Hour'), pp. 183–223.
59. Beránek and Ťupek, *The Temptation of Graves*, pp. 152–3.
60. Ibid. p. 155.
61. For a thorough analysis of these apocalyptic authors, see Filiu, *Apocalypse in Islam*, pp. 121–40.
62. Available at http://www.alhawali.com/main/5898-2-1---يوم-الغضب-هل-بدأ-بانتفاضة-رجب--.html (last accessed 9 November 2017).
63. Filiu, *Apocalypse in Islam*, p. 108.
64. Landes, 'Enraged Millennialism', p. 440.
65. Al-^{c}Arīfī, *Nihāyat al-^{c}ālam*, pp. 7–18.
66. See Juergensmeyer, *Terror in the Mind of God*, pp. 182–4.
67. Filiu, *Apocalypse in Islam*, p. 185.
68. See https://www.washingtontimes.com/news/2015/jan/5/apocalypse-prophecies-drive-islamic-state-strategy/ (last accessed 22 November 2017).
69. Landes, 'Enraged Millennialism', p. 452.
70. See, for example, Fishman, *The Master Plan*, pp. 34–7.
71. Ibid. pp. 462–4.
72. See especially Wessinger, *Millennialism, Persecution, and Violence.*
73. See the chapter entitled 'Valorizing violence at the end of days', in Pregill, 'ISIS, Eschatology, and Exegesis', pp. 17–20. Cf. also Juergensmeyer, *Terror in the Mind of God*, pp. 187–215.
74. Atwan, *Islamic State*, p. 14.
75. For inspiring considerations about 'otherness in Islam', see Morrow (ed.), *Islamic Images and Ideas*, pp. 217–27.
76. *Dabiq* 7:54–66.
77. For demonstrative examples of contemporary Islamist apocalyptic creativity, see translations of the shorter texts written by Abū Bāṣir al-Tartūsī and Jawād al-Natsha, in McCants, *The ISIS Apocalypse*, pp. 173–8.

78. Cook, 'Iraq as the Focus for Apocalyptic Scenarios'.
79. McCants, *The ISIS Apocalypse*, p. 99.
80. See http://english.ahram.org.eg/NewsContentPrint/1/0/22476/Egypt/0/Mubaraks-fall-spawns-End-of-Times-prophecies.aspx (last accessed 20 November 2017).
81. See Cook, 'Abu Mus^c^ab al-Suri and Abu Mus^c^ab al-Zarqawi'. [Grateful thanks to David Cook for supplying me with the draft of this study.]
82. Velji, *An Apocalyptic History*, p. 76.
83. Pregill, 'ISIS, Eschatology, and Exegesis', p. 8.
84. See, especially, Fishman, *The Master Plan*, pp. 37–9; Atwan, *Islamic State*, pp. 150–8. His real identity has been also discussed in McCants, *The ISIS Apocalypse*, p. 210. Cf. Fārūq, *Dā^c^ish*, pp. 145–54 and Qindīl and ^c^Abd al-Rabbihi, *al-Fikr al-islāmī al-jihādī al-mu^c^āṣir*, pp. 141–8.
85. For the English translation by William McCants, see https://azelin.files.wordpress.com/2010/08/abu-bakr-naji-the-management-of-savagery-the-most-critical-stage-through-which-the-umma-will-pass.pdf (last accessed 20 May 2017).
86. Gerges, *ISIS*, p. 38.
87. See Fārūq, *Dā^c^ish*, pp. 145–53.
88. Cf. Shandab, *Munāẓara ma^c^a ^c^aql dā^c^ish*, pp. 118–19.
89. Fishman, *The Master Plan*, p. 38.
90. For the life and thought of al-Sūrī, see Lia, *Architect of Global Jihad*. See also Filiu, *Apocalypse in Islam*, pp. 187–91; Fishman, *The Master Plan*, pp. 13–17 and pp. 166–8; Zackie, 'An Analysis of Abu Mus'ab al-Suri's "Call to Global Islamic Resistance"'. Cf. also Qindīl and ^c^Abd al-Rabbihi, *al-Fikr al-islāmī al-jihādī al-mu^c^āṣir*, pp. 385–7.
91. For the adoption of a *nom de guerre* among Jihadists, see Hegghammer (ed.), *Jihadi Culture*, p. 196.
92. Lia, *Architect of Global Jihad*, p. 4.
93. This work first appeared in December 2004 and soon spread to all jihadist websites. Currently, it is available, for example, at https://ia800303.us.archive.org/25/items/Dawaaah/DAWH.pdf (last accessed 25 May 2017). There are also three fundamental sections, translated by jihadists into English, available at https://ia600304.us.archive.org/27/items/TheGlobalIslamicResistanceCall/The_Global_Islamic_Resistance_Call_-_Chapter_8_sections_5_to_7_LIST_OF_TARGETS.pdf (last accessed 25 October 2017). For extensive key excerpts from 'The Military

Theory of the Global Islamic Resistance Call' in commented English translation, see Lia, *Architect of Global Jihad*, pp. 347–484. For an analysis and selected excerpts, see Qindīl and ^{c}Abd al-Rabbihi, *al-Fikr al-islāmī al-jihādī al-mu^{c}āṣir*, pp. 149–71.

94. Filiu, *Apocalypse in Islam*, p. 188.
95. Al-Sūrī, *Da^{c}wat al-muqāwama al-islāmīya al-^{c}ālamīya*, pp. 1517–601.
96. Ibid. pp. 77–90.
97. Filiu, *Apocalypse in Islam*, p. 188.
98. Al-Sūrī, *Da^{c}wa*, pp. 1519–45.
99. Ibid. p. 1546.
100. Ibid. p. 191.
101. Ibid. p. 1547. For this notorious *ḥadīth*, see Ayyūb, *al-Masīḥ al-Dajjāl*, pp. 282–93 and also al-^{c}Arīfī, *Nihāyat al-^{c}ālam*, pp. 136–7.
102. See Nu^{c}aym, *The Book of Tribulations*, pp. 150–87. Cf. al-Muqaddam, *Fiqh ashrāṭ al-sā^{c}a*, pp. 86–7.
103. Muslim, *Ṣaḥīḥ*, p. 937 (no. 2910).
104. Al-Sūrī, *Da^{c}wa*, pp. 1559–600.
105. Cook, 'Abu Mus^{c}ab al-Suri and Abu Mus^{c}ab al-Zarqawi'.
106. Lia, *Architect of Global Jihad*, p. 8.
107. Filiu, *Apocalypse in Islam*, p. 191.
108. Atwan, *Islamic State*, p. 41.
109. For his biography, see Brisard and Martinez, *Zarqawi*; Ḥusayn, *al-Zarqāwī*. See also Gerges, *ISIS*, pp. 50–97; Wagemakers, *Salafism in Jordan*, pp. 180–8; Fishman, *The Master Plan*, pp. 60–74; Atwan, *Islamic State*, pp. 40–5; McCants, *The ISIS Apocalypse*, pp. 7–15; Weiss and Hassan, *ISIS*, pp. 14–30. See also Byman and Williams, 'ISIS vs. Al Qaeda'; cf. Qindīl and ^{c}Abd al-Rabbihi, *al-Fikr al-islāmī al-jihādī al-mu^{c}āṣir*, pp. 383–5.
110. Brisard and Martinez, *Zarqawi*, p. 203.
111. See al-Zarqāwī, *Kalimāt muḍī^{c}a*, pp. 58–75.
112. Perhaps the only exception is his citing of the above-mentioned notorious apocalyptic *ḥadīth* about the killing of Jews in an interview in 1998. Gorenberg, *The End of Days*, p. vi.
113. See Fromson and Simon, 'ISIS', pp. 28–9.
114. Cook, 'Abu Mus^{c}ab al-Suri and Abu Mus^{c}ab al-Zarqawi.'
115. Fishman, *The Master Plan*, p. 44.
116. Ibid. p. 250.

117. See, for example, the thirteenth issue of *Dabiq*, entitled 'The Rafidah: From Ibn Saʾba to the Dajjal', which explicitly explains that the Shiites are actually led by the Antichrist.
118. Gerges, *ISIS*, pp. 81–2.
119. Ibid. p. 82.
120. Al-Zarqāwī, *Kalimāt muḍīʿa*, p. 237.
121. Bunzel, *From Paper State to Caliphate*, p. 14.
122. For Nūr al-Dīn in Mosul, see Tabbaa, 'The Mosque of Nūr al-Dīn in Mosul', pp. 340–3.
123. McCants, *The ISIS Apocalypse*, p. 9.
124. Ibid. p. 102.
125. Al-Zarqāwī, *Kalimāt muḍīʿa*, pp. 176–9.
126. Ibid. p. 151.
127. For more information about al-Maqdīsī, see Wagemakers, *Salafism in Jordan*, pp. 180–4.
128. Cook, 'Abu Musʿab al-Suri and Abu Musʿab al-Zarqawi'.
129. Ibid.
130. Al-Zarqāwī, *Kalimāt muḍīʿa*, p. 162.
131. Ibid. p. 151. Cited from an ISIS translation published in *Rumiyah* 3:26.
132. McCants, *The ISIS Apocalypse*, p. 28.
133. Cook, 'Abu Musʿab al-Suri and Abu Musʿab al-Zarqawi'.
134. See Cook, 'Iraq as the Focus for Apocalyptic Scenarios'.
135. McCants, *The ISIS Apocalypse*, p. 29.
136. Cook, 'Abu Musʿab al-Suri and Abu Musʿab al-Zarqawi'.
137. Ibid.
138. Hegghammer (ed.), *Jihadi Culture*, p. 163.

3

The Topography of the Last Days

The flag of Khilāfah will rise over Makkah and al-Madīnah, even if the apostates and hypocrites despise such. The flag of Khilāfah will rise over Baytul-Maqdis [Jerusalem] and Rome, even if the Jews and Crusaders despise such. The shade of this blessed flag will expand until it covers all eastern and western extents of the Earth, filling the world with the truth and justice of Islam and putting an end to the falsehood and tyranny of jāhiliyyah, even if America and its coalition despise such.

– *Dabiq*[1]

Symbols focus and concentrate passions. Even secularists can be infuriated by the burning of their country's flag, though they know it is arbitrary chosen to stand for an idea. But in the literalism that characterizes fundamentalism, a symbol *really is* the thing it represents. The purported violation of the mosques doesn't merely represent the West's humiliation of Islam. The world is askew because the sacred is polluted.

– Gershom Gorenberg[2]

Not surprisingly, there are many ways to explain the ISIS story: as an extreme ideological movement, as a by-product of the Iraqi disturbances and the Syrian civil war, as part of a broader social backlash against the century-old division of the Middle East into modern nation states. All of these lenses have their undeniable value; nevertheless, this chapter aims to identify another approach of 'putting ISIS on the map' in order to provide the reader with an appropriate context and to make any further interpretation more comprehensible. The first section focuses on the 'apocalyptic topography' of Syria and Iraq. Accordingly, before examining particular Muslim End-time narratives within the framework of ISIS propaganda, some geographic, historical and literary sources should be reconsidered in order to introduce fragmentary glimpses onto the actual 'stage' of ISIS apocalyptic self-presentation.

The second section attempts to contextualise ISIS messages within a broader semantic framework. The use of symbols helps us to understand the religious system at its basic level of communication. Symbols are of exceptional importance within the context of religious clashes.[3] However, while the apocalypse is more than the sum of its parts, there are continually recurring images that help us to locate the apocalyptic participant's world.[4] In other words, 'symbolism serves to communicate what are perceived to be eternal truths to the audience and enables it to visualize quickly and effectively the world of the End times'.[5] From our 'apocalyptic perspective', also of particular interest is the language and metalanguage used by ISIS propagandists.

Finally, both apocalyptic and symbolic 'maps' should be preceded by a real map, that is, a geographic and historical survey of the ISIS phenomenon. Such interpretations have been provided by several scholarly monographs, some of which were referred to in the introductory chapter. Moreover, an overview map of the Middle East, including the important toponyms related to both the history of ISIS and Muslim apocalyptic imagery, can be found in Appendix 4.

In speaking of the visual framework of ISIS self-presentation, it seems paradoxical that a group whose expressed aim is to take the world back to the days of the first generation of Muslims (*ṣahāba*) is so dependent on the most sophisticated technology; however, 'in war people use every weapon at their disposal'.[6] This claim also undoubtedly applies to the mastery of marketing and propaganda, without which the group could never have achieved its ambitions in such a short time (see 'How to Sell the Apocalypse' in Chapter 5).

From the East to Jerusalem

There is no doubt that the apocalyptic appeal of ISIS propaganda has been reinforced by the repeated promotion of links between the group's action arenas and various classical End-time references. As William McCants has succinctly pointed out, it is 'little wonder such a heady enactment of the End-Time drama on the original stage where it was first rehearsed has drawn an unprecedented number of Sunni and Shiite foreign fighters to the theatre'.[7]

From a geographical perspective, the given apocalyptic framework accords with the current distribution of forces in Middle-Eastern conflicts and that is why an 'apocalyptic reading of geopolitics' offers itself. A lot of factors serve to strengthen such an impression: the fact that a great number of military operations have occurred in the northern borderlands of Syria, that fierce battles have been waged in symbolically significant Dābiq, that the rampage unleashed by ISIS has deepened the clashes between Sunnis and Shiites and, above all, that Muslims have never been so disunited as now, are all factors that have positively played into the 'apocalyptic hand' of ISIS.

Within this overarching logic, a number of other points (violence and cruelty, torture, terror, corruption, and so on) have further reinforced the belief that the apocalyptic reading of the present is actually the only right understanding. The chief point to be made here is that a single glance at a map of the Middle East reveals that the ISIS propagandists (who are, with a few exceptions,[8] anonymous to us) do not have to possess a fertile imagination to be able to exploit their message of the Last Days, based on current realities. Needless to say, such a creative joining of the apocalypse with geopolitics has brought forth the fruits of propaganda on countless occasions throughout Muslim history.

With regard to Muslim 'apocalyptic evaluations' that relate to the advantages and disadvantages of particular regions and cities, two fundamental types of primary sources are available, the apocalyptic *aḥādīth* themselves and the so-called *kutub al-faḍāʾil* ('books of virtues'). The latter focus on the supposed merits of particular loci and, in the Middle Ages, they also played the role of specific 'travel-guides' to pilgrimage sites. However, the primary significance of the *faḍāʾil* discourse lies in 'the promotion of a culturally constructed mode of seeing and conceptual mapping'.[9]

Concerning the identification of apocalyptic events with particular sites, Nuᶜaym's renowned book is of utmost importance, containing a lot of otherwise lost traditions, full of place names that are, mostly, traceable. This is because Nuᶜaym recorded what was often discarded later as dubious:

> During the ninth and tenth centuries these traditions are gradually winnowed out, with the usual paradigm being that whatever is most specific in the earlier traditions is accepted in the canonical versions in the most generic form. Alternatively, if there are names, then they are focused upon the Muslim holy figures and locations, not allowed to be spread out to numerous other people and sites.[10]

The location of events associated with the End times is of major significance. The apocalyptists often mention the loci in which conflicts involving Muslims will take place and which are consequently denoted in binary Islamist discourse as 'the territory of the enemy'. The particular loci of apocalyptic battles are referred to in various reliable *aḥādīth*. The 'topographies of the Last Days', as depicted by the competing Muslim forces, however, may differ significantly and the mirror-like Shiite Doomsday visions (see 'Doomsday Visions of the Shiites' in Chapter 6) are just one example among many.

The following outline will introduce the large region that stretches from the Mediterranean to Iran, which is clearly identifiable in fundamentalist End-time references (see also Appendix 4). Unfortunately, such an imaginary 'mapping' exercise incurs a lot of difficulties, despite the fact that countless attempts to identify places where the main characters of the Islamic apocalypse will appear, as well as other sites of crucial events, rank as the most productive features of Muslim apocalypticism. In reality, only a general consensus exists with regard to the vague claim that both arch-enemies, the Dajjāl and the Mahdī, will arrive from the East.

Medieval sources offer an incoherent list of places where the Mahdī is destined to fight, but his very coming is shrouded in speculation (Mecca, Medina and the Khurāsān are the most frequently mentioned loci). As for the expected site of Jesus' coming, the Great Mosque in Damascus and the Dome of the Rock in Jerusalem are referred to most often. As regards the Dajjāl, the desert region between Syria and Iraq, Khurāsān, Iṣṭakhr (Persepolis), Iṣfahān, and also Syrian Baisān or Egyptian Qaws are claimed to be the sites of his presupposed emergence.[11] Finally, it is suggested that al-Sufyānī will emerge from what is today's northern Jordan, and that he will lead armies from Syria to attack the Shiites in Iraq.

Within our 'apocalyptic mapping', Syria would definitely occupy an exceptional place. Sunni prophecies laud this region as the blessed land of gathering where the final battle against the infidels will take place and as the starting point for 'the purification of Muslim countries from the filth of idolaters and the subsequent liberation of Jerusalem from Jewish hands'.[12] It is also claimed that this will serve as the gathering place for Doomsday.[13] The extraordinary role that Syria will play has been highlighted by many radicals, among them Musa Cerantonio, a notorious Australian supporter of ISIS, who told a Melbourne audience in 2012 that this country 'holds a very specific, special, and strategic place in the future'.[14]

In the medieval context, Nuᶜaym ibn Ḥammād praised Syria,[15] along with many others, reporting that the Prophet said: 'When the Syrians are annihilated, there will be no further good in my community.'[16] Since this region played a decisive role in the formative process of Muslim apocalypticism, numerous local toponyms appear in various narratives related to End-time struggles. Medieval apocalyptists knew Syria intimately and were able to refer to even smaller place names with remarkable care and accuracy.[17] It is no wonder, therefore, that some 'apocalyptic shortcuts' employed by ISIS propaganda simply offer themselves up to be utilised.

While the very name 'Syria' is of both pre-Islamic and modern provenance, medieval sources claimed a somewhat wider designation for al-Shām, one that encompassed most of the eastern Mediterranean. Jihadists, however, often equate al-Shām with the state of Syria.[18] Whatever the case, al-Shām holds a prominent place in Muslim tradition, being identified as the birthplace of many prophets, as well as the abode of forty crucial Sufi saints called *abdāl* (substitutes), by whose virtue this world supposedly continues to persist.

Put simply, there is no doubt that Syria is actually the most important apocalyptic site in Islam. Its territory, according to Cook's suggestion, needs to be subdivided into two areas: the coastal cities and the inland cities. The coastal cities are the source of a tremendous amount of apocalyptic material, the area being subjected to Byzantine attacks during the early period of Islam and this fact being reflected in the emphasis placed on the religious merits of living in such dangerous locations.[19] In addition, Muslim's *Saḥīḥ* assigns great importance to Syria as a whole.[20] As a Byzantine target, the base for counterattacks on Constantinople, the theatre of the struggle between Jesus and the Antichrist, and the final arena for the devastation caused by Gog and Magog – this land is truly central to all apocalyptic accounts.[21]

ISIS propagandists have undoubtedly been influenced by such information. The article eloquently entitled *Sham is the Land of Malahim* contains a list of names, well-known to the common Arab reader, showing the allegedly close relationship between the group's military tactics and its End-time dreams:

> Then, these nuzzā˒[22] gathered in Shām, the land of malāhim and the land of al-Malhamah al-Kubrā. Allah's Messenger has informed of battles that will occur in places within Shām and its vicinity, such as al-Ghūtah, Damascus, Dābiq (or al-A˒māq), the Euphrates River, and Constantinople (which is near Shām), as well as Baytul-Maqdis (Jerusalem), the gate of Lod, Lake Tiberius, the Jordan River, Mount Sinai, and so on. And he linked this blessed land with many of the events related to al-Masīh, al-Mahdī, and the Dajjāl . . . Indeed, the camp of the Muslims on the day of al-Malhamah al-Kubrā will be in al-Ghūtah, next to a city called Damascus, one of the best cities of

> Shām . . . Allah's Messenger said, 'I saw as if a pillar of the Book was taken from underneath my pillow, so I looked and it was a shining light extending towards Shām. Verily faith, at the time of tribulations, is in Shām.'[23]

Incidentally, the strong belief in the exceptional status of Syria within the End-time drama is also shared by opponents of ISIS. As evidence of this we can mention Muḥammad al-Yaᶜqūbī, a Western-educated Islamic scholar, who believes that 'the eschatological End game of Islam is playing out in Syria, with the Mahdi and the Sufyani soon to appear'.[24] If it is true that 'at all times the genre of apocalypse has been used to channel social frustrations from a given population',[25] one might remark that the currently civil-war-wracked Syria is an incomparable site for the flourishing of this specific genre.

The Syrian war arguably fulfils many of the salient criteria associated with the anticipated features of global conflict that will foreshadow the appearance of the Mahdī. Respected traditions state that in such a war good Muslims will fight against unbelievers, who themselves are in league with bad Muslims. This belief, shared by both supporters and opponents of ISIS, has supposedly already been fulfilled by the internationalisation of this conflict, where a broad spectrum of powerful players is currently involved.

Thus, Syria provides us with a twofold battleground – the real and the apocalyptic. A number of specific Syrian localities could be analysed from an apocalyptic perspective (among them the city of Ḥimṣ, the spiritual birthplace of Nuᶜaym's collection), but only three of them (Dābiq, al-Aᶜmāq and Damascus) are discussed below as separate items.

The second key region is modern-day Iraq, a phenomenon of several different parts. Iraq appears in ISIS propaganda as an area where 'the camp of sincerity', a revival of the caliphate, has been established.[26] A large part of current Iraqi territory pertains to what was traditionally referred to as Bilād al-rāfidayn (Mesopotamia). Iraq, and particularly the region around Baghdad, was well known to Syrian apocalyptic informants, who have provided us with a detailed account.[27] The central area is referenced in medieval traditions, generally in unsympathetic terms. Baghdad is referred to using the pejorative name al-Zawráᵓ (distorted, perverted) and is roundly cursed. However, ISIS attitudes towards the city have witnessed an improvement, with the group's spokesman repeatedly referring to it as 'the Baghdad of the Caliphate' and 'the Baghdad of al-Rashīd'. In addition, the laudatory language of Abū ᶜUmar al-Baghdādī, the ISIS first leader, speaks about 'the very home of the caliphate, the Baghdad of al-Rashīd'.[28]

Other important cities in central Iraq are also featured in apocalyptic traditions: al-Baṣra is threatened with *khasf* (being swallowed up by the earth) and metamorphosis. On the other hand, the traditions pertaining to al-Kūfa are quite positive since they emphasise the idea of an alternate Jerusalem as the messianic capital, with an ingathering of all true believers to this location. Being the site of Imam ᶜAlī's assassination, the Kūfa mosque is of enormous importance in terms of the Shiite apocalypse, since it is the place where the Mahdī is destined to make his initial appearance and from where he will launch his struggle against the forces of evil.[29] However, people are warned against living in the Sawād (the fertile alluvial plain), as they can expect to be treated harshly.[30]

As regards both former principal centres of ISIS, Mosul (Iraq) and al-Raqqa (Syria), their 'apocalyptic position' is rather marginal. While Mosul is presented as a place of battle, cursorily referred to in sermons delivered by Imam ᶜAlī,[31] al-Raqqa (home to Hārūn al-Rashīd for several years) has received only an insignificant mention as a place where a thunderbolt will strike during al-Sufyānī's apocalyptic march.[32]

When dealing with Iraq, it is surprising how little al-Zarqāwī actually used its apocalyptic symbolism in support of his own stance.[33] ISIS also concentrated its 'End-time attention' more on Syria. In any case, there is one fundamental apocalyptic tradition that relates to the area between Syria and Iraq, and which has been studiously avoided by ISIS propaganda and the group's supporters alike, even though it represents one of the most reliable *aḥādīth*.[34] The Antichrist, according to the version that instigated lengthy cyberspace disputes among Muslims,[35] will appear in this desert region, that is, precisely in the place where ISIS was originally located. In fact, this inhospitable area has a lot in common with the border between Afghanistan and Pakistan, a poorly governed region that has housed militants for decades. The open deserts of Syria and Iraq offer less topographical security than the mountains of Afghanistan and Pakistan, but the local political situation is just as dysfunctional.[36]

The third circle within our 'End-time mapping' approach is rather more ethnic than geographic. This is because the Turks, as they appear in Muslim traditions, cannot be definitely associated with their current territory, which was originally under Byzantine control. However, the Turks are important for us since the signs of the Hour would be incomplete without reference to the battle that will take place with them.[37] They are presented as just being 'out there' – a group whose origins are unclear, who are currently making and will continue to make, regular incursions into the Muslim world, for no apparent reason.[38]

In medieval sources, we find the following descriptions: small eyes, reddish cheeks, flat noses, and so on. These images are conspicuously similar to those attributed to Gog and Magog because the medieval authors commonly believed that they were of the same genesis. Wahb ibn al-Munabbih has even suggested an idiosyncratic etymology of 'Turk': When Gog and Magog were separated from civilisation by the legendary Dam (*al-sadd*), the only tribe that remained (*turikū*) behind the Wall were the Turks.[39]

The genuine role of Turks and Turkey in modern Muslim apocalyptic creativity is ambiguous. Meanwhile, the hard-to-classify contemporary Turkish author Harun Yahya suggests in his visions of the End times that Turks will play a positive role as examples to be followed. In this way, therefore, they will become the unifiers of all Muslims. Other authors (Muḥammad ᶜĪsā Dāᵓūd, for example) focus rather more on the alliance of Turkey with the Western powers, including NATO and Israel, a fact that identifies the country as one of the supposed enemies of the Mahdī.

In contemporary apocalyptic discourse, in general, most writers simply omit the battles between Muslims and Turks, today hardly contextualisable,[40] although they are foretold by a number of reliable *aḥādīth*. They would rather refer to the capture of Constantinople as a precursor of the Hour. This location is often expanded in line with the 'mental map' of some authors, since the conquest of Constantinople supposedly signifies the capture of the space and system of the 'West' caused by the Mahdī's supernatural power.[41]

Apart from the regions, a great number of other items are to be found on 'apocalyptic maps'. In Nuᶜaym's case, monasteries, springs, lakes and rivers, and even the location of prominent stones and trees are featured.[42] Nonetheless, the presence of the Euphrates (al-Furāt) among them is quite unique since this river is connected with a single prophecy of almost archetypal importance that concerns the discovery of gold in the riverbed. This final sign has been a major concern in many Arab countries; ever since Turkey built a series of dams in the upper reaches of the Tigris and Euphrates, Arabs have been reminded that their water resources are at the mercy of unpredictable foreigners.[43] Related *ḥadīth* can be found in various versions attributed to Abū Hurayra, in Muslim's *Ṣaḥīḥ*,[44] as well as in Nuᶜaym's *Kitāb al-fitan*: 'A mountain of gold will be uncovered at the Euphrates – out of every 100 ninety-nine will be killed there, and only one will remain.'[45] Not surprisingly, this point has not missed the attention of ISIS (see 'They Plot but Allah Also Plots' in Chapter 5).

Within any account of Muslim apocalyptic toponyms, Dābiq would occupy an exceptional place. This settlement location (referred to either as a town or a village)[46] occurs in the following interpretation as the expected stage for the final battle (*al-malḥama al-kubrā*). In fact, Dābiq is predicted to be the location of at least two battles between the 'Islamic vanguard' and its enemies, as the eponymous *Dabiq* magazine has expressly recorded:

> The great events unfolding now in northern Sham – in Dabiq and its surroundings – are but signs of the coming malahim [fierce struggles], inshaallah. These great events will force the Crusaders – sooner or later – to accept the terms of the Jamaᵓah [community]

> of the Muslims, a truce that is precedent to the Major Malhamah of Dabiq . . . This war of attack and withdrawal occurring in Dabiq and its surrounding areas – the minor battle of Dabiq – will inevitably lead to the Major Malhamah of Dabiq, even if a withdrawal were to precede it by Allah's decree.[47]

Essentially, the Dābiq prophecy did not figure prominently in ISIS propaganda until 2014,[48] albeit that it cursorily appeared in a speech delivered by Abū ᶜUmar al-Baghdādī.[49] The increasing relevance of Dābiq later manifested itself in the form of the major propaganda tool used by ISIS and intended for Western audiences. The motto, which is used to introduce each issue, referring to the spark that 'has been lit here in Iraq' could not express the group's intentions more clearly. Undoubtedly, Dābiq has had a crucial role to play in ISIS propaganda, with data from Google clearly showing how the group's attacks in the West have effectively fuelled apocalyptic rhetoric, and vice versa.[50] Paradoxically, as William McCants has noted, 'the inevitable defeat of the State at Dābiq, should it ever confront "Rome", would also argue against the prophecy's applicability'.[51] Yet, this narrative has itself become a certain archetypal illustration of apocalyptic prophecy.

In addition to this major prediction regarding the expected final battle, a number of other minor apocalyptic references should also be noted. The Umayyad caliph Sulaymān, remarkable for his apocalyptic dreams, was buried here and his tomb has been destroyed by ISIS soldiers, who considered the shrine to be idolatrous.[52] In the apt words of William McCants, 'the resting place of a man who wanted to fulfil prophecy by conquering Constantinople did not survive the zealotry of his modern heirs'.[53] Furthermore, this event happened more than a thousand years after the apocalyptic partisans of the Abbasid dynasty had desecrated Sulaymān's remains.

Dābiq also witnessed the epic defeat of the Ottoman army by the Mamlūks in 1516 – exactly five centuries before ISIS finally lost control over this area. As regards the occurrence of this name within classical sources, the situation is somewhat paradoxical, as David Cook clearly summarises:

> Dābiq, known from the historical and military literature of the Umayyad period as the staging ground for Muslim Arab armies invading the Byzantine Empire, is not mentioned in Nu^c^aym, although the alternate location of al-A^c^māq (the more generic one) is. The ISIS has latched on to the only occurrence of the name in all the tradition literature. Thus, it is possible for a highly Salafi and literalist group to focus upon an apocalyptic location that is outside the general 'holy sites' of Islam – Mecca, Medina and Jerusalem – in order to complete its fulfilment of the apocalypse.[54]

While Dābiq does not appear in Nu^c^aym's compendium, which is, arguably, a major source of inspiration for ISIS apocalyptists, this name can be found in Muslim's *Saḥīḥ*, as follows: 'The Last Hour will not come until the Romans land at al-A^c^māq or in Dābiq.'[55]

The former toponym refers to a pivotal apocalyptic area, the A^c^māq.[56] The A^c^māq, the plural of *^c^amq* or *^c^umq* (literally 'depth, bottom'), are the valleys of northern Syria between Ḥimṣ and the Taurus Mountains, a frequently fought-over land between the two warring empires during the first centuries of Islam. It would seem that geography had an important part to play in the development of traditions related to the A^c^māq. The whole area would seem to be the location of decisive change events, of continual battles. As David Cook's informs us, 'no one can pass through this area without being fundamentally affected'. The A^c^māq are thus one of the prime regions witnessing the battle between the godly kingdoms and the infidels.[57]

In addition to the ISIS news agency, the A^c^māq gave their name primarily to an apocalyptic cycle, fundamental to the study of Muslim apocalypticism in general, with its basic story line being repeated in most of the major traditions or used to link stories.[58] As we will see later, this cycle is also of great importance for ISIS apocalyptists, for whom it serves as an inexhaustible well of motifs. According to David Cook,

> the A^c^māq cycle is so convenient to current exploitation, since its narratives do not depict a simple straightforward conflict between Muslims and nonbelievers, but rather a sophisticated and an

> ambiguously interpreted war ... There exists a division between the two groups of Muslims so deep that the Muslims of Syria turn to the Byzantines for aid in punishing the Iraqis for their refusal to fight.[59]

In our 'apocalyptic mapping', both traditional centres, Damascus and Jerusalem, also have their own fixed roles. The eschatological importance of Damascus (*Dimashq al-Shām*) was recognised by medieval authors and, more recently, by ISIS propagandists, the following excerpt from an interview with a local military leader being an illustration of the work of the latter:

> Dabiq: You know the importance of Dimashq [Damascus] towards the future of Islam, the Malāhim, and al-Malhamah al-Kubrā. How can the Muslim support the mujāhidīn in Wilāyat Dimashq now?
> Yarmūk: Our role model and noble Messenger praised Dimashq very much, and this was mentioned in a number of authentic narrations. Dimashq is the camp of the Muslims during the great battle ... Any advance of the Khilāfah [caliphate] against the Nusayriyyah and Rāfidah [Alawites and Shiites], any manifestation of unity through new bayᵓāt [oaths of loyalty] to the Khilāfah ..., strengthens the mujāhidīn in Dimashq.[60]

Many of the apocalyptic sites referred to in ancient prophecies are located in the vicinity of Damascus,[61] with the oasis of Ghūta (the Muslim place of assembly on the day of the great battle)[62] being one significant example. Damascus is said to be the refuge of Muslims during the End-time wars and people are instructed to come to this city and fortify themselves there when the portents of the End begin to appear. When the Prophet was asked by Ibn Masᶜūd: 'How many Muslims can Damascus contain?' he said 'it will contain as many Muslims as come to it, just as the womb contains a child.'[63]

In addition to this, Damascus is one of the possible places where Jesus will return to earth.[64] The Great Umayyad Mosque of Damascus is particularly important, since one of its three minarets called Manārat ᶜĪsā (the Minaret of Jesus) is destined to serve as the site where Jesus will descend from heaven and its courtyard will act as the location of his final battle with the Antichrist, albeit that local people sometimes ascribe this privilege to the nearby minaret of al-Bāb al-sharqī (the Eastern Gate), which is not actually part of any mosque.[65] In this exact spot, according to *Risāla ilā ḥukkām al-bayt al-abyaḍ* (*The letter to the rulers of the White House*), a pamphlet written by Abū ᶜUmar al-Baghdādī, Jesus will – as expressed in medieval prophecies – 'shatter the crucifix, kill the swine, abolish the protection tax, and make wealth flow until no one needs any more'.[66]

Incidentally, it is another name of this specific minaret, al-Manāra al-bayḍāᵓ (the White Minaret),[67] that was given to the official media outlet of Jabhat al-nuṣra,[68] a jihadist organisation sharing ancestry with ISIS and utilising similar apocalyptic rhetoric, though apparently to a lesser degree and with less intensity. This media wing was founded before the group split from ISIS.[69] In any case, the symbolic value of Damascus, noticeably featuring – together with Jerusalem – in Christian eschatological imagination, is unquestionable.

As regards Jerusalem (Bayt al-maqdis, al-Quds),[70] its apocalyptic role in Islam can hardly be overstated.[71] This is the place where the Dajjāl will besiege the Muslims, Jesus will descend upon the Dome of the Rock in order to usher in the messianic kingdom, and from where the Mahdī will reign. In ISIS propaganda, the conquest of Jerusalem is primarily presented as an alleged requirement of shariah. Meanwhile, the related geopolitical motives are of secondary importance.[72] Jerusalem appears in ISI and ISIS propaganda from the very beginning.[73]

Many Muslims believe that the Temple Mount will be the place where the resurrection and last judgement will occur. Other legends consider the Rock at the Temple Mount as the pivotal place in the universe, where all souls will be gathered on the Day of Resurrection. Inter-Islamic polemics on the sanctity of Jerusalem have been in evidence throughout history. Among those Muslim authorities who have expressed their resistance to the sanctification of the city, Taqī al-Dīn ibn Taymīya, the godfather of Salafists (who lived in the fourteenth century), remains the most influential. As Gershom Gorenberg has aptly expressed in his well-written book about the eschatological dimension of the struggle for the Temple Mount, 'the Temple Mount . . . is built out of stories, not stones. Some say the world began here; more say this is where it will end.'[74]

The eschatological importance of Jerusalem is often associated with the Dome of the Rock (*qubbat al-ṣakhra*), the alleged starting point of the legendary Muḥammad's ascent to heaven (*miʿrāj*). The real reasons behind the development of this building are, however, the subject of never-ending scholarly dispute. As we are often reminded, the Umayyad caliph al-Walīd, in order to dissuade them from making the Mecca pilgrimage, allegedly told the people that the last judgement would be in the exact place from which the Prophet ascended to heaven.[75]

In ISIS propaganda, the al-Aqṣāʾ mosque – as one of the most important sacred buildings in Islam and, at the same time, an embodiment of the Muslim heritage in a Jerusalem controlled by Israel – unquestionably plays a prominent role. ISIS has invoked this grievance as an argument for defending this mosque, together with all 'that belongs to the Muslims in Palestine'.[76] Both monuments, the al-Aqṣāʾ mosque and the Dome of the Rock, have their own highly symbolic dimension. While the former is often employed as an Islamic symbol of Palestinian identity, the latter is revered as a powerful pan-Islamic manifestation of unity.[77]

Not only Jerusalem, but also Palestine (Filasṭīn) in its entirety, are referred to as having divine value and a preordained role,[78] often with particular reference being made to a mystical night journey (*isrāʾ*) undertaken by the Prophet Muḥammad, as well as to its role as the final resting places of many prophets of Islam. This point has also been highlighted in ISIS propaganda as part of the infamous video of Lt Muʿādh al-Kasāsba's terrifying execution, an act that caused outrage all over the world.[79]

Neither does Islamic apocalyptic imagery omit reference to the ultimate goals of the dreamed Muslim expansion. Constantinople and Rome often appear as part of ISIS End-time propaganda.[80] Both will be conquered as part of the final phase of history. The capture of

Constantinople (Qusṭanṭīnīya) is described in similar terms to that of Jericho (Joshua 5:13–16:21), with Muslims taking the place of the Israelites. When Muslims approach the city, they will encamp on the far side of the Bosporus. The straits will suddenly dry up and the Muslims will be able to cross over. They will cause the walls to fall by shouting *takbīr* (the cry 'Allāhu akbar').[81]

In modern apocalypticism, the role of Istanbul, today's Constantinople, as a metropolis already inhabited by Muslims, is controversial – and also difficult to explain.[82] The fact that the city has to be reconquered – because its conquest is one of the signs that the Antichrist is about to appear – is somewhat problematic. Some have sought to address this difficulty by seeking to deny that the original conquest in 1453 was actually accomplished by true Muslims. Thus, it needs to be 'reconquered' before the End. Others blame Kemal Ataturk, the founder of modern Turkey and someone who is often characterised as being a Jewish agent, for turning Turkey into a country that is subject to the ideological occupation of the West, a yoke from which it needs to be freed by means of a new conquest.[83]

In apocalyptic terms, Constantinople acts as the foreground to Rome (Rūmīya), which appears, not only in ISIS imagery (see its eponymous propagandistic magazine), as the embodiment of a remote locality that, as the Hour approaches, will finally be conquered by Muslims.[84] This motif can be found, for instance, in the speech of Abū Bakr al-Baghdādī (published in English as 'Even If the Disbelievers Despise Such')[85] and in al-Zarqāwī's address 'Riyāh al-naṣr' ('Winds of triumph'),[86] also being cursorily mentioned by Abū Ayyūb al-Miṣrī.[87]

In the medieval texts, there are no identifiable toponyms in Europe in addition to Constantinople other than the city of Rome.[88] Discussions took place in apocalyptic circles of the time as to which of the two cities would fall first. Generally, the honour was always accorded to Constantinople. Currently, Rome is often identified with the Vatican, which for modern Muslim apocalyptists symbolises either 'the capital of global idolatry' or even the seat of the Antichrist.[89]

The final, but no less significant, comment in this section concerns the traditional perspective of the world as being divided into the *dār al-islām* (abode of Islam) and *dār al-ḥarb* (abode of war), which constitutes the most general level in our 'apocalyptic mapping' model. For the vast majority of Islamic scholars, this stark division has lost its relevance in the modern period of globalisation and the migration of millions of Muslims to the West. However, this idea has survived among jihadists,[90] including those ISIS propagandists who have been attempting to revive a host of other medieval proprieties. Within the mental map associated with the group's leaders, this binary division of the world, which has undeniable apocalyptic connotations (see 'To Rome' in Chapter 4), continues to hold a significant place.

Symbolism and Imagery of the Apocalypse

This section aims to introduce the visual imagery and symbolism associated with ISIS propaganda, in general, and its apocalyptic face, in particular. Jihadist groups have had a brief but prolific history in terms of their visual self-presentation and they have created their own distinct 'genre' of Internet-based imagery, which has become a primary vehicle for the diffusion of their message.[91] There is no doubt that the self-presentation of ISIS, fully aware of the importance of the need to control the public space through its symbols,[92] shares many features in common with older jihadist attempts at indoctrination. However, there are additional points where the group's propagandists have traversed a new, so far untested path, especially in the field of 'marketing'.

As far as the visual aspect of the group's propaganda is concerned, the most revolutionary aspect is the level of its professionalism, with the glossy look of *Dabiq* being one of many examples. When compared with the often clumsy attempts of its jihadist predecessors, ISIS video messages to the world are more religiously intransigent and better developed as a spectacle of near-Hollywood quality. The End-times motifs in ISIS propaganda productions can hardly be separated from their other great themes, namely the supposed veracity of their religion and, above all, the combination of death and the afterlife. The symbolism of martyrdom constitutes one of the most prolific issues. Simply stated, ISIS has created its own way of expression, one in which the inexorable forces of religion go hand-in-hand with the pursuit of an attractive message, especially for younger audiences.

The style associated with ISIS written propaganda clearly demonstrates such an approach. Its English-speaking productions are generally characterised by an increasing use of Internet jargon ('netspeak'), indicating how the group is seeking to adapt itself to the Internet environment in order to connect with the identities of young individuals.[93] As a result, the boring delivery of self-declared Islamic purists freely mingles with efforts to be 'cool' – a remarkable result of which is a jargon symptomatic of this jihadist sub-culture. Even within English-language texts, ISIS editors deliberately retain particular Arabic terms untranslated, an act that might well contribute to the creation of a sense of dedication and a feeling of exclusivity among readers.

The designations reserved for the enemies of ISIS certainly deserve special attention since their systematic 'demonisation' is one of the most productive methods used as part of the group's propaganda machinery. Such names generally bring particular groups within the purely religious framework of a struggle between 'belief' and 'disbelief' (or even referred to as 'complete falsehood', in *Dabiq*'s vocabulary).[94] An illustration of this is the use of the term *Mājūs* (Zoroastrians, originally magicians), reserved for Iranian Shiites. Confessional and derogative terms such as *nuṣayrīs* (describing them to be 'filthy')[95] for the Syrian regime and *rāfiḍīs* and *ṣafawīs* for its Iraqi counterpart, cast both enemies within the broader terms of anti-Shiite rhetoric, that is, as being heretics and traitors with their roots deep in Islamic history[96] – all of which is relevant to the apocalyptic context.

ISIS language, reflecting the fanaticism of the group, is full of both insults and superlatives. Extreme adjectives, used together with expressive vocabulary, ultimately help to create and maintain a certain degree of community cohesion. An analysis of ISIS ideological thought through reference to linguistic specifics has proven that affiliation appears to be an increasingly important psychological motive driving the work of this group. Secondly, ISIS has sought to use an expanded body of emotions in a strategic manner.[97] Issues to do with death, females and religion have thus begun to encapsulate three of the most important ideological aspects the ISIS propaganda.[98] And all of them, as we will see below, have found their own symbolic manifestations.

The language that characterises ISIS propaganda, skilfully mixing the stark rhetoric of religious fanaticism with attempts to project a 'cool' style typical of the Internet generation, may easily lead us to the conclusion that there is no space at all for symbols. However, this is definitely not the case. On the contrary, ISIS propagandists certainly possess a well-developed sense of symbolism and – what is of most importance – they have an awareness of how to use it effectively.

It is thus inconceivable to approach ISIS propaganda narratives without the expectation that there will be a varied range of symbolic expressions. In addition to the use of medieval apocalyptic imagery, contemporary material also relies on a range of preferred motifs. Perhaps the most universal symbolic level we should consider first is represented by the motif of other and otherness. In the case of the Qur'ān, with the exception of a few verses that refer to particular categories of people – such as the People of the Book (*ahl al-kitāb*) – in a relatively positive way, the overall representation of the other is essentially negative.

Others are most often portrayed in terms and images that expose them as ignoble and accursed creatures, those who resemble mindless animals and who will soon be severely punished in hell.[99] In fact, the whole concept of otherness in Islam is highly problematic due to the fact that some Muslims themselves are categorised as others in this discourse.[100]

Enemies thus form the most significant 'subset' of the others and, as such, they are subject to the never-ending attention of ISIS. In order to explain to the group's adherents why they are so dangerous and need to be mercilessly killed, many carefully constructed – and often dehumanised – references to them are used as a means of strengthening an awareness of the importance of hating them.

Not only pejorative designations (for example Crusaders and Ṭawāghīt), but also various attributed properties (the symbolism of the cross, for instance),[101] are employed to evoke emotions of resistance and hatred. The latter designation, Ṭāghūt, invoking a Qur᾽ānic concept, describes anyone who has exceeded the limits, in this case becoming a tyrant.[102] Orange uniforms, originally designed for Muslim prisoners in Guantánamo Bay and then used as clothing for ISIS hostages, provides an example of the principle 'an eye for an eye' in its clearest form.[103] According to Admiral Mike Mullen, 'it has been a symbol, and one which has been a recruiting symbol for those extremists and jihadists who would fight us.'[104] ISIS references to Guantánamo Bay are mostly employed in an attempt to paint the United States as being tyrannical and hypocritical and in order to act as a call to arms to fellow Muslims. But they are also used in more simplistic terms, as in the case of orange uniforms.

The infamous video of the Jordanian pilot, Lt Muᶜādh al-Kasāsba, being burnt alive serves as imagery of the ISIS response to its enemies. The footage, officially entitled '*Shifāᶜat al-ṣudūr*' (which its makers translate as 'Healing the Believer's Chest') contains a whole repertoire of such expressions. For example, half a minute into the video, the producers slam the Jordanian king, ᶜAbd Allāh, as the 'Ṭāghūt of Jordan'. After almost four minutes of diatribe, the pilot appears in his orange uniform, referencing Guantánamo. His ID photo flashes on the screen with '*asīr ṣalībī*' written above it, for which the video provides the translation 'Crusader Detainee'. In addition, the United States, France and other states are described as being '*al-taḥāluf al-ṣalībī*', translated on screen as the 'Crusader Coalition'.[105]

Along with the representation of enemies, martyrdom constitutes a central theme of any jihadist self-presentation.[106] The concern of ISIS with death (often called a 'death cult') has been indicated as being one of the most important aspects of this group.[107] Death (*mawt*) is not only celebrated, but even elaborated on in broader juridical terms.[108] Simply stated, death, which is generally seen as the most chaotic aspect of reality, has the main function of opening the gate to the afterlife, around which much of the religious imagery and symbolism has been built.[109] Within ISIS propaganda, in general, death serves two different purposes, both of which incorporate additional symbolic overlaps: as a prerequisite of martyrdom and as a gate to the Next World. In the words of David Cook, 'visualizing the ideological field that is attracting and keeping fighters and "martyrs" is critical for counteracting the dangerous appeal that violent apocalyptic groups, such as Jund al-Sama', have among the larger population in Iraq.'[110] Furthermore, the martyrs introduced by ISIS propaganda are mostly young personable people, characters with whom the group's followers can easily identify.

In the visualisation of ISIS, its notorious black flag plays a crucial role.[111] Neither its colour nor its imagery was chosen randomly. In fact, they were approved by a decree issued by Abū ᶜUmar al-Baghdādī.[112] The apocalyptic appeal of this symbol goes back to the early Islamic period. According to Muslim tradition, the black banner was flown by the Prophet Muḥammad and it was historically used by Abū Muslim as the rallying symbol of the Abbasid revolution in 747.[113] Since then, black flags have often been used as a symbol of religious revolt.[114] The choice of the colour black by ISIS is definitely not innovative, since black flags have also been used by other Islamist organisations since the 1990s.[115] For example, the rise of the Taliban in 1994–6 witnessed frequent mentions of the 'black banners from the east' as part of the family of traditions that supposedly heralded the re-establishment of the caliphate.[116]

The so-called 'seal of Muḥammad' in the centre of the flag is allegedly a replica of the seal used by the Prophet on several letters sent to foreign dignitaries, currently preserved in Topkapi Museum in Istanbul.[117] There is no doubt about the apocalyptic connotations associated with the flag. According to William McCants, there is no doubt that ISIS 'was signalizing that its flag was not only the symbol of its government in Iraq and the herald of future caliphate; it was the harbinger of the final battle at the End of Days.'[118] Moreover, *Dabiq* explicitly predicts that it will soon be flying in Mecca and Medina.[119]

In the millennialist context, black banners appear in a wide variety of forms in the classical collections compiled by Ibn Ḥanbal, Ibn Māja and al-Tirmīdhī, albeit described by the latter as *gharīb* ('strange'). As the portents of the Mahdī, black banners emanating from Khurāsān, or simply 'from the East', defining 'an eschatological territory or even geography', are often referenced. Despite doubts as to their authenticity, they are often cited by modern apocalyptists. References to them can be found across the Internet within a variety of visual and audio material, mostly as an introduction to the topic of inter-Muslim warfare.

According to Nu^caym, 'black banners will appear from Khurāsān; nothing will stop them until they are raised in Jerusalem'.[120] As we already know, it is not only warriors who will be encountered on battlefields stretching from the Mediterranean to Mesopotamia but also symbols and even colours. A prophecy exists according to which 'when the black banners and yellow banners meet at the navel of Syria, then the interior of the earth is better than its exterior'.[121]

The black banners of ISIS are, in fact, a historic irony since their origin is connected with a Shiite anti-regime movement that prepared the way for the Abbasids.[122] However, the current holder of the yellow flag is Ḥizbullāh and consequently the Syrian conflict can also be viewed as a 'war of colours'. Such a perspective can be found among Shiite groups, an example being the Iranian cleric Rūḥullāh Ḥuseinian who, in connection with Syria, cites Imam Ja^cfar al-Ṣādiq who stated that a sign of the Mahdī's return would be a battle involving warriors fighting under yellow flags.[123]

The ISIS official explanation of its flag's design leaves no room for speculation: 'We ask God . . . to make this flag the sole flag for all Muslims. We are certain that it will be the flag of the people of Iraq when they go to aid . . . the Mahdi at the holy house of God.'[124] The flag thus refers, above all, to the total unity of those fighting in its shadow, acting as 'one single body'.[125] Several years ago, iconic pictures of a caravan of white pick-up trucks bearing these haunting flags[126] was broadcast as a visualisation of the 'black banners from the East' motif, revealing the updated apocalyptic face of ISIS and displaying a mixture of brutality and symbolism to the world.

One of the other favoured elements of the symbolic language used by ISIS is the image of the mosque, which points directly to Islam. In ISIS videos, this symbol often alternates with a flapping black flag.[127]

Mosques, from a common perspective, are connected with the crescent moon and serve as the symbol of Islamic identity, while also evoking 'notions of the divine and afterlife'.[128]

As well as mosques, there are many other buildings, monuments and tombs associated with holy figures or fundamental events in the Islamic tradition. Pilgrimage to local shrines is sometimes even prioritised over visits to Mecca, which is the sacred geographic centre for Muslims.[129] The reverence accorded to many of the sites is shared by all Muslims (the Kaᶜba and the Dome of the Rock for example), while others hold significance only for certain groups. ISIS has been involved in the destruction of many sites that are dear to the hearts of local populations. At one point, they even threatened to destroy the Pyramids, perceived in the Muslim tradition as an expression of human haughtiness in the face of God.[130]

Unostentatious, yet highly effective, is another aspect of the symbolic ammunition utilised by ISIS: the family. Idealised pictures of family life, especially women and children, are used as a counterbalance to the gloomy scenes of ubiquitous violence. A portrait of an ISIS warrior gently stroking a kitten has become an iconic part of the group's visual self-presentation.[131]

As regards women, they hold a very unique and powerful symbolic value within Islam in general. The increasing focus on females has been demonstrated by a quantitative linguistic analysis of ISIS propaganda.[132] The visual representation of women is also used to illustrate a feeling of peace and prosperity, although this actually applies only to Muslim women since non-Muslim women are usually depicted as being despised creatures who are participating in the social decline of the West.[133]

Muslim children raised in the caliphate, presented as 'a millenarian project',[134] are primarily used as a reference to peace and happiness and they are employed in jihadist imagery to ignite feelings of pride, but also injustice. Children killed by outside forces are utilised to inspire feelings of anger and a desire for retaliation against the enemy, a fact that can be documented through reference to many examples.[135]

In their notorious videos,[136] ISIS propagandists often blend the above-mentioned symbols and others, mostly taken from Islamic sources, with 'historical grievances and highly-produced sequences incorporating battle scenes from Hollywood war movies to legitimize themselves as Rambo Muslims for jihad'.[137] A more or less explicit apocalyptic ethos can be found in many specific examples, some of them being promoted in the group's magazines, an example of which is a video with the very apocalyptic title *Bāqūna ilā qiyām al-sāᶜa* (*Remaining until coming of the Hour*),[138] advertised in *al-Nabaᵓ* magazine.[139]

Perhaps the most eloquent apocalyptic message ever presented to the world is found in *Meeting in Dabiq*,[140] which depicts the group's vision of a global battle that concludes in Rome. The footage depicts a collection of armoured units heading towards the Colosseum, as well as to St Peter's Basilica in the Vatican. According to this disturbing video, 'believers' will fight against 'crusaders' in their own command post, a fact that is commented on by the narrator in the following way: 'This is your last crusade, the next time it is us who will take the battle to your own land.'[141] Needless to say, an important part of the Muslim apocalypse narrative claims that the final battle will take place on the territory of the enemy and what could be a better embodiment of such an expectation than the episode described above.

Another example of an apocalyptic message is provided by the gruesome ISIS video announcing the execution of Peter Kassig. This video, entitled *Law kariha al-kāfirūn* (*Although the disbelievers dislike it*; the translation offered by ISIS),[142] also contains a threat delivered by the well-known ISIS executioner in his East-London accent:

> Your forces will return greater in number than they were before. We also remind you of the haunting words of our Sheikh Abū Muṣᶜab al-Zarqāwī who told you: 'The spark has been lit here in Iraq and its heat will continue to intensify by Allah's permission until it burns the crusader army.'

Belief in an approaching global conflict that will bring ISIS forces to the gates of Western capitals was also expressed in the video of Lt

Muᶜādh al-Kasāsba's brutal execution,[143] where a song breaks out: 'Inside your own home, the wars will be waged, only for your destruction and suffering, my sword is sharpened.'[144]

Of course, it is no easy task – if indeed at all possible – to distinguish between apocalyptic rhetoric being used as a means of promoting and reinforcing a warlike agenda and situations where scenes of warfare are primarily designed to amplify apocalyptic beliefs. Such a question is raised, for instance, in relation to the video documentary *Flames of War: Fighting Has Just Begun.*[145] Much of the footage in this slickly produced piece focuses on battles in Syria, highlighting their world-historical significance. With the use of flame graphics, night vision and archive US news footage, *Flames of War* actually chronicles the ongoing insurgency of ISIS. The emotive style provides the audience with an insight into the immense ambitions of the group, which transcend simple eschatological boundaries.

ISIS videos are nothing without their traditional soundtracks. Jihadist songs, known as *nashīd*,[146] are an inherent part of ISIS propaganda. They date back to the late 1970s, when Islamic fundamentalists in Egypt and Syria started writing them to inspire their supporters and disseminate their message. Most Islamic scholars now agree that these songs are acceptable, especially during wartime. Since ISIS considers musical instruments to be *ḥarām* (forbidden), almost all their *nashīd*s are performed *a cappella*, the only accompaniment being an array of sound effects ranging from horses' hooves (symbolising the Prophet's time in the desert) to bombs.[147]

Essentially, ISIS *nashīd*s are not defensive in nature. They encapsulate a desire to change the world for ever (see the opening quote in the following chapter). They celebrate the achievements of ISIS warriors, as well as their expected triumphs, ushering in the apocalyptic times that are so colourfully depicted within the group's self-presentation, faithfully following al-Zarqāwī's impassioned intentions, as 'a vanguard of all Muslims' (*ṭalīᶜat al-umma*),[148] fully prepared to face the forces of evil.

Notes

1. *Dabiq* 5:3.
2. Gorenberg, *The End of Days*, p. vii.
3. See the chapters 'Symbolic War' and 'When Symbols Become Deadly' in Juergensmeyer, *Terror in the Mind of God*, pp. 155–63.
4. Nuᶜaym, *The Book of Tribulations*, p. xxxii.
5. Ibid. p. xxxiv.
6. Atwan, *Islamic State*, p. x.
7. McCants, *The ISIS Apocalypse*, p. 111.
8. For an official obituary of the official spokesperson of ISIS, al-ᶜAdnānī, see *al-Nabaʾ* 45:2.
9. Necipoğlu, 'The Dome of the Rock as Palimpsest', p. 80.
10. Nuᶜaym, *The Book of Tribulations*, p. xxxvi.
11. Cf. Ayyūb, *al-Masīḥ al-Dajjāl*, pp. 237–41.
12. Cf. Shandab, *Munāẓara maᶜa ᶜaql dāᶜish*, p. 133.
13. Al-Albānī, *Takhrīj aḥādīth faḍāʾil al-Shām wa-l-Dimashq*, p. 14.
14. See his 'Syria Lecture', available at https://www.youtube.com/watch?v=JklntwgnonA (last accessed 22 November 2017).
15. See the chapter 'The Center of Islam is in Syria', in Nuᶜaym, *The Book of Tribulations*, pp. 134–8.
16. Ibid. p. 124 (no. 611).
17. Ibid. p. xv.
18. McCants, *The ISIS Apocalypse*, p. 100.
19. Cook, *Studies in Muslim Apocalyptic*, p. 256.
20. See Muslim, *Ṣaḥīḥ*, pp. 927–52.
21. Filiu, *Apocalypse in Islam*, p. 18.
22. Another expression for 'strangers'.
23. *Dabiq* 3:9.
24. See his Facebook profile, available at https://ar-ar.facebook.com/ShaykhMuhammadAbulhudaAlYaqoubi/ (last accessed 27 August 2017).
25. Nuᶜaym, *The Book of Tribulations*, p. xxiv.
26. *Dabiq* 15:13.
27. Nuᶜaym, *The Book of Tribulations*, p. xvii.
28. McCants, 'Why ISIS Really Wants to Conquer Baghdad'.
29. Amanat, *Apocalyptic Islam*, p. 227.

30. Cook, *Studies in Muslim Apocalyptic*, pp. 263–4.
31. Ibid. p. 359.
32. Ibid. p. 363. Cf. Nuᶜaym, *The Book of Tribulations*, pp. 167–8.
33. Cook, 'Abu Musᶜab al-Suri and Abu Musᶜab al-Zarqawi'.
34. Cited even in al-ᶜArīfī, *Nihāyat al-ᶜālam*, p. 231.
35. An example can be found at http://mlahim.firstgoo.com/t889-topic (last accessed 25 September 2017).
36. Fishman, *The Master Plan*, p. 254.
37. See Nuᶜaym, *The Book of Tribulations*, pp. 419–25.
38. Ibid. p. xviii.
39. Al-Shahāwī, *al-Masīḥ al-dajjāl wa Yaʾjūj wa Maʾjūj*, p. 63.
40. See Bayūmī, *ᶜAlāmāt yawm al-qiyāma al-ṣughrā*, p. 66.
41. Damir-Geilsdorf and Franke, 'Narrative Reconfigurations', p. 429.
42. Nuᶜaym, *The Book of Tribulations*, p. xxxi.
43. Cook, *Contemporary Muslim Apocalyptic Literature*, p. 54.
44. Muslim, *Ṣaḥīḥ*, p. 932.
45. Nuᶜaym, *The Book of Tribulations*, p. 383.
46. For more information about this locality, see al-ᶜArīfī, *Nihāyat al-ᶜālam*, p. 227.
47. *Rumiyah* 3:25.
48. McCants, 'ISIS fantasies of an apocalyptic showdown in northern Syria'.
49. *Majmūᶜ tafrīghāt*, p. 90.
50. Available at https://www.washingtonpost.com/news/worldviews/wp/2016/10/17/the-isis-apocalypse-has-been-postponed-but-the-militants-might-still-believe-in-it/?utm_term=.50469393aff8 (last accessed 21 November 2017).
51. McCants, *The ISIS Apocalypse*, p. 105.
52. See http://www.asor-syrianheritage.org/wp-content/uploads/2015/03/ASOR_CHI_Weekly_Report_01r.pdf (last accessed 2 February 2018).
53. McCants, *The ISIS Apocalypse*, p. 105.
54. Nuᶜaym, *The Book of Tribulations*, p. xxxvi.
55. Muslim, *Ṣaḥīḥ*, pp. 932–3.
56. Cook, *Studies in Muslim Apocalyptic*, p. 257.
57. Ibid. pp. 53–4.
58. Ibid. p. 49. See also Nuᶜaym, *The Book of Tribulations*, pp. 242–80.
59. Cook, *Studies in Muslim Apocalyptic*, pp. 50–1.
60. *Dabiq* 9:72–3.

61. McCants, *The ISIS Apocalypse*, p. 100.
62. Al-Albānī, *Takhrīj aḥādīth faḍā*ᵓ*il al-Shām wa al-Dimashq*, p. 38. Cf. also al-ᶜArīfī, *Nihāyat al-*ᶜ*ālam*, p. 150.
63. Nuᶜaym, *The Book of Tribulations*, p. 245.
64. Cook, *Studies in Muslim Apocalyptic*, p. 258.
65. See al-ᶜArīfī, *Nihāyat al-*ᶜ*ālam*, pp. 298–9.
66. Al-Baghdādī, *Risāla ilā ḥukkām al-bayt al-abyaḍ*, quoted according to translation in McCants, *The ISIS Apocalypse*, p. 106.
67. For a picture, see, for example, *Dabiq* 5:4.
68. See Qindīl and ᶜAbd al-Rabbihi, *al-Fikr al-islāmī al-jihādī al-mu*ᶜ*āṣir*, pp. 465–6. Its propaganda is available at http://jihadology.net/category/al-manarah-al-bay%E1%B8%8Da-foundation-for-media-production/ (last accessed 20 November 2017).
69. McCants, *The ISIS Apocalypse*, p. 219.
70. For the ISIS view on Jerusalem, see *al-Naba*ᵓ 22:13. Cf. al-Zarqāwī, *Kalimāt muḍī*ᶜ*a*, p. 151.
71. See, for example, al-ᶜArīfī, *Nihāyat al-*ᶜ*ālam*, p. 42.
72. See *al-Naba*ᵓ 22:13.
73. See, for example, *Majmū*ᶜ *tafrīghāt*, pp. 26, 48, 52, 59-61, 99–101, etc.
74. Gorenberg, *The End of Days*, p. 61.
75. Necipoğlu, 'The Dome of the Rock as Palimpsest', p. 28.
76. See Nomani and Arafa, 'Inside the symbols and psychology of the Islamic State'.
77. See Alvanou, 'Symbolisms of basic Islamic imagery in jihadi propaganda'.
78. See Ayyūb, *al-Masīḥ al-Dajjāl*, pp. 239–41.
79. Nomani and Arafa, 'Inside the symbols and psychology of the Islamic State.'
80. See, for example, *Rumiyah* 3:26.
81. Cook, *Studies in Muslim Apocalyptic*, pp. 59–60.
82. See al-ᶜArīfī, *Nihāyat al-*ᶜ*ālam*, pp. 152–7.
83. Cook, *Contemporary Muslim Apocalyptic Literature*, p. 133.
84. See Muslim, *Ṣaḥīḥ*, p. 933.
85. 'And the march of the mujahidin will continue until they reach Rome, by Allah's permission.' Available at https://archive.org/stream/EvenIfTheDisbelieversDespiseSuch/Even%20if%20the%20Disbelievers%20Despise%20Such#page/n0/mode/1up (last accessed 21 November 2017).

86. Al-Zarqāwī, *Kalimāt muḍīʿa*, p. 151.
87. See *Majmūʿ tafrīghāt*, p. 142.
88. Nuʿaym, *The Book of Tribulations*, p. xviii.
89. Cook, *Contemporary Muslim Apocalyptic Literature*, p. 188.
90. See Qindīl and ʿAbd al-Rabbihi, *al-Fikr al-islāmī al-jihādī al-muʿāṣir*, pp. 373–4.
91. Alvanou, 'Symbolisms of basic Islamic imagery in jihadi propaganda'.
92. Beránek and Ťupek, *The Temptation of Graves*, p. 184.
93. Vergani and Bliuc, 'The evolution of the ISIS' language', p. 7.
94. *Dabiq* 2:5.
95. *Dabiq* 2:42.
96. Günther, 'Presenting the Glossy Look of Warfare in Cyberspace'.
97. Vergani and Bliuc, 'The evolution of the ISIS' language', p. 7.
98. Ibid. p. 17.
99. Morrow, *Islamic Images and Ideas*, p. 234.
100. Ibid. p. 225.
101. See *Dabiq* 15:46–63.
102. Qurʾān 4:51, 4:60, 4:76. See also Qindīl and ʿAbd al-Rabbihi, *al-Fikr al-islāmī al-jihādī al-muʿāṣir*, p. 361.
103. For particular examples, see *Rumiyah* 11, *Dabiq* 8 and 5; the ISIS photographs of Coptic prisoners; videos of Japanese hostages and a Jordanian pilot being murdered; ISIS video series 'Lend Me Your Ears' featuring British journalist and ISIS prisoner John Cantlie speaking about ISIS – in each video Cantlie is dressed in an orange uniform à la Guantánamo; video of ISIS executing American hostage Steven Sotloff, etc.
104. See http://www.humanrightsfirst.org/sites/default/files/AQ-ISIS-Propaganda-Use-of-Gitmo-Issue-Brief.pdf (last accessed 22 November 2017).
105. See Nomani and Arafa, 'Inside the symbols and psychology of the Islamic State'.
106. For the Muslim doctrine of martyrdom among Salafi jihadists, see Hegghammer (ed.), *Jihadi Culture*, pp. 151–70.
107. Vergani and Bliuc, 'The evolution of the ISIS' language', p. 16.
108. See, for example, *al-Nabaʾ* 52:13.
109. Juergensmeyer, *Terror in the Mind of God*, p. 158.
110. Cook, 'Iraq as the Focus for Apocalyptic Scenarios'.
111. For its official design, see *Mashrūʿīyat al-rāya fī al-islām*, p. 5.

112. Ibid. p. 4.
113. For a historic context, see Yücesoy, *Messianic Beliefs*, pp. 19–24.
114. Alvanou, 'Symbolisms of basic Islamic imagery in jihadi propaganda'.
115. See Kovács, 'The "New Jihadists" and the Visual Turn from al-Qaᶜida to ISIL/ISIS/Daᵓish,' pp. 47–69. See also Hegghammer (ed.), *Jihadi Culture*, pp. 87–93.
116. Nuᶜaym, *The Book of Tribulations*, p. xxxiv.
117. Aydin, *Pavilion of the Sacred Relics*, p. 101.
118. McCants, *The ISIS Apocalypse*, pp. 21–2.
119. *Dabiq* 5:3.
120. Nuᶜaym, *The Book of Tribulations*, p. 109 (no. 530).
121. Ibid. p. 147 (no. 749).
122. The current perception of the black flags of ISIS among Muslims is controversial. For an illustrative example of the related on-line disputes, see https://dawaalhaq.com/post/69109 (last accessed 25 July 2017).
123. Karouny, 'Apocalyptic prophecies'.
124. *Mashrūᶜīyat al-rāya*, p. 5. Cited from the translation in McCants, *The ISIS Apocalypse*, p. 22.
125. *Mashrūᶜīyat al-rāya*, p. 1.
126. See, for example, http://www.ronpaulinstitute.org/archives/featured-articles/2015/october/09/the-mystery-of-isis-toyota-army-solved/ (last accessed 22 December 2017).
127. See Nomani and Arafa, 'Inside the symbols and psychology of the Islamic State'.
128. Alvanou, 'Symbolisms of basic Islamic imagery in jihadi propaganda'.
129. Beránek and Ťupek, *The Temptation of Graves*, p. 3.
130. See https://www.iraqinews.com/iraq-war/isis-threatens-to-blow-up-egyptian-pyramids/ (last accessed 20 November 2017).
131. See *Dabiq* 15:9.
132. Vergani and Bliuc, 'The evolution of the ISIS' language', p. 7. For more information about the role of women in ISIS propaganda, see Mah-Rukh, *ISIS and Propaganda*.
133. See *Dabiq* 15:20–5.
134. Berger, 'The Metronome of Apocalyptic Time', p. 61.
135. See *Dabiq* 7:6.
136. For the ISIS contribution to the Jihadi cinematography, see Hegghammer (ed.), *Jihadi Culture*, pp. 124–6.

137. See Nomani and Arafa, 'Inside the symbols and psychology of the Islamic State'.
138. As far as I know, this video is currently not available.
139. *Al-Naba*ʾ 77:10.
140. Available at https://archive.org/download/MeetingAtDabiq (last accessed 22 February 2018).
141. For a thorough analysis of this notorious video, see Sophie Jane Evans, 'ISIS's chilling death march to the End of the World: Jihadists release video depicting their apocalyptic vision of a future battle culminating in Rome', available at http://www.dailymail.co.uk/news/article-3356503/ISIS-s-chilling-death-march-end-world-Jihadists-release-video-depicting-vision-future-battle-culminating-Colosseum.html (last accessed 22 November 2017).
142. Available at https://sendvid.com/ryvlns0s (last accessed 22 February 2018).
143. Available at http://video.foxnews.com/v/4030583977001/?#sp=show-clips (last accessed 22 July 2017).
144. See Nomani and Arafa, 'Inside the symbols and psychology of the Islamic State'.
145. For the full video, see https://archive.org/download/TheIslamicStateAlHayatMediaCentrePresentsTheBrilliantVideoReleaseFlamesOfWarFightingHasJustBegun (last accessed 22 November 2017). Shortened version is available at http://news.siteintelgroup.com/blog/index.php/categories/jihad/entry/287-is-releases-video-documentary-%E2%80%9Cflames-of-war-fighting-has-just-begun%E2%80%9D (last accessed 22 November 2017).
146. For an insightful introduction to the cultural meaning of the *nashīd*, see a lecture by Behnam Said, available at http://jihadology.net/2016/02/29/jihadology-podcast-nasheeds-history-and-cultural-meaning/ (last accessed 20 November 2017). For the ISIS usage of *anāshīd*, see Hegghammer (ed.), *Jihadi Culture*, pp. 60–2.
147. See https://www.theguardian.com/music/2014/nov/09/nasheed-how-isis-got-its-anthem (last accessed 21 November 2017).
148. See al-Zarqāwī, *Kalimāt muḍīʿa*, p. 178.

4

The Spark Has Been Lit Here in Iraq

Ghurabaa [sic!] do not bow their foreheads to anyone besides Allah. Ghurabaa have chosen this to be their motto of life. If you ask about us, we do not care about tyrants. We are the regular soldiers of Allah; our path is a reserved path . . . We never care about chains, rather we'll continue forever. So, let us make jihad, and battle, and fight from the start. Ghurabaa, this is how they are free in the enslaved world.

– English subtitles from a video of the song *Ghurabāʾ* ('Strangers'), an unofficial ISIS hymn.[1]

I call this process satanization . . . When the opponent rejects one's moral or spiritual position; when the enemy appears to hold the power to completely annihilate one's community, one's culture, and oneself; . . . and when there seems no way to defeat the enemy in human terms – all of these conditions increase the likelihood that one will envision one's opponent as a superhuman foe, a cosmic enemy.

– Mark Juergensmeyer[2]

The Islamic State operates like a nasty bacterial infection. The Surge and the Awakening almost killed it, but the remnants that survived emerged more resistant to the antibiotics of military force – and even more capable of recruiting widely.

– Brian Fishman[3]

This chapter attempts to examine the role of the End-time agenda in ISIS self-presentation materials. Using the group's primary sources, the first section elaborates on the development of ISIS apocalyptic rhetoric and this brief chronological introduction then enables us to carefully investigate the methods by which ISIS has utilised selected apocalyptic pointers, either events or trends, which from the perspective of the group's propagandists have already been fulfilled. These allegedly past signs serve as a powerful tool and are used to prove the accuracy of the overall 'apocalyptic approach' in relation to current affairs. This approach is aimed at the indoctrination of the audience and, above all, at the recruitment of new adherents to the cause.[4] If an individual becomes convinced that apocalyptic lenses can truly explain the past and the present, there is no reason why they should not also believe in the accuracy of future predictions (see 'The Apocalytic March' below).

Nevertheless, from the very beginning, we should not forget the epistemological limitations related to our subject. It still holds true that no one is sure as to whether the proponents of ISIS really believe in the message they broadcast to the world. As Fawaz Gerges has succinctly noted, 'ISIS's story is complex and it cannot be derived from its propaganda narrative, a narrative that some scholars take for granted at their own peril.'[5]

The following interpretation, therefore, attempts to discuss the apocalyptic dimension of ISIS self-presentation as well as its contexts and overlaps. No expressions pertaining to 'the beliefs of ISIS representatives' and the like are employed below since such a short-sighted approach might easily lead us astray. On the other hand, the author certainly does not wish to restrict his interpretation to the provision of only a description of the style of 'ISIS apocalypticism as seen from the ISIS perspective'. This is because the group's contribution to internal Muslim End-time polemics, as promoted by its propaganda, looks completely different when placed in the broader framework of contemporary Islamic apocalyptic discourse.

The Apocalyptic March

An exploration of the ISIS apocalyptic message to the world is hardly a straightforward task. In this section, the birth of the above-mentioned 'apocalyptic mutation of global jihadism', to which Jean-Pierre Filiu has so presciently referred,[6] will be discussed in order to proceed to a key question related to the genuine specifics of such an 'upgraded apocalypticism' (see 'To Rome', this chapter). The turbulent development of ISIS has been thoroughly examined by a number of scholars, and thus the story of the transformation of a tiny group of jihadists into the most frightening nightmare faced by both Westerners and the vast majority of Muslims, as well as its subsequent retreat to the margins, will not be paraphrased here. And, since the development of modern Muslim apocalypticism has already been discussed in Chapter 2, our natural starting point will be the legacy of Abū Musᶜab al-Zarqāwī, characterised by his preoccupation with the role of Iraq within the expected End-time drama.

As Brian Fishman has accurately stated, 'although Zarqawi was not primarily focused on the end-time prophecies, the Islamic State celebrates his references to eschatology, and his successors introduced apocalyptic prophecies into group overall vision'.[7] The apocalyptic agenda, in fact, is precisely linked to those aspects of Zarqāwī's thought that in no way adhered to the traditional Salafi approach. Several years later, ISIS proudly declared its loyalty to his ideological heritage, not only by adopting the famous motto that has become the title of this chapter but also by the recurrent publication of his statements in the group's propaganda.[8]

As we have already identified, the ideologies of Salafism, in general, and Wahhabism more particularly, that have generally provided the doctrinal resources for Sunni jihadist groups have historically been far less prone to any form of apocalyptic lure. The apocalyptic message of ISIS – rising, according to Cole Bunzel, from the same sources as the millennial uprising in Mecca in 1979 led by Juhaymān al-ᶜUtaybī[9] – belongs to the group's major ideological innovations. It is definitely not a 'spiritual ornament', as might be deduced from a number of otherwise knowledgeable monographs on ISIS, but a fundamental constitutive element. Continuing to use such building terminology, we can state that while the foundations of this edifice lie firmly in Salafi soil, they have been totally reshaped. In this respect, the starting points of ISIS are not particularly original, as Fawaz Gerges has correctly summarised:

> Nevertheless, far from being sui generis, genealogically and ideologically, ISIS belongs to the Salafi-jihadist family, or global jihadism, although it marks another stage in the evolution or, rather, mutation of the ideological gene pool. Its leader, Abu Bakr al-Baghdadi, not only inherited the bloody legacy of his predecessor, Abu Musab al-Zarqawi, the founder of Al Qaeda in Iraq, but also models himself on Osama bin Laden, who is for Salafi-jihadists a 'martyr' and remains the undisputed, charismatic leader of the global jihadist movement.[10]

Apocalypticism is simply 'a dish from an ideological menu' served up by ISIS, whose individual members are, of course, driven by a wide variety of forces. In fact, not all members are motivated by – or even aware of – the ideology of the group they support. Such ideology should be understood at two levels, the first being Salafi jihadism and the second being the ISIS hard-line orientation that exists within this faction, which is, to a large degree, what actually separates it today from al-Qāᶜida.[11] Nevertheless, for an important section of the group's followers, the ethos of apocalypse undisputedly pertains to some of the most attractive features of ISIS.

Al-Zarqāwī's legacy has left indelible traces on the group's ideological framework and, in their online literature and YouTube videos, ISIS propagandists often celebrate him as an icon of their generation and their first *amīr* (commander).[12] In practical terms, two of al-Zarqāwī's obsessions (hatred towards Shiites and the historical episode of the unification of Muslims against Crusaders) played a part in the formation of what might be called 'the apocalyptic face of ISIS'. The hatred towards Shiites, together with his distinctive takfiri way of thinking, head in the same unsophisticated direction: the stark division of humanity into two irreconcilable camps – the supporters of

ISIS and the rest of the world – an approach which is so symptomatic of the concept of 'cosmic war'. Needless to say, such fratricidal inter-Islamic clashes represent some of the most prominent features of the approaching Hour.

We can only speculate as to whether apocalyptic belief really drives the group's worldly activities or, on the contrary, whether it is just the unpredictable policy of ISIS that further reinforces the apocalyptic conviction of the group's followers. At a political level, the takfiri approach to fellow Muslims has already become a particular 'hallmark' of ISIS. At an apocalyptic level, such bi-polarity constitutes one of the most productive motifs of any Muslim End-time scenario, as we will see below. To the mind of ISIS followers, most of the one and a half billion Muslims are targets, not allies,[13] a fact that applies in both geopolitical and eschatological terms.

Apart from this, al-Zarqāwī's preoccupation with the personality of Nūr al-Dīn Zengī was to lead him to the dream of dominating all Muslims. Later, such a dream found its symbolic expression in a key moment in ISIS history, the declaration of the caliphate, strategically positioned in the centre between 'the Crusaders and the Jews in the Levant and the Rafidah [Shiites] in Iraq and Persia'.[14] In a presumed tribute to al-Zarqāwī, the group specifically chose the Great Mosque of al-Nūrī to make this historical statement, the very spot from which many believe Nūr al-Dīn launched his own campaign against the Crusaders. It is very likely that Abū Bakr al-Baghdādī, as the self-declared caliph Ibrāhīm, thus sought to show to the world that the initial motivations behind al-Zarqāwī's struggle were being fulfilled.

Several highly symbolic elements thus intersected at a single point: Al-Baghdādī, wearing the supposed clothing of the first Muslims, announced the revival of the caliphate, a model Islamic institution, in the same place where a medieval attempt to unite all Muslims had been undertaken, all of this highlighted by the mighty millennial message referenced in the black flags. This is the reason why these infamous banners (see 'Symbolism and Imagery of the Apocalypse' in Chapter 3) have also been adopted by ISIS as its macabre 'trademark', spreading terror wherever they appear.

If the evolution of the ISIS approaches to the End-time agenda were to be summarised into a single point, it would be the gradual shift from the unbound millennialism of the early phase to the 'tamed apocalypticism' of the caliphate. This working designation, intended for the later period, should not lead us to view the current situation as something less dangerous or less deserving of concern when compared to the earlier manifestation. Such a form of 'tamed apocalypticism' is actually designed so that it can be retained in the hands of its own creators.

It should not be assumed that this is an indication of any moderation in terms of the means to be adopted to realise objectives. On the contrary, the very ability to induce strong emotions is a necessary prerequisite of any preacher of the apocalypse – and ISIS, in this respect, is no exception. In other words, we are speaking about a certain transition from the profession of the imminent End towards the promotion of the End 'behind the horizon', still near and able to elicit emotions but not within immediate reach. That is the difference.

Within this overarching logic, ISIS propaganda has been able to establish a feeling of urgency, the first requirement of any apocalyptic movement, without losing absolute control over its undesirable side-effects in the time remaining. Furthermore, the group has conveyed and reinforced this sense of urgency with a remarkably high level of media production and dissemination, at a level that is incomparably higher than any other jihadist organisation.[15]

As far as the thematic composition of such an apocalypse is concerned, the 'tamed features' are more implicit, temporally oriented, and, above all, less supernatural in terms of origin. For instance, the establishment of the caliphate was depicted as ushering in a fundamentally new and more just era for Muslims and as creating a clean break with the past. Thus, in the first issue of *Dabiq*, immediately after an article describing the significance of the Dābiq prophecy, there are four 'more practical' pages devoted to explaining and celebrating the caliphate's birth and message.[16] This tamed apocalypticism permeates both ISIS propaganda and the informal conversations of the group's followers on the Internet. In fact, this latter level of 'nondoctrinal ideas', which might also be called 'an apocalyptic reading of the present' runs parallel to the fully-fledged millennialist narratives, mostly relying on the *malāhim* (battles) motifs.

The initial approach of 'unbound millennialism' was greatly influenced by Abū Ayyūb al-Miṣrī, also known as Abū Hamza al-Muhājir (ca. 1968–18 April 2010), the leading ideologist and minister of war for the group, killed during a US-led raid.[17] ISIS still venerates his memory.[18] Just a few months after taking the helm, al-Miṣrī attempted to fulfil al-Zarqawi's 'state-building' prediction in particular and, in October 2007, he announced the establishment of ISI. He also declared that all Iraqi Muslims should pledge an oath of allegiance to the new leader, Abū ᶜUmar al-Baghdādī (1959–2010).[19]

With this self-confident declaration, al-Miṣrī started to promote his own messianic ideas,[20] according to which the Mahdī was going to return at any moment. This was why ISI needed to be established before his return.[21] Therefore, a great number of apocalyptic messages spread by the then group's propaganda machine focused on the establishment of 'a caliphate according to a prophetic method'. This was in order to fulfil the famous *ḥadīth* describing the course of history as a descending process terminating in the establishment of the rightly guided empire,[22] which would occur prior to the coming of the Mahdī.[23] The caliphate had to be prepared in order to provide the Mahdī with a logistic background and versatile support, above all by the gathering of a Muslim vanguard under the black banner of ISI that would, in al-Miṣrī's own words, be taken over by the Mahdī.[24]

Al-Miṣrī's millennial belief was arguably inspired and fuelled by al-Zarqāwī's legacy, with the latter drawing an outline, while the former painted the full picture. At the end of his first interview, al-Miṣrī even quoted al-Zarqāwī's reference to the world-historical significance of the struggle: 'We are fighting in Iraq, but our eyes are on Jerusalem.'[25] The fundamental advantage supporting any form of Muslim millennial speculation is actually the large scale and even greater ambiguity of traditions associated with the 'End-time portents', particularly those related to the internal Muslim clashes that will take place during the final days. Furthermore, al-Miṣrī's major contribution to the apocalyptic image of ISI (as well as more latterly ISIS) has been the group's adoption of the black flag, together with the reasoning linked to the choice of colour and wording.[26]

In the case of al-Miṣrī's End-time obsession, he not only magnified existing apocalyptic speculations but he was also able to capitalise on them in political terms. And, if we borrow the title of the above-cited David Cook study, he indeed belongs to the group of 'apocalyptic practitioners'. In his Friday sermon (*khuṭba*), al-Miṣrī even made a clear reference to the classical narrative claiming that the Mahdī would appear in front of the Kaᶜba and would usher in the apocalypse.[27]

Since al-Miṣrī strongly believed that the Mahdī would come within the year, he instigated particular measures in order to welcome him. Anticipating the imminent conquest of the major Islamic cities, as foretold in apocalyptic tradition, al-Miṣrī ordered the building of pulpits (pl. *manābir*) that the Mahdī would ascend in the Prophet's mosque in Medina, the Great Umayyad mosque in Damascus, and the al-Aqṣā Mosque in Jerusalem. He undoubtedly anticipated the conquest of the whole of Iraq within a single three-month period.[28]

In a notable 2007 episode of jihadist whistle-blowing, the ISI chief jurist Abū Sulaymān al-ᶜUtaybī wrote a letter to the al-Qāᶜida leadership in Afghanistan in order to complain about his own superiors' level of apocalypticism:

> Among [ISI's] errors is the incorrect understanding of the signs of the [Final] Hour. If the issue were limited to this, it would be easy to solve, but the problem spills into [our] jihadist work in the field. For instance, [their claim] that the Mahdi will appear in less than a year led [them] to the claim that we would control the entire land of Mesopotamia [i.e. Iraq] within three months. So, they issued an order [to the fighters] against withdrawing from the battlefield until the [apocalypse] came to pass.[29]

In their response to al-ᶜUtaybī's accusations, al-Qāᶜida leaders wrote a letter to al-Miṣrī to query, among other things, his genuine views on the coming of the Mahdī. By asking this question, they indicated that they considered the accusations, at minimum, worth looking into. They got no response.[30]

In his second preserved interview,[31] al-Miṣrī referred to the American occupation of Iraq as part of a broader Jewish plan to establish 'Greater Israel from the Nile to the Euphrates', enthusiastically supported by other enemies – that is, Shiites, here referred to as Zoroastrians, *majūs* (magicians). In fact, his hatred of the Shia, as well as his penchant for conspiracy theory, also fitted well within the apocalyptic perception of an irrevocably broken world.

Unfortunately, al-Miṣrī's millennial obsession was to fully absorb him. He was convinced that his message of the imminent arrival of the Mahdī would have mass appeal, totally overturning the Middle Eastern order. Simply put, while al-Miṣrī has become a source of inspiration, at the same time, he has created specific blind alleyways in relation to Mahdist propaganda. His collected speeches[32] document his belief in his personal historic mission. The self-confident comparison he makes between the Prophet's community in Medina and ISI – as being a haven for the oppressed, thus highlighting the similarities between the beginning and end of Islam – are very characteristic of Muslim apocalyptic thinking in general. It is precisely this theme that acts as a leitmotif to al-Miṣrī's impassioned speech entitled '*al-Dawla al-nabawīya*' (The Prophetic State).[33] An impressive account of general decay, symptomatic of the apocalyptic age, is vividly described in his other addresses.[34]

His eschatological pronouncements soon started to become a cause for concern among other jihadists.[35] Al-Miṣrī's perception of the ISI struggle in Iraq as being an introductory phase of the global war that would lead to the Hour led him to the conviction that the group should also pave the road for the Mahdī's rule through the consistent implementation of shariah regulations, allegedly an inevitable outcome for all rightly guided Muslim countries. As regards the obvious counter-productivity of al-Miṣrī's millennial zeal, other members of ISI soon became aware of the 'devastating consequences it was having on the group's future development'.[36]

To be accurate and consistent, there are doubts concerning the genuineness of al-Miṣrī's belief. The real motivations of Abū Sulaymān al-ᶜUtaybī's complaints are open to question as well. Simply stated, there are a number of arguments both against and in favour of the destructive influence of the unrestrained millennialism over the early stage of ISI. Some of these ambiguities has been summarised by Brian Fishman:

> It is difficult to know what to make of Abu Sulayman's claim that Abu Hamzah rushed to establish the ISI because he thought the world would end within a year. On the one hand, Abu Hamzah said nothing of the sort when he celebrated the state's founding and immediately blessed projects to create a state-like institutional structure. The minister of agriculture and marine wealth was named only months after the ISI was established, which seems discordant if the group's leaders truly believed the world would end within twelve months. On the other hand, both Abu Hamzah and Abu Umar often referenced a final judgment day and sometimes framed their analysis of current events within the prophetical 'Signs of the Hour', which according to Islamic prophecy indicates that the final battle between good and evil is imminent.[37]

It was becoming increasingly clear that the assumed millennial obsession of al-Miṣrī resulted in the questioning of his ideological competence. In this fundamental respect, al-Qāᶜida's leaders were warned that al-Miṣrī had become too heavily focused on 'the tribulations preceding the Day of Judgment, especially regarding the Mahdī' and that ISI was 'approaching an abyss' if it remained under his control.[38] In fact, al-ᶜUtaybī even alleged that al-Miṣrī, in his rush to establish the ISI on an apocalyptic timeline, 'has invented' Abū ᶜUmar al-Baghdādī to play the role in his fixed End-time visions and ideas.[39] The subsequent 'jihadist divorce' between the group and al-Qāᶜida nevertheless resulted for a number of reasons of both an ideological and political nature – and the different opinions associated with the End-time certainly did not feature as one of the major issues raised regarding ISIS legitimacy.[40]

It should also be emphasised that the period of the group's 'millennial heyday' was the same period that witnessed its decline in military and political terms. When success was next to come to ISIS, its apocalyptic presentations had little in common with the original millennial obsessions of al-Miṣrī. Of course, a belief in the imminent arrival of the Mahdī cannot last forever and, therefore, the former 'overheated millennialism' had reaped its reward. The group started to be much more cautious. Its propagandists tried to solve the eternal problem that plagues all movements utilising the immense power of millennialism: 'how to keep hope smoldering without letting it burst into flames', referencing here the apt simile coined by Gershom Gorenberg.[41]

After 2008, ISI started to lose its support and legitimacy amongst jihadists, both in Iraq and abroad. The millennial ardour of the group was thus to gradually cool because 'the "shelf life" for any intense degree of messianic anticipation is alarmingly short, as the history of millenarian movements abundantly demonstrates'.[42] Despite this, the pursuit of apocalyptic rhetoric did not cease completely. Indeed, this was true of Abū ᶜUmar al-Baghdādī,[43] Miṣrī's former boss, who, in April 2007, had publicly stated that Iraqi troops would 'aid the Mahdi clinging to the curtains of the Kaᶜba'.[44] This is thought to be a reference to a narrative describing how tribes around the Kaᶜba would be engaged in fighting with one another, some fleeing the battle when they found a man who had buried his face in the Kaᶜba's coverings and was weeping. Because of the man's purity, they would pledge allegiance to him – with the man turning out to be the Mahdī.[45]

This enigmatic point, according to William McCants, also has another dimension, its non-canonical origins from Nuᶜaym's *Kitāb al-fitan* allegedly showing that 'ISIS's first emir succumbed to its gravitational pull is a testament to the apocalyptic fervour of the State's founders'.[46] It is an important point since Nuᶜaym's reliability and orthodoxy have been questioned by many conservative *ᶜulamāʾ*.[47]

Abū ᶜUmar al-Baghdādī, this self-declared 'commander of the faithful', also quoted the Dābiq prophecy, reminding all Muslims about what his followers were fighting for.[48] Clearly, his *Risāla ilā ḥukkām al-bayt al-abyaḍ* (*The letter to the rulers of the White House*)[49] is saturated with apocalyptic themes and contains a note about Jesus' eschatological role, as well as references to the approaching final war between Muslims and infidels.

Over time, ISIS was able to learn from its earlier mistakes. Thus, the group began to focus its ideological efforts on a more sustainable approach to apocalypticism that could attract Muslims but, at the same time, demonstrate its 'state-building qualities'. In 2014, when the notoriously secretive new leader of ISIS, Abū Bakr al-Baghdādī, alias Caliph Ibrāhīm (1971–?),[50] delivered his famous Mosul sermon, the group's propagandists were already better advised on how to deal with the explosive millennial content in order to make it 'usable' for a longer period of time. As part of the introduction of ISIS to the world, the caliphate of al-Baghdādī has been a crucial step on the path toward the battle between the forces of Islam and 'Rome' (the West), which is generally predicted to culminate in the final triumph of Islam before the Hour.

On 14 May 2015, ISIS released an audiotape with al-Baghdādī as the alleged speaker. In this recording, which was released simultaneously with transcripts in several languages, al-Baghdādī also comments on the great future that lies ahead for ISIS:

> Our Prophet (peace be upon him) has informed us of the Malahim [battles] near the end of time. He gave us good tidings and promised us that we would be victorious in these battles. He is the truthful and trustworthy, peace be upon him. And here we are today seeing the signs of those Malahim and we feel the winds of victory within them . . . You are recording the Malahim and restoring the glories of Islam.[51]

On another occasion, in his 'recruitment speech' '*Baqīya fī al-ᶜIrāq wa al-Shām*' ('Those who stayed behind in Iraq and Syria'), al-Baghdādī encouraged Muslims to come to the territory under the control of ISIS since 'great battles are about to transpire'.[52] Those great battles precede the Hour.

There is no doubt that for ISIS the return of the caliphate, the intention behind al-Zarqāwī's dreams,[53] is part of a broader millennialist narrative. The group deliberately uses this motif as a sign of the fulfilment of apocalyptic prophecies and in order to claim its own key cosmological significance. In doing so, ISIS has created a new 'jihadist paradigm', since the alleged fulfilment of the prophecy concerning the revival of Islamic rule represents the cornerstone of the group's conceptual and theoretical challenge to al-Qāᶜida.

To maintain the internal validity of this narrative, however, ISIS must continue to hold and preferably expand the territory under its control. The narrative is thus one of ISIS's greatest strengths but it also potentially creates a high level of vulnerability. ISIS, with its necessary attachment to territory, can be destroyed as an organisation in a way that al-Qāᶜida cannot be.[54]

According to Timothy Furnish, it is very likely that al-Baghdādī saw himself as preparing the way for the Mahdī's coming.[55] Pointing to al-Baghdādī's engagement in a high-stakes gamble by leaning so heavily on apocalyptic references, Aaron Zelin has characterised the group's devotion to the apocalypse in the following way: 'They're going for broke. They're putting all the chips on the table, and they think they're going to win.'[56] In any case, al-Baghdādī's impassioned speech has foreshadowed the immodest ambitions of this newly founded proto-state:

> The sun of jihad has risen, and the glad tidings of goodness have shone forth. Triumph looms on the horizon, and the signs of victory have appeared. Here, the flag of the Islamic State, the flag of monotheism, rises and flutters. Its shadow covers the land from Aleppo to Diyala. Beneath it the walls of the tyrants have been demolished, their flags have fallen, and their borders have been destroyed . . . It is a dream that lives in the depths of every Muslim believer. It is a hope that flutters in the heart of every *mujahid* [performing jihad] monotheist. Now the caliphate has returned. We ask God the exalted to make it in accordance with the prophetic method.[57]

Finally, al-Baghdādī was to announce his vision of global expansion: 'This is my advice to you. If you hold to it, you will conquer Rome and own the world, if Allah wills.'[58] The city of Rome (Rūmīya) here symbolises the utmost goal.[59] In this, ISIS actually removed its focus from the Mahdī's imminent return to emphasising the need for an established powerful state, thus preparing the path for His mission. In his famous Mosul sermon, al-Baghdādī addressed a deep tension associated with the caliphate's creation. Brian Fishman aptly formulates this as 'the fundamentally anti-establishment movement . . . trying to institutionalize itself'.[60]

In fact, in very unambiguous terms, al-Baghdādī provided a framework for a decisive conflict between the forces of good and evil, one which would be far beyond the scale of normal warfare: 'Verily, today's battle is not a mere crusaders' campaign but it is actually a war led by the countries of disbelief in their entirety against the countries of Islam.'[61] Simply summarised, the group gradually removed its attention from a focus on the eschatological Saviour to the earthly State. As a result of al-Baghdādī observing how his precursors had almost destroyed themselves because of their hastily made strategic decisions, linked to their assumed belief that the Mahdī would appear any day, he chose to make the caliphate the real locus of the group's apocalyptic imagination. This decisive shift of eschatological emphasis bought the group 'more time to govern while sustaining the apocalyptic moment that has so captivated its supporters'.[62]

The apocalyptic ethos, however, cannot only be maintained and reinforced by identifying and temporalising the End-time portents, but also by other effective means, for instance by reference to suitably chosen narratives about various historical movements that have emerged from the same millennial ground.[63] Such an indirect (retrospective) comparison of ISIS with great heroes or powers of the past can also be used to substantially support the group's appeal. In fact, this narrative technique can be found in countless examples of its propaganda.[64] Even Abū Ayyūb al-Miṣrī and Abū ᶜUmar al-Baghdādī used the comparison of their 'state' to the Prophet's emirate in Medina which, according to their argumentation, originally did not control a large territory and faced massive opposition from both internal and external enemies; yet no Muslim would consider it illegitimate. Their rhetorical trick was obvious: to doubt the legitimacy of the ISI was to doubt the Prophet Muḥammad himself.[65]

What actually makes ISIS' 'retrospective propaganda' so alluring is the fact that – in Michael Pregill's succinct terminology – it embeds the present in a kind of timeless scriptural now. The contemporary experience is not so different from that of bygone days, and the present appears as the natural culmination of the scriptural past. The oppression of evildoers in all ages is the same; the suffering of the faithful in all ages is the same. Throughout history, the pattern recurs until the time of the Mahdī.[66] In this overarching logic, it is definitely not a coincidence that the ISIS propaganda so strongly highlights the motif of the new *hijra*, that is, the recommended resettlement of all righteous Muslims in ISIS territories (see 'To Rome', this chapter).[67]

This key theme of the *hijra* (or emigration) to the new caliphate, declared by Abū Bakr al-Baghdādī as 'obligatory', also appeared in the very first issue of *Dabiq* magazine. ISIS propaganda framed this call in religious terms, but al-Baghdādī's speech emphasised more practical considerations, since he required emigrants with specific skills, namely 'scholars, legal experts and judges, as well as people with military, administrative, mechanical expertise, along with medical doctors and engineers of all specializations'.[68]

The theme of Islamic renewal through emigration also appears in the seminal book *Thalāthat al-usūl* (*The Three Principles*) by Ibn ᶜAbd al-Wahhāb, generally recognised by the group as an incontestable authority. This stress put on *hijra* issues, according to Māzin Shandab, a Lebanese expert on extremism, stems from the principle of social polarisation (*istiqṭāb*), which is supposedly a genuine driving spirit of ISIS and which also manifests itself through the black-and-white contours of the group's apocalyptic propaganda.[69]

The grandiose ethos of the caliphate naturally connects living geopolitical reality with ancient prophecies. In fact, the existence of both spheres is difficult to deny and thus ISIS, as Fromson and Simon have accurately summarised, 'has married apocalyptic prophecy to its two defining strategic priorities: declaring a caliphate and attacking its sectarian opponents, especially the Shiᶜites.'[70] Moreover, the well-known phrase 'a caliphate in accordance with a prophetic method'[71] (*khilāfa ᶜalā minhāj al-nubūwa*) has become a never-ending source of prestige. From such a perspective, ISIS supporters are not simply watching the historic fulfilment of an apocalyptic portent – they, as the architects of its fulfilment, are actually part of a great cosmologic drama.

The loudly proclaimed necessity to resettle within a community of rightly guided Muslims, which is how ISIS perceives itself, is also related to other fundamental signs of the Hour, one of which claims that 'states will encourage each other against the Islamic countries'.[72] In this respect, Abū Bakr al-Baghdādī makes a clear pronouncement:

> O Muslims! Do not be astonished by the gathering of the countries of disbelief and its states and communities against the Islamic state. This is a state of the victorious group at any time. Such a congregation will continue and trials and tribulations will intensify until two camps will be accomplished. No hypocrite will remain here and no believer will remain there. Then, be sure that God will help his believing servants. And announce good news and calm down, since your state will verily thrive. Every time when the fierce struggle of the states against your state will increase, be even more convinced of the God's help! Your state is verily on the straight path![73]

Opponents are expected to number 'eighty banners', according to *Dabiq* magazine, referring to an apocalyptic prophecy.[74] On another occasion, the self-proclaimed caliph tackled an additional basic apocalyptic prop: a total war in which the 'Muslim vanguard' should face a complete gathering of their enemies, including not only the Jews and Crusaders (*ṣalībīyūn*), but also Shiites and Apostates (*murtaddūn*), a broad term which, in ISIS 'heresiographic vocabulary', generally refers to all allegedly misguided Muslims.[75]

The extreme trauma currently existing in Syria and Iraq has perhaps created the most favourable conditions needed for apocalypticism to flourish. In its stirring messages, ISIS propaganda has been able to skilfully employ pre-existing apocalyptic schemes and evoke broader 'End-time factors' as mobilising incentives in relation to the group's supporters. The immense humanitarian catastrophe that is contemporary Syria has thus become 'the midwife in the resurgence of active apocalypticism in the Islamic, and especially jihadist, world'.[76]

Finally, on 21 June 2017, the destruction of the Great Mosque of al-Nūrī[77] – famous for its leaning minaret, al-Ḥadbāʾ ('the hunchback'),[78] and the place where the caliphate had officially been declared – symbolically foreshadowed the fall of ISIS in military terms. Yet, it would be quite unwise to dismiss this destruction as a last desperate effort by ISIS, 'a fit of rage in the face of imminent defeat', since the group has been as much engaged in a symbolic war as it has in a military one – and it is precisely this type of war that might become key in expressing the group's power and ideology.[79] Despite the fact that ISIS now operates mostly underground or by means of its scattered metastases, far away from its Iraqi birthplace, the real defeat of the group, in ideological terms, will certainly not be an easy task (see Chapter 7). Undoubtedly, the more ISIS has failed in the military field, the more its propaganda has focused on the apocalyptic message.[80]

Furthermore, even before the fall of Mosul, ISIS had started to once again change its propaganda preferences. Over time, the focus on the long-time advocated building of a state has gradually been replaced by an emphasis on fighting against the Dajjāl and his allies (namely Jews and Christians), always and everywhere.[81] According to its threatening rhetoric, ISIS will not lose the caliphate, which will continue to exist in cyberspace – and Western experts are well aware of this macabre threat.[82] Unfortunately, even such a 'digital caliphate' is likely to have enormous appeal. As Mark Juergensmeyer has noted, 'if the struggle is seen as hopeless in human terms, it is likely that it may be reconceived on a sacred plane, where the possibilities of victory are in God's hands'.[83]

As demonstrated above, the development stages through which the End-time rhetoric of ISIS has passed might be succinctly summarised as a gradual shift from an unrestrained form of millennialism (revolutionary, hot, overheated, and so on – depending on the applied terminology) into a level of so-called 'managed millennialism' (appearing, in this book, as 'tamed apocalypse'). Through reference to a number of other historical examples, we have learned that it is definitely possible for a movement permeated with a strong apocalyptic ethos to go through different 'types' or 'modes' of millennialism during various phases of its existence, as well as when exposed to totally different circumstances – which is also true in the specific case of the short history of ISIS. In this regard, we have no choice but to speculate as to whether the current 'mode' is the final one or whether there will be some further developments, perhaps derived from the group's future situation.

It is also true to say that a realistic prognosis of the group's future in political and military terms is definitely not one that is full of optimism. The current situation of ISIS was, in fact, predicted by Fawaz Gerges in 2016:

> ISIS's conduct seems suicidal, however. There is a disconnect between ISIS's limited military capabilities and the long list of regional and global powers pitted against the group . . . A more plausible scenario is that, as military pressure intensifies against ISIS in the near future, its core middle and senior leaders might melt into urban areas and wage a terrorist campaign along similar lines to that of Al Qaeda in Iraq (AQI) between 2007 and 2011 . . .[84]
>
> ISIS is a product of an organic crisis in Arab politics. Therefore, the decline and demise of the group will depend on the reconstruction of fragile state institution and genuine political reconciliation among warring ethnic and religious communities, a complex and difficult process that will take years to materialize. In the meantime, Salafi-jihadists of the ISIS variety will continue to exist.[85]

From a broader perspective, it is indeed possible that jihadism will flourish after ISIS in the same way that it did before the group's emergence. The above-mentioned 'spiritual divorce' between ISIS leaders and the pivotal authorities of current Salafi jihadist thought has further reinforced the group's actual isolation. Supporters of ISIS are increasingly on the defensive, dreaming of a future turning point that will see a shift from the current stage of 'absolute confrontation' to the achievement of 'final victory'. Brian Fishman has summarised the realistic expectations related to the future of ISIS as follows:

> That failure does not mean the Islamic State will be defeated or will cease to be significant threat. To the contrary, the same elements of the Islamic State's ideology that limit its broad appeal will help to remain resilient ... The anti-Islamic State coalition must not assume that dramatic territorial and personnel losses mean the Islamic State is 'defeated' ... Some will argue that the Islamic State's declaration of a caliphate means its ideological appeal will dissipate if it loses territory. Do not believe it ... The Islamic State will lose recruits as its battlefield position declines, but it will remain capable of unleashing terrorist attacks and continue to attract enough diehard supporters to be a terrible danger.[86]

A more general assessment of the actual impact of ISIS apocalypticism leads us to the conclusion that the End-time appeal of the group's propaganda has certainly been higher than its opponents would admit, but, at the same time, substantially lower than its promoters would wish for. Therefore, it does not make sense to pose the question of whether ISIS has succeeded in its 'End-time mission'. In fact, we should rather reflect on another question: in which aspects have they succeeded and in which have they failed? Any list outlining the group's achievements identify numerous items, including the excellent timing and positioning of their apocalyptic self-presentation, which has no adequate modern precedent. Moreover, the ISIS propaganda apparatus, as will be elaborated below, has developed a new and viable pattern of apocalyptic rhetoric, one that is capable of becoming an effective tool in the process of legitimising the group's existence and its claims regarding the caliphate.

This innovative presentation of apocalypticism has proved itself to be completely different from its traditional versions, regarded mostly as a potential source of unrest and decay. The 'state-building form of apocalypse' as developed by ISIS has had precisely the opposite effect. Moreover, ISIS propagandists have succeeded in the task of organically interconnecting the medieval ideas and narratives, common to all types of Muslim apocalypse, with the modern glossy appeal of their visual self-presentation. In the apocalyptic passages within their videos, Nu^{c}aym ibn Ḥammād's legacy joins forces with Hollywood-style Armageddon-esque scenes. It is little wonder that such a spectacle has been able to entice even those Muslims who would otherwise have no love for ISIS.

On the other side of our imaginary scales, we should emphasise that the group's instrumentalisation of the apocalyptic message has been rejected by the vast majority of Muslim authorities, including the most prominent scholars, regardless of their interpretation of Islam. All of them have repeatedly pointed in the same direction: to the non-Islamicity of its teaching and practice. In this respect, the ethos of the ISIS apocalypse has not contributed to the unification of the current Muslim *umma* but, on the contrary, has led to its further fragmentation. Once again, apocalypticism has thus confirmed its divisive nature, the reason why the *^{c}ulamā$^{\circ}$* have been so afraid of it. Furthermore, ISIS apocalypticism, as we will elaborate on in 'Sunni "Apocalypses Light"' in Chapter 6, has triggered countless responses all over the Muslim world, with apocalyptic arguments being employed against the group's original claims.

This point convincingly proves, therefore, that no Muslim has a monopoly on apocalyptic self-stylisation and that the same arguments that can be used as an effective tool against one's enemies can easily be levelled against the original disseminators. Of course, the well-organised promotion of the apocalyptic agenda serves multiple purposes. In addition to the above-discussed legitimisation of the state-forming authority of its promoters, an area in which ISIS has experienced undeniable success, it is essential to address as large an audience as possible in order to attract the maximum number of supporters. However, in this regard, the group's success is much more questionable. Simply stated, they have become more infamous than famous, with the group's wider appeal being much less successful than its renown among Muslims all over the world.

For the time being, the idea of a 'cyber-caliphate' is the latest desperate response of ISIS propaganda to the current uninterrupted wave of military failure. Whatever the ultimate fate of ISIS, it is clear that it has changed the notion of jihadism forever. The mastery it has achieved in utilising the Internet is undoubtedly one of its fundamental contributions (see 'How to Sell the Apocalypse?' in Chapter 5). In its current period of decline, the most important propaganda priority for ISIS will be 'to demonstrate that it can still attack'.[87] Only the future will show us how successful this 'underground cyber-caliphate' can be and the extent to which apocalypticism will participate in its success.

[While preparing this book for publication, the last Middle-Eastern territorial possession of ISIS – al-Bāghūz, a small Syrian town close to the Iraqi frontier – was finally conquered. The transformation of ISIS from mighty 'proto-state' to underground terrorist network is thus complete.]

From Dābiq

As we have already seen in the first section of Chapter 3, Syria is a region extremely rich in apocalyptic references. This fact has also left its mark on ISIS propaganda. End-time symbolism has thus become a certain 'hallmark' of the group's overall self-presentation. Furthermore, the noticeable links between the warlike dreams of ISIS leaders and their supposed role within the Last Days scenarios have found their eloquent expression in the very designations chosen for three major propaganda tools employed by ISIS. The above-discussed region of al-A^{c}māq gave its name to the group's news agency, which has become notorious for the spreading of news regarding the countless atrocities committed by its founders.[88]

The former group's chief organ, *Dabiq* magazine, was named after the locality of Dābiq, in general a pivotal place in Muslim apocalyptic thinking.[89] In September 2016, ISIS replaced it with another online magazine *Rumiyah* (Rome), published in English, as well as in other languages. According to common interpretation, this change was due to the undeniable failure of ISIS to keep this eponymous region of paramount symbolic importance under its control. Remarkably, the loss of Dābiq's importance was anticipated by William McCants in his book published roughly a year before the demise of the journal:

> The fact that Turkish Muslims, not infidel Romans, control Constantinople, or Istanbul, today and are working with the infidel West against the Islamic State makes the Dabiq prophecy a poor fit for contemporary events. The inevitable defeat of the State at Dabiq, should it ever confront 'Rome', would also argue against the prophecy's applicability. But in the apocalyptic imagination, inconvenient facts rarely impede the glorious march to the end of the world.[90]

However, the ISIS occupation of Dābiq, lasting for several months, had been enthusiastically celebrated. The group's soldiers, standing on a hill overlooking the area, recorded themselves as stating, 'We are waiting for you in Dābiq. Try and come and we will kill every single soldier,' while another warrior is heard claiming, 'Thirty states remain to complete the number of eighty flags that will gather in Dābiq and begin the Battle.'[91] Moreover, Dābiq was to become a sinister setting for the British militant Mohammed Emwazi, better-known as 'Jihadi John'. He was filmed with the severed head of Peter Kassig at his feet, announcing 'here we are, burying the first American Crusader in Dabiq, eagerly waiting for the remainder of your armies to arrive'.[92]

This dusty and, from a strategic perspective, insignificant settlement, lying about ten kilometres from the border with Turkey, thus became an embodiment of the excited dreams focusing on the approaching cosmic clash between two worlds.[93] However, despite earlier mentions of Dābiq in ISIS propaganda, the group's statements did not really focus on this site until April 2014, when an ISIS spokesperson mentioned 'the ill-fated village' as one of several places prophesied to fall into the hands of jihadists.[94] In fact, Dābiq had always been endowed with symbolic power, with the recent outburst of Middle-Eastern turmoil renewing its faded significance. For a certain period of time, the very name of the ISIS magazine thus managed to spread horror, or at least legitimate concern, among foreign observers.

In this section, particular apocalyptic samples taken from both the magazines, *Dabiq* and *Rumiyah*, will serve as 'stepping-stones' to an exploration of broader considerations. Based on ISIS primary sources, an attempt will be made to establish what might be referred to, with some degree of exaggeration, as 'an apocalyptic methodology'. This will suggest a set of the most productive approaches to the 'End-time agenda', as applied by ISIS propagandists, and will be summarised as an 'apocalyptic quartet' (see the following section 'To Rome' in this chapter).

In the most general terms, an effort to creatively interweave classical sources with current events, so symptomatic of modern Muslim apocalyptic thought, also drives the ISIS propaganda effort. By consistently avoiding non-Islamic elements, ISIS, in its End-time visions, relies solely on medieval Islamic sources. Coming under the constant criticism of Muslim scholarly circles, the anonymous compilers of *Dabiq*[95] always strove to support their claims by reference to supposedly solid Islamic foundations – and the group's apocalyptic efforts are definitely no exception to this.

Every issue of *Dabiq* regularly ends with an apocalyptic *ḥadīth* justifying the deeds of ISIS. This is seen as a means of fulfilling prophecy, or as a way of separating believers from nonbelievers, a division that also pertains to the predestined divine plan intended for the Last Days. In such an approach, the apocalyptic *aḥādīth* serve rather as an 'illustrative motto,' loosely framing the overall direction of the group, and this is a tactic that is hard to challenge. This renders such an approach as being both prudent and, simultaneously, psychologically effective. In the past, the easily attackable failure to achieve even partial expectations had the capacity to harm the credibility of a whole group, or a particular author, in a single moment.[96] To the contrary, the prophecies that appear on the back pages of *Dabiq* will never fail. Rather than attempt to make straightforward links between ancient references and contemporary events, *Dabiq* places the prophecies at the end of each issue instead, thus seeking to encompass the entirety of the magazine's discussion points – a tactic that is used to lead readers to quite intuitively make connections between the two.[97]

In this section, attention will be paid primarily to those portents of the Hour that are discussed as having been fulfilled or are currently in the process of being fulfilled (for the awaited signs, see 'They Plot, but Allah Also Plots' in Chapter 5). An essential contribution in this regard can be found covered in the very first issue of *Dabiq* and entitled 'The Return of Khilafah', where the articles 'Khilafah Declared' and 'From Hijrah to Khilafah'[98] appear, both of which address in celebratory terms the declaration of the caliphate in Mosul on 29 June 2014.

Through an apocalyptic lens, the history of Islam started with the *hijra*, together with the establishment of the *khilāfa*, and the End times will bring about both again in an imaginary return to the beginning. Needless to say, the prepared *khilāfa* should be organised *ᶜalā manhaj al-nubūwa* (according to prophetic methodology), a concept that was elaborated by al-Miṣrī in his speech *'al-Dawla al-nabawīya'* ('The Prophetic State').[99]

Both events, the *hijra* and the establishment of the *khilāfa*, are projected to appear on the global scene again, not only as a fulfilment of apocalyptic prophecy, but also – and above all – in order to distinguish between true believers and misguided Muslims, coupled with infidels. The *khilāfa* has to serve as an imaginary sieve, separating the wheat (Salafi jihadists) from the chaff (the rest of the world, including the rest of Muslims). It is exactly in this sense that a statement by al-Zarqāwī, supported by the authority of his two successors, has been quoted:

> The hypocrites and those who obstruct the path to Allah will say to you, 'Do you think anything of what you want will ever be achieved? Do you really think that the Islamic Khilāfah or even just the Islamic State will ever be established? That is something that can never happen and it is closer to imagination than reality.' So, if they say such to you, then remember the statement of Allah . . .[100]
>
> This attitude then was inherited by his successor, Abū Hamzah al-Muhājir, who said, 'O muwahhidīn [believers in the unity of God], . . . we will not rest from our jihād until we are under the olive trees of Rome, after we destroy the filthy house called the White House.' . . . This attitude was also echoed by the mountainous man, Abū ᶜUmar al-Baghdādī, who said, 'O soldiers of the Islamic State, O youth of Muhammad, . . . today we are upon the doorstep for a new era, a turning point for the map of the region, rather the world.

> Today we witness the end of the lie called western civilization and the rise of the Islamic giant.'[101]

The well-known speech delivered by their most famous successor, Abū Bakr al-Baghdādī, on the occasion of the announcement of the caliphate, leaves no room for doubt as to the mission of this newly declared entity, which means, according to his own words, the fulfilment of a long-held and ignored duty that is incumbent on Muslims.[102] Moreover, reference to the caliphate as an inevitable culmination of predestined historical development appears in a favourite *hadīth* cited in the same issue:

> It was always a hope the mujahidin were certain of attaining, for Allah's Messenger . . . had promised them with it. He said, 'There will be prophethood for as long as Allah wills it to be, then He will remove it when He wills. Then there will be Khilafah on the prophetic methodology and it will be for as long as Allah wills, then He will remove it when He wills. Then there will be harsh kingship for as long as Allah wills, then He will remove it when He wills. Then there will be tyrannical kingship for as long as Allah wills, then He will remove it when He wills. Then there will be Khilafah on the prophetic methodology.'[103]

In their exegetical endeavour, Muslim apocalyptists mostly share the belief that a 'tyrannical kingship' (*mulk jabrī*) generally refers here to modern rulers, not necessarily only dictators, but also leaders of various secular or nationalist regimes. 'A tyrannical kingship' thus represents the total decline of the Muslim *umma*, aptly expressed by a postscript written by Nuᶜaym ibn Ḥammād: 'So when it is like that, the interior of the earth is better than its exterior.'[104]

As far as the actual declaration of the caliphate is concerned, Muslims are fundamentally divided. The vast majority of them assume that the caliphate cannot be established unless a long process of gradual unification of Muslim states is achieved. To the contrary, ISIS leaders made a conscious decision not to wait for such a unification but to adopt a reverse procedure. In their opinion, the declared caliphate had to become the core of the unification process among orthodox Muslims.[105]

This uneasy assignment of theology to justify the caliphate was undertaken by the leading ideologist of ISIS, Turkī ibn Mubārak al-Binᶜalī (1984–2017),[106] a young jurist originating from Bahrain, whose thoughtful argumentation based, among other things, on a not very innovative exegesis of an apocalyptic prediction related to the twelve caliphs from the Quraysh, has been thoroughly examined by William McCants.[107] In fact, there have already been far more than twelve caliphs descended from the Quraysh tribe, so al-Binᶜalī chose to side with those believers who interpreted the prophecy as requiring twelve 'rightly-guided' caliphs.[108] Thus, Abū Bakr al-Baghdādī has been accorded the role of 'last just caliph', a claim that many historic figures have made before.

The articles included in the first issue of *Dabiq* introduce many of the subjects that are discussed in detail in further issues. For example, a sketchily outlined idea regarding the deepening of the division of the world into two opposing camps ('Indeed the world today has been divided into two camps and two trenches, with no third camp present: the camp of Islam and faith, and the camp of kufr, disbelief, and hypocrisy')[109] mingles here with continuous references to various manifestations of decline, also including apocalyptically tinged arbitrary approaches towards Muslim religious prescriptions (for example, 'treating the Qurᵓān as a book of chanting and recitation rather than as a book of governance, legislation, and enforcement').[110]

The overtly gloomy descriptions of current affairs, as well as the anticipated *fitan* ('there will be tribulations, each one eclipsing the one before it in severity. There will be tribulations [so severe] that the believer will say, "This will be what destroys me"')[111] are skilfully interlaced with occasional references to an unspecified but better future. As we have seen, and will continue to see, the great expectations of the Muslim apocalypse are significantly less well elaborated than strategies for achieving them. Yet, cursory glimpses of such a utopian and perfect government also appear in *Dabiq*.

> Amirul-Muᵓminin [Commander of the Faithful] said: 'Soon, by Allah's permission, a day will come when the Muslim will walk everywhere as a master, having honor, being revered, with his head raised high and his dignity preserved. Anyone who dares to offend him will be disciplined, and any hand that reaches out to harm him will be cut off.'[112]

The second issue of *Dabiq*, published under the title 'The Flood', develops the theme of a predestination that people cannot change. In the same way that the Flood (*ṭūfān*) could not be stopped during the lifetime of Nūḥ (Noah), nothing can stop the caliphate from spreading across the world or forestall the approaching Hour.[113] In this context, the ISIS attitude to the specific Qurᵓānic theme of Noah's ark, along with its use in realising propaganda objectives, is typically implicit and allusive rather than overt and direct, a point that can also be highlighted in many other exegetical attempts made by ISIS. The comparison between the Flood and the establishment of the caliphate in the twilight of history is used to intuitively convince the reader about their alleged irreversibility since both events are depicted as being part of the Divine plan, whose perfection cannot be contested.

In such a fabricated form of catastrophism, there are only two ways forward, either salvation by adhering to ISIS philosophy or destruction; there is no third way. Simply stated, if you believe in what had been preordained by Allah and conveyed to the Prophet Muḥammad in his time, there is no good reason to reject the prophecies related to the present or near future that are based on the same sources. ISIS propagandists actually do their best to create precisely such an impression. The final page of the same issue vividly illustrates this approach, that is, how to mix indisputable historical facts with anticipated developments:

> Allah's Messenger said, 'You will invade the Arabian Peninsula and Allah will enable you to conquer it. You will invade Persia, and Allah will enable you to conquer it. You will then invade Rome, and Allah will enable you to conquer it. Then you will fight the Dajjal, and Allah will enable you to conquer him.'[114]

The same issue contains an article entitled 'The Widespread Ignorance amongst the People',[115] referring to another often-recurring sign of the Hour, which is the 'withdrawal of knowledge and the spread of ignorance' (*raf^c^ al-^c^ilm wa intishār al-jahl*).[116] Of course, prophecies about the decline of knowledge can always be applied in every situation. Modern Muslim exegetes vary in terms of what is exactly meant by *^c^ilm* and *jahl*. The latter does not actually refer only to ignorance but also to crudeness, and it is precisely such an explanation that is often suggested. As regards *^c^ilm*, the question as to how one can speak about the decline of knowledge in a period of scientific progress has been repeatedly raised. A Solomonic solution has been suggested by Muḥammad Ḥisān, a modern Egyptian apocalyptic author, who has stated that what is referred to is not knowledge in general but a more specific concept which has religious education at its heart.[117]

Whatever the case, the never-ending sharp criticism of supposedly malevolent or misled scholars by ISIS fits well with Muslim apocalyptic patterns. Specific evidence that such criticism does not issue from mere moralising but has an eschatological context is provided by the appearance of the rare Arabic archaism, *ruwaybida*, in the text of *Rumiyah* magazine.[118] As apocalyptic predictions repeatedly mention, the End times will be stigmatised by fraud, when the truthful will lie, the liar will be right, the faithful will betray others and, in such a situation, *ruwaybida* is due to speak. The term *ruwaybida* denotes an insignificant person, a miserable creature. The speech of *ruwaybida*, therefore, metaphorically refers to the total upending of social norms in the time before the Hour.[119] From a general perspective, the denunciation of allegedly ignorant Muslim leaders, as well as misguided scholars, constitutes the most productive agenda ever for *Dabiq*. For example, an article entitled 'The Traits of Evil Scholars'[120] meticulously elaborates various 'kinds of ignorance' of which such Muslim authorities are accused.

The apocalyptic decline has a number of manifestations and one of them is all-encompassing moral decay, referred to by another End-time narrative from the same issue:

> On the authority of ᶜImrān Ibn Husayn who stated that Allah's Messenger said: 'The best of my Ummah are those of my generation, and then those who follow after them, and then those who follow after them.' ᶜImrān said: 'I do not remember whether he mentioned two or three generations after his generation.' Then the Prophet added, 'There will come after you, people who will bear witness without being asked to do so, and will be treacherous and untrustworthy, and they will vow and never fulfil their vows, and obesity will appear among them.'[121]

The third issue of *Dabiq* ('A Call to Hijrah') is arguably one of the most apocalyptic in nature. Among the developed motifs are the *hijra* in its millennial meaning (once even presented as a chance to escape 'modern-day slavery')[122] and the first appearance of *ghurabā*ᵓ ('strangers'). Both of these crucial notions are further discussed below. In principle, the *hijra* is an inevitable condition required for the further progress of the believer, since – in the words of Timothy Furnish – 'only by fleeing to the Ark of the Islamic State can Muslims be saved from baathism, secularism, liberalism, democracy or anything else that would contradict the essence of *tawhīd*'.[123] Nevertheless, the main attention of *Dabiq* is paid to the apocalyptic battles which are the subject of another, already mentioned, article entitled 'Sham is the Land of Malahim'.

In fact, the very existence of ISIS is a 'marvel of history that has only come about to pave the way for al-Malhamah al-Kubrā'.[124] Principally, the *hijra* of the *ghurabā*ᵓ to the Middle East is depicted as a necessary prerequisite to their decisive involvement in the approaching drama of the apocalyptic wars, universally described in a 'timetable style'. A topography of the Last Days here comes to life in the contours of an austere narrative, endowed with unexpected factuality, as an anonymous author from *Dabiq* eloquently illustrates.[125]

These colossal battles will usher in the coming of two major Muslim apocalyptic figures, the Dajjāl and Jesus, whose clash will dwarf all worldly wars. ISIS propagandists perhaps knew anecdotally what the Pew Research Center data proved empirically in 2012: that apocalyptic belief across the Muslim world was neither marginal nor even extreme. Moreover, the millennial conviction seemed to be especially strong in Iraq, the country of key importance with regard to the fate of ISIS. What might be somewhat surprising is the fact that the frequently referenced Muslim clash of good and evil is not connected, at least in ISIS versions, with the Mahdī, who, according to tradition, will inevitably lead the army of the orthodox believers. However, the locality of Dābiq recurs here as a major battlefield:

> The name of our magazine was taken from the area named Dābiq in the northern countryside of Halab [Aleppo], due to the significant role it will play during the events of al-Malhamah al-Kubrā (The Grand Battle) against the crusaders. Abū Hurayrah reported that Allah's Messenger said, 'The Hour will not be established until the Romans land at al-Aᶜmāq or Dābiq (two places near each other in the northern countryside of Halab).[126]

The fourth issue of *Dabiq* ('The Failed Crusade') further examines the phenomenon of the aforementioned 'strangers', who have proven their appeal among jihadist circles. 'Strangers', as a model to be followed, are introduced through al-Zarqāwī's exegesis of a related *ḥadīth*:

> 'Verily Islam began as something strange, and it will return to being something strange as it first began, so glad tidings to the strangers.' Someone asked, 'Who are the strangers?' He said, 'Those who break off from their tribes'. Imām Abū Musᵓab al-Zarqāwī said, 'Allah has described these strangers with a number of characteristics, among them being that they are nuzzāᵓ of the people, or nuzzāᵓ from the tribes. The word nuzzāᵓ is the plural of nazīᵓ and nāziᵓ, which refers to a stranger who breaks off from his family and tribe [meaning he departs and distances himself from them], and the nazāᵓiᵓ of the camels are the outsiders. Al-Harawī said, "By this he [the Prophet] is referring to the muhājirīn who have abandoned their homelands and migrated to Allah."'[127]

Nevertheless, the most fundamental contribution of this issue to the apocalyptic agenda of ISIS is the article 'The Revival of Slavery before the Hour', relating to the enslavement of the Yezidi women after the group had occupied the Sinjar Mountain in northern Iraq.[128] After the international outrage caused by the event, ISIS propagandists did not try to apologise for the crimes that had been committed. However, they chose to present the return of slavery as an inevitable condition that had to be fulfilled before the End. In his thoughtful analysis, Younus Mirza argues that the ISIS exegesis of related apocalyptic *ḥadīth* considerably diverges from the authoritative medieval approaches. He concludes:

> The very specific interpretation that the ISIS author ascribes to 'the slave girl will give birth to her master' tradition will be rejected by those who are sceptical of apocalyptic traditions in general or who may agree with the alternative or broad interpretation of the hadith. However, for a select few, there is an appeal to the idea of participating in the end of times and the movement's hypersexuality and militancy.[129]

Within the argumentation published by *Dabiq*, the ISIS author relies on an enigmatic *ḥadīth* according to which the End will not come until 'a slave girl will give birth to her own master'. This can be interpreted in a number of completely different ways: for example, metaphorically, as a reference to the contemporary rise of disobedience in children, where they behave towards their own mothers as if they were slaves,[130] or as a vague prognosis of moral decay leading to an increase in the number of single mothers, whose children, therefore, will actually stand higher in comparison to them.[131] In this respect, medieval Muslim scholars mostly point to the spread of concubines because, in Islamic law, the master's child from a female slave is deemed to be free and of equal status in relation to his other children.[132]

After conducting an investigation into a variety of explanations, involving the opinions of relevant medieval authorities,[133] the article rejects all allegorical and metaphorical approaches that avoid slavery in its real meaning, and concludes that this sign must be interpreted and understood quite literally.

> An-Nawawī explained the hadīth by saying, 'The majority of scholars say that this foretells the increase of concubines and their children in numbers, because the child of a concubine has the status of her master' [Sharh Sahīh Muslim]. Ibn Hajar commented . . ., 'But this suggested interpretation is questionable, because a slave girl giving birth was an occurrence that existed in the era when the statement was made. Also, most of the conquests of the lands of shirk [idolatry], the enslavement of their families, and the taking of their women as concubines, occurred at the beginning of the Islamic era' [Fathul-Bārī]. Again, it appears that those who drift away from the literal interpretation of slavery do so because it was already existent and common in their era in such a manner that they found it hard to understand it as referring to actual slavery. But after the abandonment of slavery by Muslims and its subsequent revival, this literal interpretation becomes much more plausible.[134]

The ISIS propagandist, according to Younus Mirza, thus presents a new understanding of the report, one that is unique within the history of Islam.[135] As further strong evidence that such an interpretation was correct, the ISIS author of the article suggests another apocalyptic reference that emerges in the cries of Roman warriors to Muslims as they prepared themselves for the battle at Dābiq: 'Leave us and those who were enslaved amongst us so we can fight them.' According to *Dabiq*, resting once again on the authority of Imam al-Nawawī, the cited part of the short discussion between both opposing forces before the bloody final battle clearly points to the existence of slavery on the Muslim side.[136] The implementation of the enslavement of Yezidi women,[137] according to the article, clearly fits into the apocalyptic framework, not only as the fulfilment of a particular sign of the Hour, but also as recompense for what was earlier neglected. In this perverted understanding of ISIS, the very existence of Yezidis in the land of Muslims does not meet shariah requirements.

> Upon conquering the region of Sinjar in Wilāyat Nīnawā, the Islamic State faced a population of Yazidis, a pagan minority existent for ages in regions of Iraq and Shām. Their continual existence to this day is

> a matter that Muslims should question as they will be asked about it on Judgment Day, considering that Allah had revealed Āyat as-Sayf (the verse of the sword) over 1400 years ago. He taʿālā [God] said, 'And when the sacred months have passed, then kill the mushrikīn [worshipers of idols] wherever you find them . . .'[138]

The analogous and perverse argument of the supposed recompense for former iniquities has been repeatedly offered as an explanation for the destruction by ISIS of historical monuments,[139] together with the practice of *taswīyat al-qubūr* (literally the 'levelling of graves', the destruction of aboveground structures denoting a place of burial). Such a stance is actually inherent in Salafi tradition, and therefore its apocalyptic reading (putting things to rights before the Hour) must be seen as a secondary explanation that supports a different original motivation. In fact, advocates of the 'levelling of graves' are driven by the conviction that they are acting in the name of pure monotheism, considering graves to be structures that must be levelled so that they will not be venerated.[140] Furthermore, the destructive behaviour of ISIS in relation to monuments, including funeral structures, can also be interpreted as a highly effective method of producing powerful visual imagery.[141]

Another 'apocalyptic aspect' favoured among them is a general tendency to escalate all contrasts between the powers of good and evil, so symptomatic of the Last Days atmosphere. ISIS, as the self-styled protector of moral values, does everything in order to protect its supporters against the temptation to adultery, even at the price of renewing the concept of slavery as being the only legal justification for the use of concubines in Islam. The consistent attempt to cling to the alleged requirements of shariah law, including elements considered by most Muslims to be anachronisms, leads to a further deepening of the divisions between the followers of ISIS and the rest of the world. In this twisted way of thinking, the apocalyptic context of the enslavement of Yezidi women has been discussed by *Dabiq* as follows:

> Before Shaytān reveals his doubts to the weak-minded and weak hearted, one should remember that enslaving the families of the

> kuffār [unbelievers] and taking their women as concubines is a firmly established aspect of the Sharīʾah that if one were to deny or mock, he would be denying or mocking the verses of the Qurʾān and the narrations of the Prophet . . ., and thereby apostatizing from Islam. Finally, a number of contemporary scholars have mentioned that the desertion of slavery had led to an increase in fāhishah [adultery, fornication, etc.], because the sharʾī alternative to marriage is not available, so a man who cannot afford marriage to a free woman finds himself surrounded by temptation towards sin. In addition, many Muslim families who have hired maids to work at their homes, face the fitnah [temptation] of prohibited khalwah (seclusion [with a member of the opposite sex]) and resultant zinā [adultery] occurring between the man and the maid, whereas if she were his concubine, this relationship would be legal. This again is from the consequences of abandoning jihād and chasing after the dunyā [this world].[142]

In addition to the scattered references to miscellaneous End-time topics throughout all its issues, *Dabiq* magazine also offers monothematic articles devoted to particular apocalyptic expectations. The excerpts from two such texts, entitled 'The Islamic State Founders on Signs of the Hour'[143] and 'Shaykh ᶜAdnānī's Words on the Crusade',[144] can be found in Appendix 3. What follows in this section is merely a brief outline of the most important points.

An absolutely vital contribution to the development of the thesis on the sharpening of all contrasts prior to the great battle is conveyed in the seventh issue ('From Hypocrisy to Apostasy: The Extinction of the Grayzone'). The motto promoted by this issue is: what is supported by Islam is not pacifism but fighting. Nevertheless, this ostensibly straightforward militarism also has its apocalyptic overtones. The Qurʾānic verse 2:216 quoted by *Dabiq* in this context says: 'Fighting has been ordained for you, though it is hard for you. You may dislike something although it is good for you, or like something although it is bad for you: God knows and you do not.'[145] To sum up, the *ᶜulamāʾ* living before the Hour are generally believed to have a propensity to choose from Islam only such elements they like and neglect whatever else, including armed *jihād*. However, Islam, as ISIS propagandists emphasise, is indivisible. In other words, those Muslim leaders proclaiming pacifism help to fulfil part of the apocalyptic plan, while proving themselves to be the lowest of the religious authorities.

Although the corresponding article does not state this explicitly, many Muslim apocalyptists believe that before the End people will try to bypass various Islamic imperatives through advocating their symbolic reading – for example, *jihād* will not be understood in terms of fighting but rather as a mere spiritual endeavour. Another manifestation of such an apocalyptic tendency is the lesser sign of the Hour known as 'frauds concerning alcohol' (*al-taḥāyul ᶜalā al-khamr*), which can be interpreted as an attempt by some Muslims to call alcohol by other names, for example *mashrūbāt rūḥīya*, which is a common practice all over the Arab world. The genuine objective is always the same, to bypass an apparent ban by the employment of various forms of quibbling.[146] It is believed that the Final Days will witness a number of similar manifestations.

The tenth issue of *Dabiq* ('The Law of Allah and the Laws of Men') is full of uncompromising criticism in relation to all non-Islamic impacts on the thinking and behaviour of today's Muslims. It points to other frequently mentioned apocalyptic portents, the return of idolatry and the imitation of unbelievers. The reference to idols that will be the object of worship should, according to Muslim apocalyptists, be read allegorically. In the ISIS view, such portents can be generally associated with disproportionate human attention being devoted to worldly vanities, as well as the subsequent marginalisation of religion.

Furthermore, the short article 'Decisiveness or Division', published in the twelfth issue and symptomatically entitled 'Just Terror' again focuses on the supposedly approaching *fitan*, which once more will endanger the fragile unity of the *umma*:

> Allah's Messenger said, 'Whoever gives bayᵓah by offering the promise of his hand and the truthfulness of his heart, then he must obey the ruler as much as he can. If another person comes disputing the

> ruler's authority, then strike that other person's neck.' . . . Allah's Messenger also said, 'If bayʾah is given to two caliphs, then kill the second of them.' . . . Prophet said, 'There will be tribulation and tribulations. So whoever comes to divide the matter of this Ummah while it is united, then strike him – whoever he may be – with the sword.' . . . In another narration, he said, 'Whoever comes to you wanting to break your strength or divide your unity while your matter is altogether under a single man, then kill him [i.e. the agitator].'[147]

As we are incessantly reminded, the Hour will be foreshadowed by a number of clashes that will further undermine the already disturbed solidarity of Muslims. In this respect, the individual apocalyptic authors suggest various specific signs or their subdivisions, supposedly encompassing such tendencies. For example, Sheikh Muḥammad al-Shaᶜrāwī has also included in his 'apocalyptic account' an item entitled 'the strong will eat the weak' (*yaʾkulu al-qawī al-ḍaᶜīf*), referring to the increase in the struggle for power when people are expected to forget all the rule-keeping prescriptions of shariah.[148] Needless to say that such vague prophecies can be applied at all times and in all situations.

The ISIS millennial arsenal also contains apocalyptic references that cannot be found in the group's official publications. This is true in the case of the sign of the Hour known as 'the truthfulness of the Muslim's dream' (*ṣidq ruʾyat al-muslim*).[149] Although lies are expected to prevail before the Hour, apocalyptists believe that there will be one significant exception – the occurrence of visionary dreams. The related prophecy says, 'when time contracts, the *ruʾya* of the believer will not lie'.[150] The term *ruʾya* means either a visionary dream or a vision in general. According to al-Shaᶜrāwī's interpretation, this sort of dream will prevail during the Last Days, in the same way that it was distinctive at the very beginning of the Prophet Muḥammad's mission.[151] This remarkable 'return to the beginning' motif appears as part of the defunct Twitter handle 'End of Time Dreams' as well as among its extant followers, and convincingly documents the respect paid to visionary dreams and the strong motivational factor behind such dreams in relation to the expected eschatological rewards.[152] Essentially, the jihadists pay attention to their dreams – there is no doubt about that.[153]

Simply stated, the apocalypse has already become part of the spiritual experience of many Muslims.

To Rome

The magazine *Rumiya*, published from mid-2016 onwards, follows the lead of *Dabiq*, not only in the effectiveness of its lay-out, but also in terms of its End-time message. The very title of this magazine reveals an apocalyptic inspiration that is further demonstrated on the cover page by the citation of Abū Hamza al-Muhājir's[154] words, 'O muwahhidin, rejoice, for by Allah, we will not rest from our jihad except beneath the olive trees of Rumiyah (Rome).' Rome (see 'From the East to Jerusalem' in Chapter 3), whose conquest will foreshadow the victorious coming of the Mahdī. Traditionally, this was identified with Constantinople, the centre of the Eastern Roman Empire. However, although according to ISIS propagandists, this prophecy refers to the actual Rome (as indicated in brackets), they primarily mean the Vatican, that is, the centre of the Roman Catholic Church.

From a number of relevant apocalyptic items, one point holds extraordinary popularity among the anonymous authors of this journal: the intransigent criticism of 'wicked scholars', often explained as being part of the decline in education and presented, in various stages of development, in all issues of *Rumiyah*. Issue four, for instance, references a prophecy about the time when Islam will become an 'empty shell', which acts as a certain archetype of apocalyptic references to a 'flourishing facade covering a content in decay':

> Abul-Hasan ᶜAli Ibn Abi Talib said, 'There shall soon come upon the people a time in which nothing of Islam remains except its name and nothing of the Quran remains except its script. Their masajid [mosques] will be built with splendor while they are ruins, void of guidance. Their scholars will be the worst creatures under the sky. Fitnah arises from them and is only due to them.' . . . Indeed,

the fitnah began from their mouths and from upon their pulpits, for after they prohibited jihad for Allah's cause and considered it a crime, they began to call the people to join falsehood, kufr [disbelief], and the fight under the banners of the tawaghit, doing so to achieve the pleasure of their rulers and keep their wealth and prestige safe. The loser is he who loses his religion by following their desires and preserving their dunya, for whoever does not busy himself with truth, Shaytan busies him with falsehood.[155]

Other apocalyptic narratives often point to the overturning of all values, either religious or social. Virtue will disappear, while various vices will spread as never witnessed before. The humble submission (khushūʿ), mentioned in the following, is just one particular example. According to Sheikh al-Shaʿrāwī, a sign of the Hour referred to as 'the first thing taken away from this Community will be humility' (awwal shayʾ yurfaʿ min hādhihi al-umma al-khushūʿ) is, in fact, the very first item from a long series of signs of complete moral decay.[156] The second part of this citation reveals another fundamental dimension of this total breakdown of values and relates to the appearance of rightly guided scholars acting as supposed bearers of genuine knowledge.

> ʿUbadah Ibn as-Samit said, 'Shall I tell you what will be the first part of knowledge to be lifted from the people? It is khushuʾ (humble submission, especially in prayer). A time will soon come where you will not find a single man with khushuʾ inside any major masjid.' . . . Thus, seeking knowledge from those who are 'the worst creatures under the sky' and those who are from 'the callers to the gates of Jahannam' [hell] is not praiseworthy. As for following the path of pages, during an era in which the scholars have disappeared – save those on the frontlines, in prisons, or in caves – then such is praiseworthy, according to the traditions.[157]

Quite surprisingly, the apocalyptic message of both *Rumiyah* and *Dabiq* is not as easily decipherable as might be deduced at first sight. The apocalyptic titles of both periodicals, followed by a selection of apocalyptic mottos, and the fact that all content items finish with End-times prophecies on the rear cover pages, are indications of related expectations: dreams full of promises and a future that can never be verified. Such 'apocalyptic tasting' can never disappoint. On the other hand, in spite of the care taken by the group, ISIS, when compared with other jihadists, continues to speak about apocalyptic battles as though they are imminent, thus 'setting the appropriate conditions to fight them'.[158] The apocalypse thus looks like part of a strategic plan rather than a religious agenda.

A closer investigation of both magazines reveals that their apocalyptic nature actually results much more from their ethos than from particular explicit statements or any straightforward analysis conducted in the 'what-has-been-fulfilled' style, which is so characteristic of an important section of modern Arab apocalyptic authorship. Moreover, the millennial message of many passages is definitely not obvious at first glance, and this is why the perception of an uninitiated reader may be completely different from the impression gained by a reader who is familiar with the Muslim apocalyptic repertoire. For the latter group of readers, both magazines would certainly prove to be more attractive reading than would be the case for the former group. And this is precisely why experts, both Muslim and non-Muslim, differ so significantly in their evaluation of the relevance of apocalypticism in ISIS propaganda.

An illustrative example explaining this point is provided by the above-mentioned article 'The Extinction of the Grayzone'.[159] The grey zone for ISIS is a state of hypocrisy (*nifāq*) that exists not only in the West, but also in the Arab world. In fact, the grey zone is epitomised by those Muslims who find their own individual accommodation between their spiritual identity and loyalty to the state. So, the hypocrites are actually all those Muslims whose actual beliefs do not match with those of ISIS. It is a case of us or them; there is no third way, as *Dabiq* resolutely implies:

> The grayzone is critically endangered, rather on the brink of extinction. Its endangerment began with the blessed operations of September 11th, as these operations manifested two camps before

> the world for mankind to choose between, a camp of Islam – without the body of Khilāfah to represent it at the time – and a camp of kufr – the crusader coalition. Or as Shaykh Usāmah Ibn Lādin . . . said, 'The world today is divided into two camps. Bush spoke the truth when he said, "Either you are with us or you are with the terrorists." Meaning, either you are with the crusade or you are with Islam' . . . The operations quickly exposed the different deviant 'Islamic' movements, the palace 'scholars,' and the deviant duʾāt [preachers], not to mention the apostate tawāghīt, as all of them rushed to serve the crusaders led by Bush in the war against Islam. And so, the grayzone began to wither.[160]

The escalation of dualism when taken to the extreme, which is the subject discussed in the given article, can be viewed either within an earthly (geopolitical, strategic, societal, and so on) framework – which, by the way, perfectly corresponds to al-Nājī's martial visions[161] – or in purely eschatological terms. The former, 'more practical', understanding primarily highlights the psychological attraction of such a simplistic perception, further multiplied by the extreme rhetoric of ISIS, exploitable because it recruits supporters precisely from such 'grey-zones'.[162] An informed comment from *The Telegraph* heads in this direction:

> Daesh's obsession with the 'extinction' of the grey zone lies in the value of this narrative to its recruitment purposes. If it can convince impressionable and disgruntled Muslims that they cannot possibly live as Muslims in Europe, and that Daesh somehow embody the actualisation of Islamic ideals in the form of a utopian 'state', then potential adepts may feel squeezed into choosing a camp, a choice which Daesh seeks to facilitate with promises of redemption and uber-machismo and by playing on real concerns over the religious freedom of European Muslims.[163]

Having considered a number of particular apocalyptic manifestations within official ISIS propaganda, primarily designed as a 'showcase' for Western audiences, let us now turn to an attempt to create a generalisation of ISIS methodology.

Firstly, an apocalyptic reading of 'The Extinction of Grayzone' reminds us of the lesser signs of the Hour that refer, in various ways, to the sharpening of current contradictions. And, it is exactly this broader tendency that can be understood as the primary common denominator underpinning the group's millennial messaging and, thus, the first part of our imaginary 'quartet' of ISIS 'apocalyptic methodology'. As expected, before the Hour, the current boundaries should cease to exist together with any existing perception of what is 'normal' and 'acceptable'.

In a similar vein, violence is projected to become more violent, killing more widespread, and such an escalation, according to the apocalyptic prophecies, will also reach current levels of contradiction in geopolitical terms. A major part of ISIS End-time narratives focuses on the separation of the group from the rest of the world in the period prior to the Hour and does so by sticking as closely as possible to a supposedly faithful understanding of the Tradition. For ISIS, there can be no other acceptable way of living or governing. Those who share such an attitude are on the side of absolute good (white) and the rest of the world is completely black; there is simply no grey in-between option.

Such an uncompromising approach actually pertains to the main features of Muslim apocalypticism in general, that is, commonly depicting 'Islam' and 'the West' as two irreconcilable worlds, while often adding that such an insurmountable division will immediately precede the emergence of the Dajjāl.[164] Within such an overarching logic, many Muslim apocalyptists – despite their loudly declared opposition to Huntington's idea about a 'clash of civilizations' – use terminology that is strikingly similar to his[165] and this fully applies to ISIS propaganda too.[166] Such an unsophisticated perspective allows them to divide the world into starkly contrasting categories and to bolster a worldview in which the West and Islam are in total opposition, now and forever.[167] Moreover, unlike al-Qāᶜida, enemies of ISIS are not manifestly specified,[168] with their 'unveiling' being a very flexible activity.

'In apocalyptic traditions there is an intense desire for the lines between belief and unbelief to be clearly drawn.'[169] This succinct remark of David Cook, in relation to the Middle Ages, is equally applicable to the contemporary context. The notion of a grey area is simply superfluous, since in the End-time 'travel maps' no compromise is deemed possible. An all-encompassing decline, symptomatic for most of the world, is thus confronted with an expected utopian perfection, returning to the beginnings of Islam and characteristic of the chosen Muslim vanguard – the supposed best of Islam. According to Charlie Winter's analysis, this kind of utopianism is by far the most important narrative within ISIS propaganda, being the most alluring in terms of recruitment.[170]

This black-and-white perspective or, in Mark Juergensmeyer's aptly expressed phrase, a 'dichotomous opposition on an absolute scale',[171] has left a significant impact on the practice of *takfīr*, so symptomatic of ISIS. This point represents the main cause of controversy between Bin Lādin and al-Zarqāwī and, later, between ISIS and al-Qāᶜida. Supporters of ISIS have been warned against intermingling with 'nonbelievers' for fear that their belief will be weakened.[172] In fact, the takfiri perception is not limited only to Shiites; a lot of Sunni leaders and scholars have also been denounced by ISIS as 'apostates' (sg. *murtadd*) or 'heretics' (sg. *zindīq*).[173] Such a willingness to not only harm other Muslims, but to make use of various rhetorical instruments to deny their status as Muslims in order to justify violence against them perfectly fits into the black-and-white apocalyptic contours of ISIS ideologists.[174] It should be highlighted again and again that for them most other Muslims are not 'brothers in faith', but rather are legitimate targets. And the proximity of the Hour further magnifies this conviction.

The ubiquitous and sinister effort of ISIS to dehumanise its enemies can also be interpreted within the concept of 'cosmic war', which places any earthly conflict within the metaphysical framework of an eternal clash between good and evil. This is because the cosmic war, as Juergensmeyer has stated, is 'intimately personal, but can also be translated to the social plane. Ultimately, though, they transcend human experience.'[175] Thus, scapegoating – so skilfully and systematically utilised in the group's propaganda – has its own incontestable apocalyptic overlaps. This particular increase in brutality as committed by ISIS fighters can, in turn, be understood as a prophesised *fitna* sent to people by God in order to distinguish between 'true' Muslims and 'hypocrites'.

Within this logic, the group's propaganda may be seeking to use such a reading of extreme violence as a 'test for the Hereafter' in the expectation that it will achieve the longed-for annihilation of the 'grey-zone' between the followers of God and Satan. In its undisguised promotion of cruelty and brutality, ISIS faithfully follows the strategic principles that have been authoritatively formulated by al-Nājī: recommending the use of extreme brutality as a means of destroying the existing unhealthy order and setting up a new one. From the ISIS perspective, brutality is in fact both inherent to a divinely inspired legal code and, above all, a tool to sort 'true' Muslims from supposed 'apostates'.[176] In their perverse worldview, according to the succinct words of Fawaz Gerges, jihadists thus are actually 'the vanguard best equipped to trigger an apocalypse or an end to apostasy, an end to the world as we know it, and a religious rebirth'.[177]

ISIS warriors have only two options, to win or die; nothing else is acceptable, as the article 'The Pledge to Fight to the Death' clearly summarises.[178] ISIS propagandists, when encouraging individual terrorist attacks abroad, know only too well that these brutal acts are likely to reinforce the already existing prejudice against local Muslims, regardless of their true level of radicalisation. So, many Western Muslims, prone to the lure of integration, will thus find themselves the objects of hate merely because of their religion. ISIS, until now having been for them an object of disdain, can assume the role of uniquely competent advocate. When speaking about the sharpening of current contradictions, we should be totally aware of this aspect.[179]

The second fundamental feature symptomatic of the ISIS apocalypse (as well as Muslim apocalypticism in general) – that is, all-encompassing decline – is closely related to the first, since it further deepens the existing division of the world into two antagonistic blocks. The particular manifestations of this universal tendency include various religious, societal and political aspects, containing such signs of the Hour as, for instance, the appearance of impostors, the widespread corruption of governments, the growth of ignorance, the arbitrary treatment of religious prescriptions, the decay of moral values, the severing of family relationships, the spread of lasciviousness, and so on.[180] In fact, most of the lesser signs of the Hour depict decline in its various forms, many of them recurring, as indicated below. Without this decline, no excellence would be visible, as also defined in Muslim apocalyptic dreams.

The idea of an imaginary return to the very roots of Islam as being a shared leitmotif in relation to many apocalyptic signs is the third feature of our proposed 'apocalyptic methodology'; this further reinforces the belief held by ISIS supporters that they are the chosen vanguard of Muslims in the period when the contrast between the worlds of believers and infidels is about to reach an archetypal degree. In the overwhelmingly dualistic ethos of ISIS propaganda, the ancient pagans of *jāhilīya*, as bearers of all conceivable aspects of corruption, are usually likened to contemporary hypocrites (*munāfiqūn*), which is, in the group's vocabulary, a derogatory designation aimed at an important section of the *umma*.

On the other hand, the celebrated virtues of the first generation of Muslims (*ṣaḥāba*) have to be reflected in the high standards of ISIS followers, who are presented self-confidently as 'the best of Allah's slaves'.[181] As David Cook expresses it, 'what was once will be yet again. Glory will be returned at the end of the world, because of divine justice.'[182] Perhaps not surprisingly, an idealised past thus draws an idealised future. This evidence of a more general validity should be highlighted here since historians of religion have long since observed the parallels between primordial time and the end of time in apocalyptic myths. As they have realised, the apocalypse often envisions a utopian future, devoid of terrestrial decay and parallel to our pure primordial existence.[183]

Staying with these broader considerations, a sense of cyclical renewal is perhaps inherent to millennialism within all Middle Eastern religions, not only Islam. These cycles are absolutely vital, as Abbas Amanat has summarised:

> It may be argued that they are far more essential for continuity of the sacred and its perpetual renewal than our modern utilitarian notion of linear time and the concept of progress. Time cycles thus may be seen as regulatory means of placing utopian and eschatological aspirations, and whatever is associated with the Beginning and the End, within a humanly conceivable time frame.[184]

Perhaps the most illustrative example pertaining to this category is the phenomenon of 'the strangers', which deserves closer attention.[185] The corresponding Arabic term (*ghurabāʾ*, singular *gharīb*) not only refers to the foreign fighters supporting ISIS but its general meaning points to any unusual person, someone who deviates from their surroundings. In our apocalyptic context, 'strangers' refers primarily to the well-known saying of the Prophet Muḥammad: that 'Islam began as a stranger, and will return to being a stranger (*badaʾa al-islām gharīban wa sayaʿūdu gharīban kamā badaʾa*), so blessed are the strangers before the Hour.'[186] When asked to define such 'strangers', the Prophet mentions the 'minority of Muslims in the world full of evil'.

The existence of the *ghurabāʾ* can also be thus interpreted as a consequence of the never-ending *fitan* that will accompany the Last Days, when most Muslims are expected to fail and to be led astray.[187] For obvious reasons, this *ḥadīth* has become a favourite among jihadists around the world,[188] including al-Zarqāwī, who also adopted the *nom de guerre* al-Gharīb on arriving in Afghanistan in 1989.[189] As Brian Fishman has commented:

> But Zarqawi took the *gharib* identity to an extreme: criticism was not simply to be disregarded; it actually confirmed that he was on the right path. Public disparagements were a test of commitments to God's will. Muhammad had been similarly tested, Zarqawi reasoned, so his group must not compromise its values because 'true' Muslims were 'the good few among the evil many'.[190]

Convinced that being held in good esteem is likely to lead to worldly attachment, the 'strangers' choose to always remain alone since, as an eponymous ISIS song proclaims,[191] they are the chosen ones. It is no wonder that al-Sūrī's training camp in Afghanistan has been named *muᶜaskar al-ghurabāᵓ* ('the strangers' camp'). Moreover, within Salafi theology, the term *ghurabāᵓ* is often used synonymously with other favoured designations referring to the state of being chosen, such as 'the saved sect' (*al-firqa al-nājiya*) or 'the victorious group' (*al- ṭāᵓifa al-manṣūra*).[192]

Ibn ᶜAbd al-Wahhāb has even proclaimed that it is difficult to find Islam in its pristine form since 'the Islamic religion today is among the strangest things' (*dīn al-islām al-yawm min aghrab al-ashyāᵓ*).[193] The sentiment of *ghurba* (estrangement, alienation) occurs quite often in Sunni reformist literature, giving the overall impression of a rotten society in need of essential socio-religious reform – and here we should keep in mind that there is no better reformer than the Mahdī.

Significantly, the inward identification of jihadists with the concept of 'strangers' has been best expressed in the above-mentioned song (*nashīd*),[194] which has become a particular jihadist hymn all over the world, often also serving as a video soundtrack.[195] (Its verses form the opening quotation of this chapter.) The authorship of this text is traditionally ascribed to Sayyid Qutb, although there is no proof for such a claim. It is little wonder that ISIS ideologists are happy to accept the original message of this crucial concept, albeit sometimes suitably adapted to meet their own needs, as *Dabiq* reveals in the following definition:

> Strangeness is a condition that the Muslim living in the West cannot escape as long as he remains amongst the crusaders. He is a stranger amongst Christians and liberals. He is a stranger amongst fornicators and sodomites. He is a stranger amongst drunkards and druggies. He is a stranger in his faith and deeds, as his sincerity and submission is towards Allah alone, whereas the kuffar (nonbeliever) of the West worship and obey clergy, legislatures, media, and both their animalistic and deviant desires . . . Thus, the Muslim in the West is in a constant struggle. His fitrah [natural disposition] is at war with the deviant drifts of the kuffar surrounding him. The battle

> to preserve his fitrah and faith knows no ceasefire. If he wants to preserve what mustard seed of faith he has been blessed with, he must exhaust himself to the utmost so as to remain just a Muslim, never mind a Muslim striving for jihad.[196]

The objectives of ISIS propaganda as they relate to 'strangers' can be summarised in the following ways: to overcome tribal hostilities, which is particularly important in the case of Iraq; to attract further supporters from among jihadists and extremists scattered around the Islamic world who identify themselves with the concept; and to address outsiders among second- or third-generation Muslims settled in the West who might be attracted by the illusion of exclusivity as offered by ISIS. The series of propaganda videos intended for recruitment purposes, entitled *Al-Ghuraba, the chosen few*,[197] introduce idealised portraits of such 'reborn' converts.[198]

The *ghurabāʾ* have no need to contend with society's laws and limitations when they obey a higher authority and expect the rewards of heaven. In this regard, they fit perfectly within the strategy of a 'cosmic war'.[199] Because of its crucial importance, the concept of *ghurabāʾ* is further elaborated or referred to in many other passages of ISIS written propaganda.[200] A related speech delivered by the official spokesperson of ISIS, Abū al-Ḥasan al-Muhājir, leaves no room for doubt:

> O troops of Iraq and Sham! O ghuraba of Islam! The encampment of falsehood has been duped by the temporal world, been deceived by desire, and become self-conceited. Shaytan has blown arrogance into its nose. Thus, it rose recklessly, manifested itself conceitedly, foamed angrily, and tremored with fear, and launched a campaign – the likes of which history has never seen in past eras – against the abode of Islam and the land of Khilafah.[201]

In order to become a genuine *gharīb*, one has to undertake a *hijra*, which is actually much more than an ordinary trip. The article 'Siyaha of Jihad',[202] discussing the phenomenon of *siyāḥa* in terms of 'traveling for religious purposes'[203] and distinguishing between its misleading perception (as the imitation of monasticism) and its more praiseworthy manifestations, clearly demonstrates the importance of religiously motivated resettlement within the ISIS discourse:[204]

> Therefore, whoever wishes to be from among those who practice the siyahah of the Sunnah, as understood by the Salaf, must perform hijrah and jihad, must strive against himself for Allah's sake by adhering to zuhd [asceticism] and dhikr [devotional acts in which short phrases are repeatedly recited] in the course of his ribat [steadfastness in faith] and combat as much as he can, and must abandon what Allah dislikes of wrongs and sins, both hidden and manifest, including pride, arrogance, backbiting, slander, and fighting for the sake of attaining booty or achieving fame.[205]

The high praise accorded to religious exclusivity, superseding other values such as family and property, as well as the perception of this word as a realm of faithlessness and barbarism, repeatedly occurs throughout the history of modern Islamic thought. The related notion of 'emotional solitude' (*ᶜuzla shuᶜūrīya*) has been elaborated by Sayyid Qutb, who highlights the need for inner withdrawal from an outward and corrupted world, which will lead in turn to spiritual deliverance.[206] Such ideas have had a significant impact on many Islamist groups, whose followers, mostly youths and idealists, often long to participate in the great ('cosmic') duel between good and evil.

In the case of ISIS, references to the feeling of spiritual election are mostly used for the practical purposes of recruitment and strengthening the group's solidarity. This feeling of being chosen can be further reinforced in various ways, among them being the gesture of a single raised index finger, that has on occasion attracted the attention of the world's media. In its ISIS usage, this well-known sign of victory has acquired a second and more sinister meaning, referring to the *tawḥīd* (a belief in the 'oneness' of God) or, more specifically, to its ISIS interpretation, which rejects any other views as being a form of idolatry. When ISIS supporters use this gesture, it is to affirm an ideology that demands the destruction of the West, as well as any form of pluralism, and openly indicates their apocalyptic belief in world domination.[207]

Finally, conspiracy, the last but not least pillar of the ISIS 'apocalyptic quartet', freely mingles with the aforementioned three tendencies. It constitutes a hidden factor that lies behind the sharpening of current contradictions and simultaneously contributes to the notion of universal decline, often seen as a by-product of a worldwide plot. Despite the group's officially declared rejection of conspiracy, which will be discussed later,[208] ISIS propaganda essentially employs conspiracy in both its fundamental forms: as a subject that invariably attracts the attention of readers ('conspiracy revealed') and as a method of argumentation ('conspiracy between the lines'). Conspiracy as a topic can be found, for example, in several *Dabiq* articles devoted to supposed Jewish-Shiᶜite plots.[209] In turn, conspiracy as a method of argumentation, characterises many contributions focused on the relentless criticism of the West.

As we have already seen, conspiracy theory has become a crucial constitutive element in the formation of modern Muslim apocalyptic creativity, and therefore the fondness of ISIS for a continuous 'unveiling of hidden truth' in relation to the enemies of Islam is definitely no surprise. From the ISIS perspective, the Dajjāl is particularly associated with both Shiites and Jews. In an eerily similar manner, modern Muslim apocalyptists claim that a worldwide conspiracy against Islam is being directed by Jews, while ISIS proclaims that the Dajjāl is systematically using Jews and Shiites as he seeks to destroy pristine Islamic traditions. In this regard, the article 'The Rāfidah: From Ibn Sabaᵓ to the Dajjal'[210] provides us with an excellent introduction to this deeply-rooted hatred and accusation of conspiracy that is directed against Shiites, who are not even deemed to be true Muslims.

On the pages of ISIS periodicals, conspiracy often goes hand in hand with the practice of excommunication (*takfīr*). The group's opponents are routinely referred to as 'idolaters' (*ṭawāghīt*, singular *ṭāghūt*) in the case of rulers, 'apostates' (*murtaddūn*, singular *murtadd*) in the case of representatives of rival organisations, or 'crusaders' in the case of Western non-Muslims in general. The exalted hatred levelled against Shiites, who are always referred to pejoratively as *rāfiḍa* (renegades), has become a particular hallmark of ISIS. Shiites are actually perceived as being part of a Jewish plot aimed at undermining Islam from the inside. As such, they often appear in ISIS propaganda,[211] which seeks to inform audiences that the hatred against them results from a true understanding of their history and so there is no reason to suppress it. The diabolical nature of Shiites, as *Dabiq* explicates,[212] can be unveiled through reference to the very roots of their history, thus also having an impact on apocalyptic teaching.

> The Tābiʾī ash-Shaʿbī . . . said, 'I warn you against the followers of deviant desires. And the worst of them are the Rāfidah, as they are the Jews of this Ummah. Some of them are Jews who fake Islam to spread their deviance, just as Paul of the Jews faked Christianity to spread his deviance, hoping the Jews would become victorious. The Rāfidah hate Islam just as the Jews hate Christianity. They did not enter Islam longing for Allah or fearing Him, rather out of spite for the people of Islam and so as to inflict harm upon them . . . Amongst them was ʿAbdullāh Ibn Sabaʾ, a Jew from the Jews of Sanaa, who was banished to Sābāt.' He also said, 'Indeed, the calamity of the Rāfidah is the same as the calamity of the Jews. The Jews say that only a person from the lineage of Dāwūd is suited for kingship. The Rāfidah say that only a person from the lineage of ʿAlī is suited for imāmah [leadership of Muslims]. The Jews say that there is no jihād until the Messiah comes forth and a sword descends from the heavens. The Rāfidah say there is no jihād until the Mahdī comes forth and a caller calls out from the heavens saying, "Follow him."'[213]

As ISIS propaganda does not fail to remind us, the classical Sunni descriptions attributed to the expected Dajjāl are, in fact, very similar to those associated with traditional Mahdī portraits that appear in Shiite sources. On this point, ISIS apocalyptists, however, are simply following common modern Arabic eschatological narratives, as *Dabiq* clearly demonstrates:

> The Prophet warned very much of the Dajjāl, even ordering the Muslim to seek refuge with Allah from the evil fitnah [temptation] of the Dajjāl five times a day. The Prophet also described many of the

> Dajjāl's attributes. In the Sunnah, the Dajjāl is described as having red in his skin tone and being bulky . . . Undoubtedly, these fabricated narrations falsely attributed to Ahlul-Bayt [the Prophet's relatives and descendants] actually describe the Dajjāl – the 'Messiah' of the Jews. Despite these reports all being fabrications, the Rāfidah [Shiites] strive to follow what the lies dictate, as they consider them the greatest pillar of their religion. Were these reports fabricated by Jews following the footsteps of Ibn Sabaʾ? Were they the plots of the Dajjāl conveyed to the Rāfidah through his network of shayātīn [devils]? Were they revealed to the Rāfidah by the shayātīn as dreams?[214]

Although a proper understanding of ISIS propaganda without referencing conspiracy is hardly conceivable, the group's official statement in *Dabiq* suggests something else. Conspiracy theory is sharply denounced as being an attempt 'to describe the enemies of Islam with attributes bordering on *rubūbīya* (Allah's lordship)',[215] quoting here from an article entitled 'Conspiracy Theory: Shirk'.[216] According to its message, 'the extreme belief in conspiracy theories varies between minor and major shirk, depending on the degree of power, knowledge, and ownership attributed by its believer to the kuffār'.[217] In everyday practice, only ISIS propagandists have sought to distinguish between what they refer to as 'conspiracy' and – more acceptably – 'unveiling hidden truth'. Such arbitrariness has considerably facilitated their agenda and, at the same time, has been able to convincingly explain inconsistencies in their approach to conspiracy.

The ISIS narrative relies on skilfully employing the above-discussed 'apocalyptic quartet' (i.e. the escalation of contradictions, general decline, a return to the beginning and conspiracy) and, moreover, often utilises episodes and motifs taken from the so-called al-Aᶜmāq cycle.[218] Essentially, the group's End-time messages derive their argumentative power from being linked to historical precedents, as well as from being constantly reproduced, re-iterated and re-framed and, as such, they help to support and justify the immense levels of violence perpetrated by ISIS.[219] This group has been able to depict Western powers as being a true fulfilment of the medieval Last-days traditions. In addition, the cycle roughly covers the area where ISIS operates, as well as an area of current and approaching conflicts. From the ISIS standpoint, these modern conflicts allegedly follow medieval schedules, reflecting other – and this time real – wars and clashes between Muslims and Byzantines. Since we are aware of how such former battles occurred, their imaginary repetition has the capacity to easily ignite a sudden wave of energy and enthusiasm across the 'Muslim world'.

ISIS' self-presentation as a Muslim vanguard can, in fact, be neither verified nor denied. Both triumph and defeat can be interpreted as part of a broader narrative that will result in a happy ending and, within such a framework, even the destruction of ISIS might be explained as a success. In this respect, ISIS has been able to effectively capitalise on the politics of both Western and Muslim governments, unlike its jihadist predecessors. As *Dabiq* and *Rumiyah* reveal, rather than the eventual removal of foreign forces from Middle Eastern battlefields, ISIS has succeeded in encouraging additional attacks from the West in order to redirect them to its apocalyptic story. From the group's perspective, the basic epic line of the al-A^{c}māq cycle has become a perfect guiding template with regard to the presentation of its millennial expectations.

Moreover, the mystery associated with some of the traditions belonging to this cycle enables ISIS to flexibly adjust its interpretations according to current requirements, a fact that should certainly not be underestimated. Essentially, any action taken by their opponents can be used by ISIS apocalyptists for their own benefit. The appearance of Western troops in Syria thus only serves to magnify the group's appeal, regardless of its actual military success or failure. In this respect, any response to the perpetration of violent acts, as Mark Juergensmeyer writes, 'will enhance the credibility of the terrorists within their own community'.[220]

Yet, apocalyptic battlefields have little in common with earthly ones. Perhaps, this is the reason why *Dabiq* and *Rumiyah* so often focus on a comparison between current failures and idealised messianic dreams. Needless to say, the acceptance of the above-depicted dichotomy inevitably leads to an attempt to correct the erroneous present in order to achieve the dreamed of ideal future. As we may conclude, at least for now, ISIS apocalyptic propaganda has unquestionably played an important role in strengthening such motivations. Furthermore, two of the most discussed sources, *Dabiq* and *Rumiyah*, are not merely simple and straightforward propaganda material; instead, they represent an outward-looking articulation of ISIS visions of the caliphate and an effort to explain why ISIS is religiously superior to all its rival Islamist organisations.

Whatever the case, the eschatological clock, which also operates in ISIS propaganda, continues to tick and the different potential forms of 'apocalyptic countdown' are the subject of the following chapter.

Notes

1. Available, for example, at www.youtube.com/watch?v=TjzxYdbiLk4 (last accessed 9 May 2017).
2. Juergensmeyer, *Terror in the Mind of God*, pp. 182–3.
3. Fishman, *The Master Plan*, p. 259.
4. For the jihadist recruitment strategy, see Al Qaᶜidy, *A Course in the Art of Recruiting*.
5. Gerges, *ISIS*, p. x.
6. Filiu, *Apocalypse in Islam*, p. 193.
7. Fishman, *The Master Plan*, p. 71.
8. For example, in *Dabiq* 3:6; 4:4; 4:33–7; *Rumiyah* 4:24–5; 8:20–5; 8:42; 9:12–16, etc.
9. Cited in Berger, 'The Metronome of Apocalyptic Time', p. 68.
10. Gerges, *ISIS*, p. 26.
11. Bunzel, *From Paper State to Caliphate*, p. 7.
12. Atwan, *Islamic State*, p. 42.
13. Fishman, *The Master Plan*, pp. 251–2.
14. *Dabiq* 15:13.
15. Berger, 'The Metronome of Apocalyptic Time', p. 63. Cf. also Fishman, *The Master Plan*, p. 227.
16. See the articles 'Khilafa Declared' and 'A New Era Has Arrived', in *Dabiq* 1:6–9.

17. See Qindīl and ^{c}Abd al-Rabbihi, *al-Fikr al-islāmī al-jihādī al-mu^{c}āṣir*, pp. 409–10. See also https://english.aawsat.com/theaawsat/news-middle-east/who-was-the-real-abu-omar-al-baghdadi (last accessed 29 September 2017).
18. See *Dabiq* 4:35–6.
19. *Dabiq* 4:4 and 4:33–7.
20. For his public speeches, see *Majmū^{c} tafrīghāt*, pp. 128–218.
21. McCants, *The ISIS Apocalypse*, p. 122.
22. See *Dabiq* 1:34.
23. See Cook, *Contemporary Muslim Apocalyptic Literature*, pp. 126–49.
24. *Majmū^{c} tafrīghāt*, p. 134.
25. See https://ia902605.us.archive.org/16/items/Archive-Of-Abo-Hamzah-Talks/first-interview_text.pdf (last accessed 29 September 2017).
26. McCants, *The ISIS Apocalypse*, p. 123. Cf. *Mashrū^{c}īya al-rāya fī al-islām*, pp. 4–5.
27. McCants, *The ISIS Apocalypse*, p. 22.
28. Ibid. p. 32.
29. Fromson and Simon, 'ISIS', p. 37.
30. Fishman, *The Master Plan*, p. 114.
31. See https://ia802605.us.archive.org/16/items/Archive-Of-Abo-Hamzah-Talks/second-interview_text.pdf (last accessed 29 September 2017).
32. For audio recordings of his speeches, see https://archive.org/details/Archive-Of-Abo-Hamzah-Talks (last accessed 29 September 2017).
33. Al-Muhājir, *al-Dawla al-nabawīya*, p. 5.
34. See *Majmū^{c} tafrīghāt*, pp. 145–8.
35. Fishman, *The Master Plan*, pp. 113–16.
36. McCants, *The ISIS Apocalypse*, p. 38.
37. Fishman, *The Master Plan*, p. 116.
38. McCants, *The ISIS Apocalypse*, p. 40.
39. Fishman, *The Master Plan*, p. 113.
40. For this 'jihadist divorce', see, especially, Fishman, *The Master Plan*, pp. 110–18; Gerges, *ISIS*, pp. 222–59; McCants, *The ISIS Apocalypse*, pp. 47–71. Cf. also Ibrāhīm and al-Najjār, *Dā^{c}ish*, pp. 25–7 and Fārūq, *Dā^{c}ish*, pp. 48–53.
41. Gorenberg, *The End of Days*, p. 47.
42. Amanat, *Apocalyptic Islam*, p. 250.

43. *Dabiq* 4:4. For his collected speeches, see *Majmūᶜ tafrīghāt*, pp. 3–127.
44. *Majmūᶜ tafrīghāt*, p. 19.
45. Cf. Nuᶜaym, *The Book of Tribulations*, p. 193 (no. 953).
46. McCants, *The ISIS Apocalypse*, p. 143.
47. See, for example, al-Muqaddam, *Fiqh ashrāṭ al-sāᶜa*, pp. 158–62.
48. Ibid. p. 103.
49. See al-Baghdādī, *Risāla ilā ḥukkām al-bayt al-abyaḍ*.
50. For his succinct biography, see McCants, 'The Believer'. See also Fishman, *The Master Plan*, pp. 149–55; Atwan, *Islamic State*, pp. 104–15; Zelin, 'Abu Bakr al-Baghdadi'.
51. See https://yolandaelvira.wordpress.com/2015/05/15/march-forth-whether-light-or-heavy/ (last accessed 20 November 2017).
52. See al-Baghdādī, *Baqīya fī al-ᶜIrāk wa al-Shām*.
53. Al-Zarqāwī, *Kalimāt muḍīᶜa*, p. 151.
54. Petit, 'Eschatology in the ISIS Narrative', p. 6.
55. Furnish, *Ten Years' Captivation with the Mahdi's Camps*, p. 38.
56. See https://www.washingtontimes.com/news/2015/jan/5/apocalypse-prophecies-drive-islamic-state-strategy/ (last accessed 22 November 2017).
57. Cited from the translation in McCants, *The ISIS Apocalypse*, pp. 121–2.
58. Atwan, *Islamic State*, p. 1.
59. Cf. also al-Baghdādī, 'Even If the Disbelievers Despise Such', p. 4.
60. Fishman, *The Master Plan*, p. 205.
61. *Al-Nabaᵓ* 11:2.
62. McCants, *The ISIS Apocalypse*, p. 143.
63. See, for example, *al-Nabaᵓ* 17:14; 18:11; 19:15; 22:14; 85:8–9.
64. See, for example, https://archive.org/details/TheRiseOfTheKhilafahReturnOfTheGoldDinar_201509 (last accessed 12 September 2018).
65. Fishman, *The Master Plan*, p. 91.
66. Pregill, 'ISIS, Eschatology, and Exegesis', p. 7.
67. See *al-Nabaᵓ* 49:8–9; 97:14; 98:13, etc.
68. Fishman, *The Master Plan*, p. 207.
69. Shandab, *Munāẓara maᶜa ᶜaql dāᶜish*, pp. 11–20.
70. Fromson and Simon, 'ISIS', p. 30.
71. Cf., for example, *Dabiq* 1:33.
72. Al-Shaᶜrāwī, *Aḥdāth nihāyat al-ᶜālam*, pp. 157–8. Cf. al-ᶜArīfī, *Nihāyat al-ᶜālam*, pp. 112–13.

73. *Al-Naba*ʾ 11:2. Cf. also *al-Naba*ʾ 29:14.
74. *Dabiq* 4:56.
75. See *al-Naba*ʾ 53:8–9.
76. Petit, 'Eschatology in the ISIS Narrative', p. 23.
77. For an overview of the monuments in Mosul destroyed by ISIS, see Melčák and Beránek, 'ISIS's Destruction of Mosul's Historical Monuments', pp. 389–415.
78. See Tabbaa, 'The Mosque of Nūr al-Dīn in Mosul', p. 351.
79. See http://theconversation.com/destroying-mosuls-great-mosque-islamic-states-symbolic-war-to-the-end-80002 (last accessed 20 November 2017).
80. See, for example, the eight-part 'apocalyptic series' published in *al-Naba*ʾ magazine: 120:8–9; 117:8; 114:8; 110:8; 109:8; 108:8; 107:8. See also *al-Naba*ʾ 131:8; 130:8; 128:8; 125:8; 123:8, etc.
81. See, for example, *al-Naba*ʾ 147:9.
82. See http://www.newsweek.com/isis-cyber-caliphate-biggest-threat-amid-fears-christmas-lone-wolf-attacks-740125 (last accessed 2 January 2018).
83. Juergensmeyer, *Terror in the Mind of God*, p. 162.
84. Gerges, *ISIS*, pp. 286–7.
85. Ibid. p. 290.
86. Fishman, *The Master Plan*, p. 248.
87. Ibid. p. 255.
88. For the role of extreme violence in ISIS propaganda, see Atwan, *Islamic State*, pp. 147–58.
89. *Al-Naba*ʾ 50:8–9.
90. McCants, *The ISIS Apocalypse*, p. 105.
91. Ibid. p. 104.
92. Available at https://sendvid.com/ryvlns0s (last accessed 22 February 2018).
93. For its symbolic dimension, see Gambhir, *Dabiq*, pp. 2–3. Cf. Fārūq, *Dāʿish*, pp. 113–19.
94. McCants, *The ISIS Apocalypse*, p. 103.
95. There are some exceptions to this rule, e.g. its editor-in-chief Abū Sulaymān al-Shāmī. However, we mostly only know what ISIS wants to be revealed; for example, the article in *Rumiyah* (8:43), which clearly describes how *Dabiq* came into existence: 'So Dabiq was released with

its name chosen by Shaykh Abu Muhammad, in order to frustrate the Crusaders of Rome and convey to them their inevitable end.'

96. For a long list of the failed prophecies of Muslim apocalyptists, see al-Muqaddam, *Fiqh ashrāṭ al-sāᶜa*, pp. 89–95.
97. Musselwhite, *ISIS & Eschatology*, p. 153.
98. *Dabiq* 1:6–9, 34–41.
99. See *Majmūᶜ tafrīghāt*, pp. 164–81.
100. *Dabiq* 4:4.
101. Ibid.
102. For this speech with English subtitles, see https://www.youtube.com/watch?v=LOiN9boAmoI (last accessed 17 April 2017).
103. *Dabiq* 1:34.
104. Nuᶜaym, *The Book of Tribulations*, p. 42.
105. Fromson and Simon, 'ISIS', pp. 30–1.
106. For more information on Binᶜalī, see Gharīb, *Minnat al-ᶜAlī bi-thabāt shaykhinā Turkī al-Binᶜalī*. For the English translation of excerpts from his short treatise devoted to the establishment of the caliphate, see McCants, *The ISIS Apocalypse*, pp. 179–81.
107. McCants, *The ISIS Apocalypse*, pp. 114–19.
108. Ibid. p. 116.
109. *Dabiq* 1:10.
110. *Dabiq* 1:24.
111. *Dabiq* 1:28.
112. *Dabiq* 12:2.
113. Cf. Gambhir, *Dabiq*, pp. 1–12. Cf. also Fārūq, *Dāᶜish*, pp. 118–19.
114. *Dabiq* 2:44.
115. *Dabiq* 2:10–11.
116. Cf. Nuᶜaym, *The Book of Tribulations*, pp. 21–6.
117. Ḥisān, *Aḥdāth al-nihāya*, p. 393.
118. *Rumiyah* 4:17.
119. Abū Mālik, *ᶜAlāmāt al-sāᶜa*, p. 27. Cf. al-ᶜArīfī, *Nihāyat al-ᶜālam*, pp. 107–8.
120. *Rumiyah* 5:26–8.
121. *Dabiq* 2:11.
122. *Dabiq* 3:29.
123. Furnish, *Ten Years' Captivation with the Mahdi's Camps*, p. 58.
124. *Dabiq* 2:6.

125. *Dabiq* 3:9.
126. *Dabiq* 3:15.
127. *Dabiq* 4:6.
128. See Mirza, '"The Slave Girl Gives Birth to Her Master"', pp. 1–23.
129. Ibid. p. 19.
130. Abū Mālik, *ᶜAlāmāt al-sāᶜa*, p. 22.
131. Bayūmī, *Nubuᵓāt al-nabī*, p. 48.
132. See al-ᶜArīfī, *Nihāyat al-ᶜālam*, p. 67.
133. See Mirza, '"The Slave Girl Gives Birth to Her Master"', pp. 12–17.
134. *Dabiq* 4:17.
135. Mirza, '"The Slave Girl Gives Birth to Her Master"', p. 2.
136. *Dabiq* 4:17.
137. See Mah-Rukh, *ISIS and Propaganda*, pp. 17–20.
138. *Dabiq* 4:14.
139. For an overt ISIS justification of the destruction of monuments, see *al-Nabaᵓ* 20:12–13.
140. Melčák and Beránek, 'ISIS's Destruction of Mosul's Historical Monuments', p. 399.
141. Beránek and Ťupek, *The Temptation of Graves*, p. 180.
142. *Dabiq* 4:17.
143. *Dabiq* 4:35–7.
144. *Dabiq* 4:37.
145. Qurᵓān 2:216.
146. Ostřanský, 'The Lesser Signs of the Hour', p. 257.
147. *Dabiq* 12:24.
148. Al-Shaᶜrāwī, *Ahdāth nihāyat al-ᶜālam*, p. 167.
149. On the other hand, the portents of the Hour also include an opposing phenomenon: the total absence of people's dreams during the Last Days; cf. Nuᶜaym, *The Book of Tribulations*, pp. 21–6.
150. Quoted according to Kabbani, *The Approach of Armageddon?*, p. 109.
151. Al-Shaᶜrāwī, *Aḥdāth nihāyat al-ᶜālam*, p. 157.
152. See Edgar, 'The Dreams of Islamic State', pp. 72–84.
153. See Hegghammer (ed.), *Jihadi Culture*, pp. 139–50.
154. That is, Abū Ayyūb al-Miṣrī.
155. *Rumiyah* 4:7.
156. Al-Shaᶜrāwī, *Aḥdāth nihāyat al-ᶜālam*, p. 69.
157. *Rumiyah* 4:18.

158. Gambhir, *Dabiq*, p. 3.
159. *Dabiq* 7:54–66.
160. *Dabiq* 7:54.
161. See Shandab, *Munāẓara ma*ᶜ*a* ᶜ*aql dā*ᶜ*ish*, pp. 118–19.
162. Cf. also *al-Naba*ᵓ 11:2–3; 15:12–13; 24:13.
163. See http://www.telegraph.co.uk/news/worldnews/islamic-state/12002726/The-grey-zone-How-Isis-wants-to-divide-the-world-into-Muslims-and-crusaders.html (last accessed 6 April 2017).
164. See, for example, Ayyūb, *al-Masīḥ al-Dajjāl*, p. 228.
165. Cf. Ibrāhīm and al-Najjār, *Dā*ᶜ*ish*, pp. 95–102. Cf. also Shandab, *Munāẓara ma*ᶜ*a* ᶜ*aql dā*ᶜ*ish*, pp. 49–62.
166. See, for example, *Dabiq* 15:13.
167. Cook, *Contemporary Muslim Apocalyptic Literature*, pp. 5–6.
168. Shandab, *Munāẓara ma*ᶜ*a* ᶜ*aql dā*ᶜ*ish*, p. 153.
169. Cook, *Studies in Muslim Apocalyptic*, p. 15.
170. Winter, *The Virtual 'Caliphate'*, p. 6.
171. Juergensmeyer, *Terror in the Mind of God*, p. 148.
172. See, for example, *Dabiq* 3:32.
173. See, for example, *Dabiq* 14:8–17.
174. For the apocalyptic dimension of ISIS takfirism, see Pregill, 'ISIS, Eschatology, and Exegesis', pp. 9–12.
175. See Juergensmeyer, *Terror in the Mind of God*, p. 146.
176. See Fishman, *The Master Plan*, p. 193.
177. Gerges, *ISIS*, p. 40.
178. *Rumiyah* 4:24–5.
179. Cf. Rapoport, 'The Islamic State Wants the West to Over-React and Hasten Apocalypse'.
180. Ostřanský, 'The Lesser Signs', pp. 235–84.
181. *Dabiq* 3:11.
182. Nuᶜaym, *The Book of Tribulations*, p. xxiv.
183. Velji, *An Apocalyptic History*, p. 22.
184. Amanat, *Apocalyptic Islam*, p. 23.
185. See Günther, 'Presenting the Glossy Look of Warfare in Cyberspace'.
186. Nuᶜaym, *The Book of Tribulations*, p. 93 (no. 458).
187. Al-ᶜArīfī, *Nihāyat al-*ᶜ*ālam*, p. 45.
188. For the concept of the *ghurabā*ᵓ among jihadists, see Hegghammer (ed.), *Jihadi Culture*, pp. 30–1.

189. McCants, *The ISIS Apocalypse*, p. 101.
190. Fishman, *The Master Plan*, p. 65.
191. See, for example, www.youtube.com/watch?v=TjzxYdbiLk4 (last accessed 9 May 2017).
192. Lia, *Architect of Global Jihad*, pp. 251–2.
193. Quoted according to Beránek and Ťupek, *The Temptation of Graves*, p. 81.
194. For an Arabic version with English subtitles, see www.youtube.com/watch?v=TjzxYdbiLk4 (last accessed 11 April 2017).
195. The motif of *ghurabāʾ* appears on YouTube in many versions and languages. For a new English version, see https://www.youtube.com/watch?v=2EhP9ZtGbeM (last accessed 12 April 2017). For more information about the phenomenon of *nashīd* itself, see http://jihadology.net/2016/02/29/jihadology-podcast-nasheeds-history-and-cultural-meaning/ (last accessed 20 November 2017).
196. *Dabiq* 12:29–30.
197. The portrait of Abū Muslim al-Kanadī (originally André Poulin), as an illustrative example, is available at http://jihadology.net/2014/07/12/al-%E1%B8%A5ayat-media-center-presents-a-new-video-message-from-the-islamic-state-al-ghuraba-the-chosen-few-of-different-lands-abu-muslim-from-canada/ (last accessed 10 November 2017).
198. For the role of recruitment campaigns within ISIS propaganda, see Atwan, *Islamic State*, pp. 171–81.
199. See Juergensmeyer, *Terror in the Mind of God*, p. 217.
200. See an interview with the head of 'the *hijra* department', in *al-Nabaʾ* 49:8–9.
201. *Rumiyah* 4:4.
202. *Rumiyah* 5:20–1.
203. Cf. *al-Nabaʾ* 59:8.
204. For the motif of *hijra* in ISIS propaganda, see Gambhir, *Dabiq*, pp. 4–5.
205. *Rumiyah* 5:21.
206. See Qindīl and ʿAbd al-Rabbihi, *al-Fikr al-islāmī al-jihādī al-muʿāṣir*, pp. 66–70.
207. See https://www.pri.org/stories/2014-09-04/isis-has-new-hand-sign-and-it-means-far-more-we-re-1 (last accessed 20 November 2017).
208. See *Dabiq* 9:15.
209. *Dabiq* 11:16–17 and 13:32–45.

210. *Dabiq* 13:32–45.
211. Cf. *al-Nabaʾ* 89:8–9.
212. *Dabiq* 13:32–45.
213. *Dabiq* 13:33.
214. *Dabiq* 13:45.
215. *Dabiq* 9:15.
216. *Dabiq* 9:14–19.
217. *Dabiq* 9:16.
218. See Cook, *Studies in Muslim Apocalyptic*, pp. 49–54. Cf. Nuʿaym, *The Book of Tribulations*, pp. 242–80.
219. See Günther, 'Presenting the Glossy Look of Warfare in Cyberspace'.
220. Juergensmeyer, *Terror in the Mind of God*, p. 237.

5

The Countdown to the Apocalypse

As for you, O knights of tawhīd, monks of the night, lions of the jungle, may Allah reward you on behalf of us and the Muslims with every good. For I have seen war and its men, and I testify by Allah, I testify by Allah, that our ummah in the land of the two grand rivers (Iraq) did not skimp on bestowing its best sons and most truthful nobles upon us . . . I do not doubt for a moment – and Allah knows such – that we are the army that will pass on the banner to the slave of Allah the Mahdī. If the first of us is killed, then the last of us will pass it on to him.

– Abū Hamza al-Muhājir, also known as Abū Ayyūb al-Misrī[1]

Religious ideas have given a profundity and ideological clarity to what in many cases have been real experiences of economic destitution, social oppression, political corruption, and a desperate need for the hope of rising above the limitations of modern life. The image of cosmic struggle has given these bitter experiences meaning, and the involvement in a grand conflict has been for some participants exhilarating.

– Mark Juergensmeyer[2]

The recurrent reference to allegedly already fulfilled End-time prophecies, as we have seen, represents the most frequently deployed rhetorical strategy in terms of apocalyptic literature. Within ISIS propaganda, which has mostly been disseminated via cyberspace, End-time motifs often act as a means of 'sense-making' by transforming a list of disconnected events (individual portents) into a unified story, ultimately to be synthesised along with various other sources and conspiracy theories.[3] In this chapter, our attention will be focused primarily on the thematic composition of such an integrated story, which might, with some degree of exaggeration, be referred to as 'a map to the future'.

Careful analysis of ISIS End-time references has led us to adopt the notion of so-called 'tamed apocalypticism', which was introduced in the opening section of Chapter 4. This is regarded as a practical, even necessary, step, because 'ruling with an eye toward the end of the world is not conducive toward establishing the kinds of daily services required to secure the long-term consent of the governed – particularly since most of its subjects do not share ISIS's abbreviated eschatological time frame'.[4] In this way, jihadists have simply avoided the trap of having to precisely date the Hour, even though they are familiar with the associated speculation.

Thus, while End-time expectations have not completely been abandoned, they have been exploited in order to bestow legitimacy on the ruling power in the present. This cautious approach to the treatment of apocalyptic material[5] largely stems from the bitter experience of over-heated millennial expectations – in the case of ISIS represented chiefly by the group's forerunner, Abū Ayyūb al-Miṣrī. In a broader sense, the always-contradictory nature associated with temporalising End-time events has been aptly described by Abbas Amanat:

> Playing an active part in temporalizing the apocalyptic scenario, the participants view their role, and that of their opponents, as divinely ordained though not entirely devoid of human initiatives and strategies. This curious mix of the scripted and the improvised, the providential design and its human deciphering, is germane to most apocalyptic currents.[6]

As far as ISIS strategy is concerned, the gradual shift from looking at the future towards the reinterpretation of the present as an effective solution to the 'Mahdist trap' – that is, how to preserve the immediacy of End-time expectations while, at the same time, ensuring 'state-building qualities' – is definitely nothing new. The same problem has had to be solved by many earlier movements, for example by the Fatimid dynasty, which 'translated expectations of the Mahdī into a successful empire' with the help of *taʾwīl*.[7] Clearly, ISIS apocalyptists are unable to resort to 'an esoteric interpretation', which is the common meaning of *taʾwīl*, since this option has been made impossible by their own self-imposed ideological straitjacket. However, the group has been able to identify other tools, equally reliable and effective, which can be used to suppress expectations of the imminence of the expected Utopia, without losing its appeal. Their overall ethos might thus be summarised as a single basic principle: where there is no concreteness, neither is there disappointment.

Through providing a depiction of the group's role as historical precursor of the dreamed-of Utopia, as predicted in medieval prophecies, its propagandists have been able to repress expectations of the imminence of the Mahdī's appearance in favour of a reader-friendly examination of particular tendencies that will be observed prior to this crucial event. Additionally, such an effort is much easier to envision if we admit that we are living in the final phase of history, and this is why an elaboration of the harbingers of the Hour match considerations devoted to current affairs.

Moreover, ISIS's preferred depiction of itself as the historic saviour of Muslims, ready to face the challenges of worldwide bankruptcy and evil, may not necessarily be regarded as tantamount to the figure of the eschatological Saviour, the Mahdī. The mere belief that the former power is already paving the way for the latter has the capacity to effectively galvanise the apocalyptic imagination of ISIS adherents, regardless of the closeness of the Hour.

Despite the unquestionable fact that the vast majority of apocalyptic signals emitted by the ISIS propaganda apparatus are directed not at the future, but rather at the present or past, the diversity of ideas relating to the expected final clash between good and evil cannot simply be ignored. Intuitively, it is clear that apocalypticism without reference to the future can never be fully-fledged apocalypticism. Consequently, the future will not be neglected in this study. Thus, our attention in this chapter will chiefly be directed towards those phenomena that are expected to be witnessed, according to ISIS apocalyptists, in the future or, more precisely, those signs that are expected to occur prior to the End.

According to the prevailing opinion of the *ᶜulamāᵓ*, when compared to those that have already been fulfilled, the number of unfulfilled signs is very limited. If ISIS propagandists truly believe in what they have been announcing publicly regarding the approaching Hour, at least some of the issues outlined below should appear as the focus of their increased attention and exegetical endeavour. This can be demonstrated through reference to a number of specific examples. To correctly contextualise such interpretations, our attempt to create an 'End-time map' will be followed by an overview that focuses on the spreading of the group's apocalyptic ideas via the media and cyberspace.

They Plot, but Allah Also Plots[8]

The final period of history is usually characterised by Muslim apocalyptists as the ever-deepening decline of a people who are oblivious to God's rules. Specific portents of the approaching End have been revealed to the people in order to reassure them that even in the face of such decay in religious and moral values, this should be recognised as part of God's preordained plan.

Various accounts of yet unfulfilled signs of the Hour can be found in many modern Muslim apocalyptic pamphlets. For instance, Muḥammad al-Bayūmī has summarised the expected events as eleven points:[9] (1) apostasy from Islam and the worshipping of idols; (2) a surplus of property; (3) the Euphrates uncovering a mountain of gold; (4) wild animals and inanimate things speaking to people; (5) the spread of public fornication; (6) the Moon expanding; (7) the Earth issuing its treasures; (8) Muslims contending with Jews; (9) fighting between Muslims and Turks; (10) a man from Qaḥṭān appearing and leading the people by his stick; and (11) tribulations. Muḥammad al-ᶜArīfī, a popular Saudi preacher, has even identified forty-six signs that are yet to be fulfilled.[10]

All these expected events can, for our purposes, be divided into three categories: (1) societal and religious, that is, the deepening of moral and religious decline; (2) geopolitical, mostly referring to the sharpening antagonism between orthodox Muslims and the rest of the world; and (3) natural, pointing to unprecedented phenomena on earth and in heaven. In such a scenario, the first two categories share a religious dimension – while the former considers a decline in religious education to be part of a broader level of bankruptcy (that is, religion as a subject), within the latter, we can find religion presented as a mighty dividing power, resulting in geopolitical clashes that will precede the Hour (religion as an agent).

Since Muslim apocalyptists, both medieval and current, enjoy moralising, the never-ending references to moral and religious decline represent some of the most numerous segments of any Islamic apocalyptic screenplay. Essentially, the various 'portents of the Hour' traditions are the primary vehicle used by modern apocalyptic authors in their attempt to admonish and warn. As regards the real impact of such moralising, David Cook writes:

> Since messianic and apocalyptic movements have been and continue to be active throughout the history of Islam, this material could always be used to 'prove' that the Hour was at hand. This would be especially effective in Muslim society where the sense of history is undeveloped, and the belief that earlier ages were better than the present is virtually ubiquitous, and strongly supported by the *ḥadīth* literature.[11]

Regardless of modern innovations (see 'Modern Muslim Apocalyptic Creativity' in Chapter 2), accounts of the portents that will foreshadow the End that appeared in the Middle Ages are essentially the same as those compiled more recently – and an attempt to introduce some of the apocalyptic tidings proclaimed by ISIS will be made within this section.

With regard to the deepening of moral decline and the sharpening of antagonism between rightly guided Muslims and the rest of the world, the concept of 'cosmic war', introduced by Mark Juergensmeyer, should be taken into consideration. This is because such a notion can help us to understand and interpret the current conflicts as part, continuation and result of legendary and mythical clashes led by members of particular religious traditions in the past. This notion performs a number of functions, above all in relation to the orientation of disoriented individuals through an explanation as to why they are suffering and who their real enemies are. The imagining of a 'cosmic war' has the remarkable capacity to justify the use of violence against opponents while dehumanising them to the level of being mere representatives of evil. From such a perspective, one's own violence can be reinterpreted as praiseworthy self-defence. Even a hopeless situation can be seen as a mere obstacle on the long journey towards prophesised victory.

In current Arabic academia, the concept of social polarisation as both the goal and vehicle of ISIS propaganda has been thoroughly investigated by Māzin Shandab in his stimulating study *Munāẓara maᶜa ᶜaql dāᶜish: Ḥawla istrātījīya istiqṭāb al-nisāᵓ wa al-rijāl* (*Polemics with the Understanding of ISIS: About the Strategy of the Polarization of Women and Men*). Moreover, escalated antagonism and stark dualism indisputably pertain to the most important form of apocalyptic realisation. This point also applies to the opponents of ISIS (see 'Sunni "Apocalypses Light"' in Chapter 6).

Before we proceed to the individual End-time portents, the fundamental issue of whether it is possible to 'hotwire the apocalypse' should at least be raised. Although this attractive idea can easily captivate the attention of apocalyptists in general, the related speculation in Islam remains rather constrained. Essentially, the vast majority of Muslims (with the remarkable exception of *ḥujjatīya*, a traditionalist Iranian Shiite religious organisation)[12] concur in the belief that the Hour cannot in anyway be hastened or postponed. Though knowledge of the timing of the Hour belongs solely to God, people should be aware of its approach through observing the harbingers. From a gnoseological perspective, respecting the unknowability of the Hour while dreaming about its acceleration may not necessarily be contradictory.[13] It is precisely such a way of thinking that has been attributed to ISIS by Timothy Furnish, who assumes that 'ISIS has passed into the realm of trying to hotwire the apocalypse' and, according to whose suggestion, 'ISIS atrocities . . . are, in effect, "bizarre rituals intended to bring about the end of the world"'.[14]

To return to the yet-unfulfilled apocalyptic portents, their expected societal and religious components (i.e. our first imaginary category) mostly develop already described apocalyptic themes and visions. However, they manage to bring them into much sharper focus. Among the most frequent manifestations of the all-encompassing decline, three narrower narrative patterns can be further distinguished. The predicted widespread immorality is scheduled to reach an unprecedented level when people, as foretold by the prophecies, 'fornicate in the street as donkeys'. It is no wonder that sexual transgressions constitute the most frequently occurring issues in apocalyptic imagery. In this regard, *Dabiq* proves to be no exception:

> Allah's Messenger said, 'Never does sexual perversion become widespread amongst a people to the point that it's openly practiced, except that they will be overtaken by plague and disease that had never afflicted their ancestors who came before them.'[15]

As being the main source of various supposed perversities, both Western influence and Muslims who have been 'led astray' stand equally accused. However, 'sexual perversion' is just the tip of the iceberg. In fact, we are talking about the total obliteration of moral values and the severing of family relationships, both of which have been considered to be an unchangeable certainty for many centuries.

The predicted signs of moral turpitude also encompass, for example, bearing false witness, the concealment of truth, an abundance of greed, greetings reserved for acquaintances, the spreading of lasciviousness, people pretending not to know each other, and so on.[16]

As regards the sources of social decay, the article entitled 'The Fitra of Mankind and the Near-Extinction of the Western Woman'[17] recapitulates a number of the destructive effects that people are currently exposed to and, at the same time, elaborates on the fundamental Islamic notion of *fitra* (natural disposition):

> So this fitrah is what causes man to distinguish between monotheism and polytheism. It also aids him in generally distinguishing between pureness and filthiness, between decency and obscenity, between mercy and cruelty, between justice and tyranny, between truth and falsehood, and between right and wrong.[18]

It is unnecessary to add that it is precisely this inner disposition that is responsible for correct conduct that is destined to disappear as the world approaches the Hour.

Another distinctive feature of End-time decline narratives is the corruption of true knowledge.[19] Today, given the existence of the so-called information revolution, it is difficult to understand why Muslim apocalyptists are so obsessed with this idea of ignorance (*jahl*) dominating the world. In fact, it is because they usually resort to an explanation that highlights the genuine nature of knowledge, rather than its quantity or speed of dissemination.[20] As most exegetes believe, the decrease in knowledge thus refers particularly to the religious sciences, not to scholarship in its universal sense.[21] This point, paradoxically, also manifests itself in the contemporary boom in the sale of Arabic apocalyptic literature written by totally incompetent authors.[22]

The incessant stress placed on 'genuine Islam' cannot only be investigated through reference to ISIS-controlled media. Textbooks manifestly reveal the group's true ideological position.[23] According to Jacob Olidort, both ISIS textbooks and other publications strive to 'justify the group's quartet of aims of encouraging violence, driving an apocalyptic narrative, establishing a purist "Islamic" state, and labeling it a caliphate'.[24] Olidort has also introduced the concept of so-called 'ISization', referring to the group's effort to impose on the people its own worldview by emphasising the caliphate, Islamic state-building, violence, and the apocalypse.[25]

The group's emphasis on supposedly authentic Islamic knowledge is often compared with the corruption allegedly characteristic of the rest of the Muslim world. As an archetypal example, a fool giving advice appears as the theme in a number of apocalyptic prophecies:

> He [the Prophet] also said, 'Indeed, Allah does not seize knowledge by taking it from His slaves, but He seizes knowledge by seizing the scholars until, when no scholar remains, the people appoint ignorant leaders. When they are asked, they pass verdicts without knowledge, by which they mislead and are misled.'[26]

Various other references, either implicit or explicit, to misguided Muslim authorities and the related devaluation of authentic religious values constitute some of the most frequently utilised themes in ISIS propaganda.[27] Furthermore, among the allegedly corrupt scholars, a number of radical Islamists are to be found.[28] For ISIS, the belief that during the Last Days false and malevolent leaders will emerge to corrupt Islam simply appears to be a self-fulfilling prophecy.

In ISIS propaganda practice, being led astray as an apocalyptic concept intertwines with its opportunistic deployment within internal Muslim conflicts. The fear of being tricked by seductive and duplicitous leaders and misguided believers, as repeatedly expressed by the Prophet Muḥammad, has been diligently utilised and developed by ISIS.

> Rasulullah [Muḥammad] said: 'Indeed, what I fear most for my Ummah is every articulate hypocrite.' These articulate hypocrites are amongst the misleading scholars mentioned in another hadīth. Abū Dharr narrated that while he was walking with the Prophet, the Prophet said three times, 'Indeed, there is something I fear for my Ummah more than the Dajjāl.' Abū Dharr asked him, 'What is this that you fear for your Ummah more than the Dajjāl?' He responded, 'The misleading imāms.'[29]

Finally, the spread of idolatry appears as perhaps the most instrumentalised narrative pattern pertaining to this first category of social decline. Recurrent apocalyptic prophecies generally speak of the worshipping of idols. In fact, such idols are generally not real idols but anything that might conceivably seduce Muslims from following the right path – an extremely wide set of items. The related notion of *shirk* thus refers not only to real idolatry or polytheism, but also to the alleged 'deification' or 'worship' of anyone or anything other than Allah. And it is the Salafists who are extraordinarily strict in terms of what has the potential to violate their perception of *tawḥīd*.

In addition to its apocalyptic dimension, the stark antagonism that exists between 'idolatry' and 'believing in God and deeming idolatry unbelief' (*al-kufr bi-l-ṭāghūt*) is also used by ISIS as a catch-all term for many of the group's political arguments. The agents whom the group accuses of spreading idolatry are the 'people of unbelief' and the 'hypocrites' (this generally means Muslims who are in partnership with the West)[30] and such a division further strengthens the black-and-white contours of the End times. The ubiquitous infection with idolatry often also emerges in ISIS periodicals:

> This past century saw a surge in migrations from historically Muslim-majority lands to mushrik-majority countries, especially in the West. Instead of seeking Allah's pleasure by waging defensive jihād in their own lands against the nearer apostate enemies, the immigrants sought comfort in this worldly life by residing peacefully in the lands of Islam's oldest enemies. As a result of their negligence towards their obligations and their exposure to Western kufr, their identity was altered. Their children learned the values and beliefs of their new homelands. The kufr of liberalism and democracy was instilled and a new breed of 'scholars' was born, becoming a major part of the West's very own imāms of kufr.[31]

It is not only Western borrowings, but anything that takes Muslims away from their religion that can be considered as being an 'idol'. In such an understanding, even adherence to this world is a certain kind of *shirk*. According to apocalyptic tradition, when the Hour approaches, people will, paradoxically, no longer think about the Hereafter but, on the contrary, they will choose to adhere to this world and its delights. In Islam, however, this world is described as a perishable place, a testing ground for the Other Side, and it is exactly this wisdom that will be forgotten in the Last Days, as the official spokesperson for ISIS, Abū al-Ḥasan al-Muhājir, reminds us in *Rumiyah*:

> Be steadfast and rejoice, for, by Allah, you will be victorious. This tribulation that you are passing through is merely an episode of tribulations by which Allah grants His mercy to His slaves and thereby distinguishes the wicked from the good and thereafter prepares you for a great truth and larger responsibility . . . You have passed through tribulations that if the anchored mountains were exposed thereto, they would have flattened them.[32]

Any discussion about *shirk* would not be complete without mentioning the cross and Christianity, which represent a significant theme and great challenge for Muslim apocalyptists in general. The unconcealed hatred of the cross is a recurring polemical topic throughout modern Muslim apocalyptic literature.[33] And, therefore, the unceasing attacks in ISIS propaganda against Christians[34] can be perceived and interpreted within the context of the group's intolerance as well as within the apocalyptic framework.

The references that fall into the second, geopolitical, 'category' – pointing mostly to the sharpening of antagonism between rightly guided Muslims and the rest of the world – perhaps constitute the most frequently encountered. For the purpose of our overview, they can be further divided into two subsets: the antagonism between Muslims and non-Muslims, heading towards the foretold great wars that will occur before the Hour, and various inter-Muslim clashes, generally preceding and accompanying the former category of conflict.

All apocalyptic violence is predicted to lead inevitably to a strengthening of the conviction of all parties that they own the truth; there will be no room for compromise. When religious cultures portray warfare as something that is acknowledged and ultimately controlled, they are, in Juergensmeyer's succinct expression, 'presenting an almost cosmological re-enactment of the primacy of order over chaos'.[35]

In such a bipolar worldview, the very act of belonging to the party that has right on its side can justify all means of violence used against enemies, including extreme cruelty. Additionally, ISIS supporters are encouraged to deal with most Muslims not as brothers in faith, but as legitimate targets.[36] The recklessness of the group's followers has been presented as a virtue. Even the spread of torture can thus be explained as the inherited part of an apocalyptic plan.[37] A number of works tie in ritual observances with adherence to ISIS, portraying them as part of the same religious requirement.[38] Loyalty is thus depicted not in political but religious terms.

As regards these 'outward struggles', the lesser signs include clashes between Muslims and Jews and wars between Muslims and Turks.[39] While the latter are completely beyond the focus of ISIS propagandists, the former constitute the most fundamental part of ISIS presentations. Apocalyptists usually distinguish between the battle against Jews who are the followers of the Antichrist ('eschatological conflicts') and the clashes with them that are part of the preparatory phase of a global war that will conclude the lesser signs phase ('earthly conflicts') and precede the emergence of the Mahdī.[40]

In this context, we should highlight the notorious *ḥadīth*: 'Judgement Day shall not come until the Muslim fight the Jews, where the Jews will hide behind trees and stones, and the tree and stones will speak and say, "Muslim, behind me is a Jew. Come and kill him."'[41] This has also been quoted by personalities having no interest in the apocalypse, who have used it merely as an expression of their anti-Jewish sentiment (Bin Lādin, for example).[42] Within the apocalyptic framework, Jews are not only depicted as warriors facing up to Muslims but, above all, as the people who are fully responsible for the never-ending hatching of plots against the *umma*,[43] starting with the early attempts to assassinate the Prophet, continuing with the alleged establishment of Shia as their original contribution to the diabolic anti-Islam plan, and for the establishment of Israel.[44]

To summarise, Jews together with other allies of the Dajjāl are accused of being responsible for the main weakness experienced by Muslims – their fragmentation – to which al-Zarqāwī has referred in his mobilising speech 'Then the Final Outcome is Theirs':

> This sickness has devastated the entire body, which was thrown to the ground and tied to a post, so the beasts and wolves of the world rushed madly upon it, as its limbs were cut to pieces by claws and canines. Such was the saying of the Prophet, as reported by Ahmad and Abu Dawud from Thawban, that he said, 'Allah's Messenger said, "The nations will soon call upon each other from every horizon, just as diners call each other to eat from a dish." We said, "O Messenger of Allah, will it be because we are few on that day?" He said, "On that day, you will be many, but you will be scum, like the scum of a flowing torrent. Awe will be removed from the hearts of your enemy, and wahn (feebleness) will be put into your hearts." We said, "What is the wahn?" He said, "The love of life and the hatred of death."'[45]

Most modern interpreters understand this mysterious reference within the context of various conspiracy theories, particularly those connected with strong anti-Jewish sentiment. In Rabīᶜ al-Zawāwī's opinion, for example, the Jews, unable to face Muslims directly, have made a decision to encourage their internal disputes.[46] Many apocalyptists see in this prediction an allegorical reference to the so-called 'clash of civilizations', in which Muslims are destined to be defeated not because of their weakness but because of their love of life, and mainly due to their self-destructive adherence to disunity. It is with reference to the various internal disputes that divide Muslims all over the world, not only on the Syrian and Iraqi battlefields, that an article in *Rumiyah* magazine speaks:

> Today, the old discords are being renewed within the ranks of the enemies of Allah. The Crusaders of the West oppose the Crusaders of the East and their murtadd [apostate] allies oppose one another. The Turks oppose the Kurds, the Sahwat[47] of Turkey oppose the Sahwat of Jordan, the Rafidah oppose the Kurds of Iraq, the Kurds of the west oppose the Kurds of the east, and the Nusayriyyah oppose the Kurds of Sham . . .[48]

In addition to the diverse manifestations of fragmentation, references to contradictory tendencies can also be found among the lesser signs. Perhaps, the most well-known of them is an enigmatic reference to 'a man from Qaḥṭān, who will appear and lead people by his stick'. In Muslim tradition, Qaḥṭān was the grandson of Noah (Nūḥ) and the fabulous ancestor of the southern Arabs. His appearance might indicate that before the Hour everything will return to the beginning. His identification is controversial and his leadership (whether good or evil) is questionable. Common approaches identify al-Qaḥṭānī with the figure referred to as Dhū al-suwayqatayni ('a man with thin weak legs'), an evil character known as the Abyssinian (al-Ḥabashī), whose emergence, however, is one of the greater signs of the Hour.[49] An attempt to exploit this portent occurred in 1979 (1400 AH), when the rebels led by Juhaymān al-ᶜUtaybī occupied the Holy Mosque in Mecca and declared their comrade-in-arms, al-Qaḥṭānī, to be the awaited Mahdī. With regard to ISIS, no attempt to exploit this apocalyptic image has yet been identified, at least not in its official propaganda.

Finally, our third apocalyptic category – natural – generally refers to unprecedented phenomena on earth and in heaven. Although the apocalyptic nature of these signs is utterly apparent to the extent that such catastrophes are usually perceived synonymously with the apocalypse itself, their effective deployment in an engaged Muslim End-time narrative appears rather problematic. This is because falling stars or the sun rising in the west do not fit too well with the otherwise moralising and geopolitical focus of most contemporary apocalyptic pamphlets. Moreover, the metaphoric reading of this kind of event is, substantially, limited and therefore their expected fulfilment is largely useful only as a means of verifying aspects of the broader eschatological screenplay of which these signs are a part. As such, they are aids rather than genuine aspects of the apocalypse, more distinctive ornament than construction pillar.

Muslim authors have recorded a number of items, mostly enigmatic, pertaining to this category; for example: the outbreak of fire in Hijāz (usually identified as a volcanic eruption); a number of earthquakes; the earth releasing its treasures; the appearance of being swallowed up by the earth (*khasf*), deformation (*maskh*) and throwing (*qadhf*);[50] heavy rains; the inflation of crescents; meadows and rivers returning to the Arabian Peninsula; the extinction of mountains; the Euphrates uncovering a mountain of gold.[51] Some of them (e.g. the fire in Hijāz) are considered by the prevailing opinion of the *ᶜulamāᵓ* as having been fulfilled, while others (e.g. the extinction of mountains) are hardly conceivable and, as such, hard to use. Others (e.g. heavy rains) are hardly exploitable for precisely the opposite reason: they are banal to the extent they could be applied almost always and in every situation.

An illustrative example of this sort of prophecy can be found in the uncovering of gold from the Euphrates and the subsequent fierce battle that will ensue between the finders. In a sense, this sign, which is predicted to immediately precede the emergence of the Antichrist,[52] has become the archetype of unfulfilled prophecy. *Dabiq* summarises its content as follows:

> Allah's Messenger said, 'The Euphrates is on the verge of uncovering a mountain of gold. He who is present there should not take anything from it.' . . . In another narration, he said, 'The Hour will not be established until the Euphrates uncovers a mountain of gold over which the people will fight. Ninety-nine out of each one hundred will be killed, but every man amongst them will say, "Perhaps I myself will survive."' . . .[53]

From an exegetical perspective, this sign can be understood either allegorically (in which case it has been already fulfilled or will soon be fulfilled), or literally. Either way, the idea of the Euphrates uncovering gold enjoys enormous popularity among modern apocalyptic authors, particularly because of the variety of sophisticated possible meanings. According to al-Shaᶜrāwī's interpretation, based on the authority of the medieval polymath al-Qurtubī, this event will happen at the very conclusion of history and will be closely related to another enigmatic forecast about the abundance of property. Thus, this sign will immediately precede the coming of the Mahdī.[54] Since it is said that this excess of money will occur after the coming of Jesus, both as a result of the newly discovered gold and as a result of Muslim war booty, it is sometimes suggested that this portent should be classified as one of the greater signs.[55]

Other modern apocalyptists (Ḥisān and Abū Mālik, for example) remind us that the uncovered gold will be real gold, which will result in a fight breaking out that will see ninety-nine out of every one hundred men dying. As Bayūmī suggests, the word *inḥisār* (uncovering) also means the denudation of something – such as after soil disappears – and therefore this forecast could be simply explained as a shift in the Euphrates riverbed, together with the ensuing erosion.[56] Al-ᶜArīfī, in turn, points to the lowering of the river's water level.[57]

On the other hand, other exegetes (Kabbani and Yahya, for instance) view this phenomenon figuratively, as being a reference either to revenues from the hydroelectric power plants built on the Euphrates in Syria and Turkey,[58] or to the discovery of the oil fields in southern Iraq.

The above-mentioned *aḥādīth* also refer to the subsequent fighting that will erupt among the finders of the gold. This classic narrative only gained popularity during the late twentieth century due to the wealth that oil had brought to the Middle East. Prior to this point in history, the Euphrates narrative actually attracted little attention. Its inclusion in *Dabiq*,[59] however, may point to the influence that modern Muslim apocalyptic literature has had on the region during the past two decades. In his brochure *Kanz al-Furāt* (*The Treasure of the Euphrates*), Muḥammad ᶜĪsā Dāwūd, an influential Egyptian author, has pointed out the likely connection between the detection of Euphrates gold and the American invasion of Iraq. Perhaps it is because of this that these particular *aḥādīth* have become so widespread in countless Muslim fictions.[60]

Within the context of ISIS apocalypticism, reference to finding golden treasure in the riverbed of the Euphrates is totally unusual, due to its straightforwardness. According to the Arabic website *Nujum masriya* (Egyptian Stars), ISIS claims that the discovery of the golden treasure has been achieved by the lowering of the water level behind the dam. This shocking announcement was used to affirm that we are currently living in the final phase of history. Moreover, the promotion of this supposedly uncovered gold was intended to justify ISIS terrorist activities since this portent will inevitably and immediately precede the greater signs of the Hour – the very first item of which is the appearance of the Mahdī.[61]

A meticulous exegesis devoted to the golden hill (*jabal min dhahab*) in the Euphrates has been suggested by, among others, Abū ᶜAbd Allāh al-Dhahabī.[62] The importance of this sign was also underlined by its own item in Arabic Wikipedia, as well as a great number of individual entries on the Internet.[63] The popularity of this mystery has also been proven by a YouTube lecture that succeeded in achieving almost two million views.[64] According to an often suggested hypothesis, the discovery of gold in the Euphrates will be preceded by the lowering of the river, resulting from the construction of dams in Syria and Turkey, which is a fact that essentially resonates with ISIS's own announcement.[65] It is no wonder that there has been speculation as to whether ISIS, by taking this step, intends to pave the way for the Mahdī.[66]

The Islamic Armageddon

From a general perspective, attention paid to the dreamed-of Utopia that features in any Islamic apocalyptic scenario – the Mahdī's perfect kingdom of peace and justice – cannot, by definition, be completed without due diligence being devoted to the partial harbingers of his appearance. This is also true of ISIS propaganda, in whose eschatological messaging the great wars of the Last Days significantly outweigh the effort spent on introducing the Mahdī himself. While the nature of his rule is mostly depicted in broad idealised terms, martial episodes concomitant to the final clash are often described in considerable detail. In the images of cosmic war, this triumph is predicted to transcend all worldly limitations.[67]

The harmonious circumstances of the messianic empire (the wolf and the ram will dwell together, children will play unharmed with scorpions and snakes, lives will be longer, and so on) will replace the above-depicted scenario, which is generally characterised by ubiquitous violence and brutality.[68] This is referred to in an apocalyptic *ḥadīth*: 'A time is about to come upon the people in which death is preferable to the learned one than red gold.'[69] According to another Utopian description presented by *Dabiq*,

> thereafter, kufr and its tyranny will be destroyed; Islam and its justice will prevail on the entire Earth. Then, it will be said to the earth, let your fruits grow and yield your blessings. On that day, a group will eat from a single pomegranate and take shade under its bowl-shaped peel. Milk will be blessed so much so that the young female camel will suffice a very large group of people, and a young female cow will suffice a tribe of people, and a young female sheep will suffice a clan of people . . . The sky will be permitted to pour its rain and the land to yield its plants, so even if you were to plant a seed on a stone, it would spring. There will be no rivalries, no envy, no hatred, to the point that a man will pass by a lion yet it won't harm him, and step on a snake yet it won't harm him . . . The Earth will be filled with peace just as a jar is filled with water . . .[70]

In the wars preceding the Mahdī's emergence, Muslims are informed that, in accordance with medieval tradition, they will engage in combat with Turks. However, according to ISIS apocalyptists, Turks will not represent the main enemy, this role being fulfilled by other allies of the Antichrist, for example Jews and, above all, Shiites. Both groups actually appear in countless depictions of the End-time conflicts promoted by the group's propaganda. Even the genocide of the Yezidis has been presented by ISIS as part of the inevitable End-time spate of clashes.[71] Omitting completely the battles between Muslims and Turks, ISIS propagandists (together with the majority of modern Muslim apocalyptic authors) more often refer to the capture of Constantinople that occurred in 1453. Since that time, the city has been under the government of Turks (i.e. Muslims) and this is why its expected re-conquest remains a mystery. From the limited amount of information we have, it can be assumed that the predicted seizure of both Constantinople and Rome will be a privilege accorded to orthodox Muslims, among whom ISIS supporters primarily rank themselves:

> Are the believers today better to Allah than that first generation of men, those who were tested and shaken greatly until their hearts reached their throats?! And whoever thinks that the conquests of

> Rome and Constantinople will be made through empty words – not wounds – is confused and mistaken! . . . Indeed such victory and conquest is near, as we find the wind of our blessed Khilafah blowing from east to west, despite the claims of the enemy.[72]

Of course, the control of Rome and Constantinople depends on the Great Battle which has irrevocably captured the main attention of ISIS propagandists and which has also been depicted as the termination of 'hypocrisy on the level of calls and movements'.[73] In the modern Muslim apocalypse, its traditional Arabic designation, *al-malḥama al-kubrā*, is often used interchangeably with a modern borrowing, *Harmajidūn* (Armageddon), often described as 'a global clash involving also nuclear weapons'.[74]

The extraordinary ideological significance of this theme has also been echoed by the former chief spokesperson of ISIS (and an early Zarqāwī recruit from Syria), Abū Muḥammad al-ᶜAdnānī,[75] in his inflammatory speech:

> And so we promise you [O crusaders] by Allah's permission that this campaign will be your final campaign. It will be broken and defeated, just as all your previous campaigns were broken and defeated, except that this time we will raid you thereafter, and you will never raid us. We will conquer your Rome, break your crosses, and enslave your women, by the permission of Allah, the Exalted . . . If we do not reach that time, then our children and grandchildren will reach it, and they will sell your sons as slaves at the slave market . . . Finally, this certainty is the one that should pulse in the heart of every mujāhid from the Islamic State and every supporter outside until he fights the Roman crusaders near Dābiq.[76]

To be accurate, the mentioned 'great battle near Dābiq' was only actually emphasised for a limited period. Following failures on local battlefields, the theme was gradually marginalised and finally disappeared altogether. During the time of its victories, the battle of Dābiq was mostly presented as a necessary condition (or the last step) before the appearance of the Dajjāl. This stance can be seen, for example, in the following excerpt: 'Amongst these best shuhadaʾ [martyrs] are the third of the army killed in the epic battle at Dabiq prior to the emergence of the Dajjal. Allah's Messenger said about them: "They are the best shuhadaʾ with Allah."'[77]

In apocalyptic wars, quantity is definitely not a decisive factor. As we can repeatedly observe in the medieval tradition, even a tiny minority of rightly guided people, even when substantially outnumbered by their enemies, can still win. This principle issues from the very essence of Muslim apocalypticism, favouring, in David Cook's words, 'small groups, even single people over the collective action of the community'.[78]

The escalation in hatred against both Jews and Shiites appears as one of the constitutive elements within ISIS End-time narratives. The irony here – one that the group's propagandists would surely not appreciate – is that, in this move, they have specifically recapitulated the discursive gestures associated with a Shiite sect that engaged in a successful medieval state-building project, referred to as the Fatimid Empire.[79] Put simply, the same 'apocalyptic methodology' can be shared even by mutually adversarial forces, as we will see in Chapter 6 ('Sunni "Apocalypses Light"'). In the case of ISIS, there is no doubt that it was the sectarian anti-Shiite ethos that was the main driver behind the group's swift expansion, as well as its appreciable popularity.[80]

In its eleventh issue, *Dabiq* contains the article 'The "Mahdi" of the Rafidah: The Dajjal',[81] which thoroughly elaborates on the great battles of the Last Days and this is of crucial importance for any consideration of the apocalyptic dimension of this periodical. In its overall meaning, this global conflict should emerge as a natural consequence of the sharpening of all contradictions, so symptomatic of the end of history (see 'To Rome' in Chapter 4). Only two polarised forces will supposedly remain: absolute good and absolute evil, corresponding to true belief (*īmān*) and disbelief (*kufr*). The Antichrist thus constitutes a perfect embodiment of the latter:

> Rasūlullāh [The Messenger of God] said, 'When the Dajjāl emerges, a person from the believers leaves for him. The armed guards of the

Dajjāl encounter him and then say to him, "Where are you going?" He says, "I am going to see this person who has emerged." They say to him "Do you not believe in our lord?" He says, "There is nothing obscure about our Lord!" They say, "Kill him." Then some amongst them say, "Has your lord not forbidden you from killing anyone without his permission?" Thus, they take him to the Dajjāl. When the believer sees him, he says, "O people, he is the Dajjāl whom Rasūlullāh spoke of." The Dajjāl then orders for him to be placed upon his belly; the Dajjāl then says, "Take hold of him and beat him until he bleeds." His back and belly are then extensively beaten. Then the Dajjāl asks him, "Do you not believe in me?" He says, "You are the liar Messiah." The Dajjāl then orders him to be sawn in half from the parting of his hair until his legs are separated. Thereafter, the Dajjāl will walk between the two halves. He then says to him, "Arise." He then stands erect. The Dajjāl then says to him, "Do you not believe in me?" The believer replies, "My insight concerning your reality has only increased." The believer then says, "O people, he will not do the same as he did to me with any person after me." The Dajjāl then takes hold of him to kill him. What is between his neck and collarbone is then made into metal, thus the Dajjāl finds no means to kill him. Therefore, he takes hold of him by his hand and feet and throws him. The people think that he has thrown him into Hellfire whereas he has been thrown into Paradise.'[82]

In the Islamic apocalypse, the Dajjāl's primary function is to lead Muslims away from God.[83] In ISIS propaganda, the Dajjāl often appears as a depersonalised figure or power and, as such, can be easily projected onto anything classified as being 'un-Islamic'. The stark dualism associated with the End-time thus manifests itself in never-ending polemics between 'Islamic' and '*dajjālist*' forces. Some authors have even warned that a 'Dajjāl-system' would actually precede the arrival of the figure of the Dajjāl. This is because the 'Dajjāl-system' is portrayed not necessarily as one that incorporates moral decay, but rather as one that contains the connotation of a political force that is setting out to control the world.[84] Apocalyptic diction merges, in this context, with moral criticism of contemporary social relations, political conspiracy theories and stereotyped constructs of the 'enemy'. In all cases, ISIS presents itself as a sole power that is able to stop the current followers of the Dajjāl.

In an earlier online ISIS forum,[85] *al-Minbar al-iᶜlāmī al-jihādī* (The Jihadist Information Pulpit), a thread called *al-Dawla al-islāmīya tuḥāribu al-dajjāl al-aᶜwar wa al-niẓām al-ᶜālamī al-jadīd* (the Islamic State fights the one-eyed Dajjāl and the new world order) advocated the caliphate of al-Baghdādī as the adversary elect of the Dajjāl. A remark from a user who referred to himself as *ṭayr al-ᶜuqāb* (eagle) states: 'All prophets have warned of the Dajjāl, whereas our prophet thus bears witness to us about him, like no one before him did . . . He shows himself to the public as a human being – a faithful follower and saviour of the Jews, as the one who built the [Zionist] entity and to whom the Palace of the Kingdom of Saudi Arabia belongs, in order to monitor the White Palace [the White House].'[86] In ISIS ideology, even misguided Muslims can be labelled as being part of a broader *dajjālist* conspiracy and the apocalypse thus constitutes a powerful vehicle through which the legitimacy of Saudi Arabia, as well as other Muslim countries, can be successfully challenged.[87]

Within Internet discussions, various attempts to identify the Dajjāl with a particular figure have been recorded.[88] For instance, ISIS followers have suggested Sheikh ᶜAbd al-ᶜAzīz ibn Bāz, the blind Grand Mufti in Saudi Arabia, as a likely candidate for this role.[89] Previously, theories circulated on-line that Ḥusnī Mubārak, the deposed president of Egypt, had actually been the Antichrist.[90] At a more official level, the leader of Ḥizbullāh, Ḥasan Naṣrallāh, appears as 'the agent of the Antichrist' (*al-ᶜamīl al-dajjāl*) in an article entitled 'The Crusade serving Iran and Russia', based on an audio-message provided by Abū Ayyūb al-Miṣrī.[91] These are just a few examples of many. However, such attempts at the 'satanization of enemies', symptomatic of 'cosmic wars', in itself, may not necessarily refer to the apocalypse.[92]

Strange rumours circulated on the Internet, mostly during September 2014, that a baby born with a rare birth defect known as cyclopism was the Dajjāl (who is actually described as being blind in his right eye – not a cyclops)[93] belong in this peculiar category. It is difficult to identify who was behind the spread of such photographs but analysts suggest that similar 'End-of-times memes' have helped ISIS in its recruitment strategy, being used as a means of persuading young Muslims that the Hour is nigh. While this specific episode can be viewed as a calculated propaganda campaign, it also demonstrates the increasing level of jihadist creativity.[94] The photographs of the alleged infant Dajjāl showed, in reality, a child born in 2008 in Bolivia, as well as another child from India, but the disseminators of the images claimed that the baby was born in Israel,[95] perhaps because it is predicted that the Dajjāl will lead an army of Jews in a war against the Muslims.[96] Such pictures have garnered hundreds of thousands of views.[97] Naturally, Shiites (generally seen by ISIS as apocalyptic allies of Jews) are not unfamiliar with such opinions.[98]

As Sabine Damir-Geilsdorf and Lisa Franke have accurately summarised, the dichotomous interpretations attributed to the Dajjāl, be it a person or a system, and usually identified as a contradiction of 'true Islam', have the following main functions:

> They simplify complex or incomprehensible facts by providing precise schemes with a clear identification of who is a friend and who is a foe. Through the construction of the 'other' being, equipped with demonic powers, they do not simply make distinct accusations, but also make the power of the hostile 'other' explicable. They upgrade their own 'we-group' and allow the strength of the 'other' to appear as actual weakness.[99]

Moving on, it should be noted that the second coming of Jesus and his victorious battle with the Dajjāl also constitute one of the most popular motifs of ISIS apocalyptists. What should be stressed here is the fact that for most Muslims the coming of the Mahdī and the return of Jesus are two separate events. Of course, there are disputes as regards the relationship between them, as well as the chronology of their activities.[100] Nevertheless, Jesus, in prevailing Muslim opinion, will have subordinate status when compared to the Mahdī and, at the same time, the Mahdī's tenure will coincide with the coming of Jesus. As is generally believed, the Mahdī, who according to Nuᶜaym 'will pass the rule over to Jesus son of Mary',[101] will rid the world of all undesirable innovations (*bidᶜa*) and re-establish the genuine Sunna.[102] There is no consensus as to the length of time either the Mahdī or Īsā will reign or how long after their deaths the Hour will arrive. Some predictions even indicate a series of descendants of the Mahdī, who himself is said to rule for five, seven, or nine years.[103] The establishment of his rule will immediately follow his battle with the Antichrist, in which Jesus will support the forces of good.

As an eschatological saviour who invokes a break with the existing order, the figure of the Mahdī is perfectly suitable as a subject to be instrumentalised for political purposes – and bestsellers.[104] This is why the histories of Muslim countries refer back to many Mahdī pretenders, some of whom have been quite successful. Speculation by misguided Muslims regarding the identity of the Mahdī has been sharply criticised by ISIS propagandists,[105] as well as their conservative Muslim scholar opponents.[106] In any case, as Sheikh al-ᶜArīfī has argued, various opportunistic fabrications related to the figure of the Mahdī have nothing to do with the truth regarding this eschatological character.[107] However, we should emphasise that current Sunni Islamists almost never explicitly refer to the Mahdī. Nor are Muslim apocalyptists in general particularly interested in the detail associated with this happy outcome. Thus, the visions we are granted of the messianic world are curiously poorly defined and principally taken from the West itself.[108]

Within current Sunni discourse, the Mahdī is simply marginalised or even goes unmentioned. Moreover, in discussion forums on the Internet and online fatwa services, Sunnis regularly ask whether the Mahdī actually exists in Sunni Islam.[109] Some of the 'practical reasons' why ISIS chose to divert its focus from this apocalyptic hero have already been examined in Chapter 4 ('The Apocalyptic March'). Another motive behind such marginalisation probably relates to the fact that he is so closely associated with the hated Shia. Furthermore, Sunni End-time narratives often emphasise the fact that any belief in the Mahdī should not lead to a state of passive waiting.[110] The Mahdī is depicted as a 'normal human being', who will establish a just but mundane order. Thus, his role seems to be rather limited and underestimated.

Yet, the theme of the Mahdī (often in the form of criticism of his allegedly erroneous perception among heretics) occasionally also appears in the ISIS media, mostly as part of a broader explanation.[111] As the group's magazine *al-Nabaʾ* overtly states, 'the issue of the Mahdī verily belongs among the most important topics which are exploited by the people of straying from the right path for marketing of their own errors'.[112] The ISIS portrayal of the Mahdī contains rather generally formulated features, which relate to his actual origins, appearance and mission, with a particular emphasis on the fact that he will undoubtedly be recognised and followed by all true believers when the time comes.[113]

To summarise, if the Mahdī is actually mentioned, the narratives mostly revolve around the victory of Muslims as a group.[114] He thus embodies, above all, the final triumph of Islam, as clearly pronounced by Abū Bakr al-Baghdādī: 'Soon, by Allah's permission, a day will come when the Muslim will walk everywhere as a master, having honour, being revered, with his head raised high and his dignity preserved.'[115] Abū Ayyūb al-Miṣrī even stated explicitly that 'we are the army that will hand the flag to the Mahdī'.[116]

Thus, the Mahdī does not often act as the genuine objective of a narrative, but rather as a symbol of victory or a pretext for broader consideration. This is also true of ISIS propaganda. The crucial theme of the Muslim apocalypse is much more to do with fighting in all its conceivable forms: fighting against one's own vices and sins, fighting against the internal enemies of the *umma* and, finally, fighting against the Dajjāl and his partisans. And the readers of Muslim apocalyptic texts, including ISIS outputs, are attracted by vague descriptions of a messianic Empire and, simultaneously, frightened by never-ending threats. Their message can easily capture the attention of the masses since such narratives are fully comprehensible and, what is more important, they are able to offer hope and establish conviction in relation to the meaning of human suffering. In such a situation, the character of the Mahdī remains an extremely powerful symbol – nothing more and nothing less.

How to Sell the Apocalypse?

The apocalyptic self-presentation of ISIS would not be as visible and impressive without the group's perfectly stage-managed propaganda effort, one that utilises a plethora of methods to disseminate its various messages. ISIS has published several on-line periodicals, intended for both Arab readers (*al-Nabaʾ*) and a non-Arabic audience (*Dabiq*, *Islamic State News* in English, *Dar al-islam* in French, *Istok* in Russian, *Konstantiniyye* in Turkish, etc.), all of which are also distributed in a number of electronic-format propaganda brochures. An analysis of ISIS official output[117] reveals that they clearly reflect the group's ups and downs. Over a short space of time, general dreaming about world triumph was gradually replaced by specific instructions on how to use a knife or a car as an effective tool in individual attacks.[118]

The deeply rooted ideological indoctrination that is a fundamental objective of ISIS propaganda cannot only be found in their magazines, videos and the so-called guidance literature, but even on the pages of textbooks.[119] Nonetheless, neither a review of the ISIS media network, nor an analysis of its propaganda activities lie within the scope of this monograph.[120] For the moment, we must restrict ourselves to the brief remark that besides on-line periodicals and its own news agency,[121] the group owns at least one publishing house, with multiple divisions, which produces literature that reinforces 'the notion that ideas do matter on some level for its legitimacy, if not its survival'.[122] As regards its digital agenda, al-Furqān ('criterion') is a media wing of ISIS, responsible primarily for spreading its message in cyberspace.[123]

The apocalypse undoubtedly reinforces the group's appeal. In this regard, utopianism plays a crucial role because ISIS has grown accustomed to presenting itself as having achieved its Utopian objectives. In his attempt to provide a taxonomy of ISIS propaganda, Charlie Winter has summarised its key features in the following way:

> By declaring the re-establishment of the 'caliphate' when it did, Islamic State seized the extremist Islamist initiative. It asserted itself above all other jihadist groups as *the* utopia that they all aspired to create. As such, its propagandists need to keep the idea afloat and, seeking to amplify it, further capitalize upon the strand of Islamic eschatology that is central to so much of the organisation's official rhetoric. Routinely, the nearing apocalypse is emphasised to increase the sense of urgency . . . The message is simple: join now or face an eternity in Hell. Eschatological allusions are not a novel introduction to jihadist propaganda. However, the amount that Islamic State media emphasises this idea *is* new.[124]

The importance of the Internet as a mighty tool by which to effectively spread their message was identified by jihadists from the very beginning. Following initial mistrust, largely stemming from general Salafi wariness of innovation and novelty, a fruitful connection has been made between medieval sources and modern technology.[125] In this regard, we can truly speak about the phenomenon of 'e-mail ethnicity', in the sense of a transnational network of 'people tied culturally despite the diversity of their places of residence and the limitations of national borders'.[126]

The new media outlets have provided enormous opportunities that allow discussions to be more open, liberal and democratic, while at the same time it has become easier to express and find alternative interpretations and voices that question the established order.[127] ISIS propaganda presents a demonstrative example of the latter approach, taken to the extreme. Abdel Bari Atwan writes,

> the Internet has given Islamic State opportunities that its predecessors neither fully exploited nor understood. By clever use of social media and digital film making, it has eclipsed the counterweight mainstream media to broadcast its bloody deeds, its triumphs and its caliphate. By using every tool the Internet puts at their disposal, the tech-savvy cyber jihadists have been able to attract frustrated, marginalised and vulnerable young people to its ranks and to convince them of its world vision, predicated on reviving the golden age

of Islamic conquest, resisting American hegemony and pitting the 'believers' against the 'infidels' and 'crusaders'.[128]

The powerful resource that is the Internet, particularly in relation to its value as a medium for broadcasting the millennial message, has also been revealed by numerous Muslim activists, including apocalyptists,[129] and currently most 'apocalyptic clashes' among competing interpretations of Islam actually appear in cyberspace (see 'Sunni "Apocalypses Light"' in Chapter 6).

In the case of ISIS apocalypticism, professional marketing and the advanced command of new technologies is on display, interlaced with a superficial knowledge of shariah (this point is typical of most takfirists).[130] Nevertheless, this has the capacity to reach out to many sympathisers for whom earlier jihadist attempts were not tempting or intelligible enough. Such an 'apocalypse in a gift package' can thus become attractive, not only for its very message but also thanks to its 'cool' format.

The urgency of ISIS communication has frequently been enhanced by its dramatic presentation approach, passionate delivery, the use of expressive pictorial attachments to accompany texts, the creation of a sense of exceptionality and, in the case of videos, by the use of an emotive soundtrack.

Jihadist music supported by *nashīd* motifs (see 'Symbolism and Imagery of the Apocalypse' in Chapter 3) has proven itself to be an effective strategy for exciting and indoctrinating people, since – in the apt words of Phillip Smyth – 'it is like Wagner being set to *Apocalypse Now*'.[131] The overall result of such factors is a millennialist atmosphere where it is possible to shape a mind-set and where the desire for martyrdom is normalised and death is sought and celebrated. This is the jihadists' most potent weapon since a soldier who does not fear death is, in fact, an invincible enemy.[132] It is unnecessary to state that death seems to be even more desirable if presented as part of a great transpersonal apocalyptic story that inevitably leads to a happy ending.

At an unofficial level, a peculiar manifestation of the millennialist ethos among ISIS-inspired social media users, which confirms the above-mentioned observation, is the act of tracking the number of countries that have officially joined the coalition against the group. This is because of the content of the following apocalyptic *ḥadīth*: 'They [the Romans] will then gather for the Malhamah . . . They will come for you under eighty banners, with each banner there will be twelve thousand people.'[133] Based on this prophecy, the group's followers erupted with joy online every time the number of ISIS opponents edged towards the prophesised 'eighty banners'.[134]

Without digital technology, it is unlikely that ISIS would have ever come into existence, let alone been able to survive and expand.[135] The main benefits of the Internet for jihadists have been succinctly summarised by Thomas Heghammer:

> It is a faster, cheaper, longer-range, and more scalable communication technology than most analogue alternatives. It can dramatically reduce the transaction costs of key rebel tasks such as propaganda distribution, recruitment, fundraising, reconnaissance, and operational coordination. In practice, however, terrorist groups have never been able to tap the Internet's full potential, because of government countermeasures such as denial, surveillance, infiltration and counter-messaging. In the face of online repression, rebels face several problems, including an access problem (making sure they are not blocked from online services), a security problem (making sure police is not listening in on communications), a trust problem (making sure their interlocutors are not infiltrators), and a saturation problem (making sure their propaganda is not drowned out by competing messages).[136]

From a global perspective, the current online Arabic-language 'jihadosphere' far outpaces similar activities in other languages. When top-tier jihadi forums are shut down, usage on lower-tier forums is able to fill some of the vacuum.[137] ISIS has actually written a new chapter of jihad on the Internet and, thus, has proven its unsuspected potential. Unlike the experience of its militant precursors, the cyber jihad promoted by ISIS is no longer limited to Arabs and – the factor that expands its actual range – is no longer bound by clumsy ways of presentation, characteristic of the pioneers of this discipline. The one feature that until recently would have seemed unimaginable – a complicated and proficient combination of utmost religious fanaticism and visual energy that produces a 'cool look' – now represents a common starting point for all ISIS self-presentations.

The cyber jihad waged by ISIS has, essentially, two interconnected faces: official, shaped by the group's propaganda, and unofficial, created by its followers. Most ISIS business is, in fact, conducted online, from self-promotion to battlefield instructions. Social networks play a crucial role for them. What the jihadists lack in terms of sophisticated weaponry, they more than make up for in their online expertise.[138] As Christina Schori Liang has summarised it,

> Islamic State has a sophisticated and effective communication strategy that uses online media tools to disseminate its multidimensional propaganda. It has populated social media platforms and has attracted a global network of supporters that articulate, magnify and circulate its violent extremist messages worldwide. IS is strategically recruiting young men and women worldwide, using Internet sites, online magazines but mostly social media tools, including Facebook, YouTube, Twitter, Instagram, and AskFM.[139]

ISIS also makes use of Twitter to spread its propaganda, although this strategy often works against the group's actual intentions. Various attempts to mock the favourite motifs of ISIS propaganda experts can be found all over the Muslim world. Since the original ISIS account was suspended in 2014, there has been a constant attempt to deter recruitment by blocking related accounts, and this is why investigating the official ISIS Twitter accounts since 2015 has become nearly impossible. This fact has led ISIS followers to establish a 'virtual diaspora', where official ISIS representation no longer exists. Therefore, many accounts have begun to claim that they are official ISIS spokespersons, a situation that has left scholars with limited capacity to decipher between those legitimately associated with the group and those that are fake.[140]

In the realm of virtual battlefields, ISIS has again proven itself more than capable of complex coding, even creating its own applications such as a Twitter app accorded the apocalyptically sounding title *The Dawn of Glad Tidings* (*Fajr al-bashāʾir*).[141] The jihadists have also practiced 'live tweeting' during fighting, reporting injuries and deaths 'in raw uncensored prose'.[142] In support of its cyber jihad, ISIS has even made a post aimed at 'recruiting IT specialists'. Furthermore, the group's social media activists are well versed in the most effective 'brand sharing' strategies.[143] Their Twitter presentations are written in perfect English and some messages are bilingual in order to reach a wider audience. ISIS distinguishes itself from other Islamist groups on Twitter through the use of hashtags that identify them as an ISIS production and allow them to hijack trending topics. For instance, during the football world cup in 2014, hashtags such as *#Brazil_2014* were attached to ISIS propaganda as part of a strategy aimed at attracting new supporters.[144]

In January 2015, ISIS dominated the world headlines because of the activities of a group of hackers calling themselves the 'Cyber Caliphate'.[145] Young ISIS cyber-warriors have certainly been working hard to devise ways of compromising the military superiority their opponents enjoy. In fact, experts are still arguing about the actual degree of danger posed by ISIS hackers. On the one hand, it is argued that despite the significant attention devoted to them, their real skill level is still quite low.[146] On the other hand, it is claimed that 'ISIS activists are able to be brazen online because they understand security issues and keep one step ahead of government agencies and service providers seeking to close them down'.[147] In this respect, Abdel Bari Atwan notes:

> The battle in cyber-space is not going the way of governments . . . It is one that ISIS . . . can continue to dominate, so long as the world's most tech-savvy youth – who hold the key to the codes required for effective cyber warfare – do not want to fight in the same trench as the authorities.[148]

Facebook profiles have also been used by ISIS fighters to recruit their friends. While Twitter, YouTube and Facebook have sought to suspend accounts held by ISIS followers, the group has continued to fight back, calling on jihadists worldwide to kill Twitter employees, proclaiming: 'Your virtual war on us will cause a real war on you.'[149]

While ISIS, at least in military terms, has been almost completely defeated, its on-line activities continue, including the publication of *al-Nabaʾ* magazine.[150] Although the threat of a 'virtual caliphate' still persists, it is still too early to assess its actual level. Within the group's otherwise professional propaganda effort, one weakness indisputably remains: the total lack of a sense of humour, a point that ISIS shares with other fundamentalists all over the world.

Notes

1. *Dabiq* 4:35.
2. Juergensmeyer, *Terror in the Mind of God*, p. 242.
3. Damir-Geilsdorf and Franke, 'Narrative Reconfigurations', p. 412.
4. Fromson and Simon, 'ISIS', p. 37.
5. For the need to adopt a cautious approach when studying apocalyptic texts and their abuse, see, for example, *al-Nabaʾ* 107:8 and 108:8.
6. Amanat, *Apocalyptic Islam*, pp. 23–4.
7. Velji, *An Apocalyptic History*, p. 4.
8. Qurʾān 8:30. – The heading has been borrowed from Picthall's translation, adapted to today's writing.
9. Al-Bayūmī, *ᶜAlāmāt yawm al-qiyāma al-ṣughrā*, p. 71.
10. Al-ᶜArīfī, *Nihāyat al-ᶜālam*, pp. 28–31.
11. Cook, *Studies in Muslim Apocalyptic*, p. 231.
12. For this religious organisation, see Amanat, *Apocalyptic Islam*, pp. 67–8, 222–5.
13. Furnish, *Ten Years´ Captivation with the Mahdi's Camps*, p. 95.
14. Ibid. p. 47.
15. *Dabiq* 7:42.
16. The cited designations have been borrowed from al-Shaᶜrāwī's *Aḥdāth nihāyat al-ᶜālam*.
17. *Dabiq* 15:20–5.
18. *Dabiq* 15:21.
19. Cf. Nuᶜaym, *The Book of Tribulations*, pp. 21–6.
20. See, for example, al-ᶜArīfī, *Nihāyat al-ᶜālam*, p. 98.
21. Ostřanský, 'The Lesser Signs', p. 261.
22. Al-Muqaddam, *Fiqh ashrāṭ al-sāᶜa*, pp. 6–11.

23. See, especially, *al-Siyāsa al-sharʿīya* and also *al-ʿAqīda*.
24. Olidort, *Inside the Caliphate's Classroom*, p. xi.
25. Ibid. p. 15.
26. *Rumiyah* 4:17–18.
27. Cf. *al-Nabaʾ* 111:8 and *Dabiq* 14:8–17.
28. *Dabiq* 14:16–17.
29. *Dabiq* 8:50.
30. Olidort, *Inside the Caliphate's Classroom*, p. 14.
31. *Dabiq* 14:13.
32. *Rumiyah* 4:4.
33. Cook, *Studies in Muslim Apocalyptic*, p. 51.
34. See, for example, *Dabiq* 15:46–63.
35. Juergensmeyer, *Terror in the Mind of God*, p. 159.
36. See the article 'Kill Imams of Kufr in the West' in *Dabiq* 14:8–17. The Muslim authorities who should be killed include not only Sufis and liberals, but also (not exhaustive) radical Salafists such as Bilal Phillips and Pierre Vogel.
37. Another frequently quoted prediction speaks about 'people who have whips like the tails of oxen, with which they beat people'. The common reading of this mysterious *hadīth* is that leaders will engage in torture and human rights abuses as they seek to keep themselves in power. Kabbani, *The Approach of Armageddon?*, p. 121.
38. Olidort, *Inside the Caliphate's Classroom*, p. 29.
39. See Nuʿaym, *The Book of Tribulations*, pp. 419–25.
40. Ostřanský, 'The Lesser Signs', p. 261.
41. Muslim, *Ṣaḥīḥ*, p. 940 (no. 2922).
42. Gorenberg, *The End of Days*, p. vi.
43. *Dabiq* 1:10.
44. See, for example, al-Zawāwī, *al-Mufsidūn fī al-arḍ: Yahūd* and ʿAbd al-Ḥakīm, *Laʿbatu al-mutanawwirīn*, pp. 66–70.
45. *Rumiyah* 8:20–1. For this specific prophecy, see also al-ʿArīfī, *Nihāyat al-ʿālam*, pp. 112–13.
46. Al-Zawāwī, *al-Mufsidūn fī al-arḍ*, p. 25. Cf. Bayūmī, *ʿAlāmāt yawm al-qiyāma al-ṣughrā*, p. 47.
47. Literally 'awakening'; for ISIS, this term refers to its enemies from the more moderate Islamist movements. See Qindīl and ʿAbd al-Rabbihi, *al-Fikr al-islāmī al-jihādī al-muʿāṣir*, pp. 360–1.

48. *Rumiyah* 3:24.
49. Ostřanský, 'The Lesser Signs', p. 273.
50. The last point can also be interpreted as meteorites. See al-ᶜArīfī, *Nihāyat al-ᶜālam*, pp. 131–2.
51. These examples have been borrowed from al-Shaᶜrāwī's *Aḥdāth nihāyat al-ᶜālam*.
52. See Ayyūb, *al-Masīḥ al-Dajjāl*, p. 228.
53. *Dabiq* 12:65. Cf. Muslim, *Ṣaḥīḥ*, p. 932 (no. 2894, 2895).
54. Filiu, *Apocalypse in Islam*, p. 39.
55. Al-Shaᶜrāwī, *Aḥdāth nihāyat al-ᶜālam*, p. 209.
56. Al-Bayūmī, *ᶜAlāmāt yawm al-qiyāma al-ṣughrā*, p. 63.
57. Al-ᶜArīfī, *Nihāyat al-ᶜālam*, pp. 138–9.
58. See Cook, *Contemporary Muslim Apocalyptic Literature*, p. 54.
59. *Dabiq* 12:65.
60. Musselwhite, *ISIS & Eschatology*, pp. 157–8.
61. Available at https://www.nmisr.com/arab-news/%D8%A8%D8%A7%D9%84%D8%B5%D9%88%D8%B1-%D8%AF%D8%A7%D8%B9%D8%B4-%D8%AA%D8%B2%D8%B9%D9%85-%D8%A7%D9%86%D8%AD%D8%B3%D8%A7%D8%B1-%D9%86%D9%87%D8%B1-%D8%A7%D9%84%D9%81%D8%B1%D8%A7%D8%AA-%D9%88%D8%A8%D8%AF (last accessed 27 May 2017).
62. See https://saaid.net/Doat/Althahabi/11.htm (last accessed 28 November 2017).
63. Available at https://ar.wikipedia.org (last accessed 28 November 2017) and, for example, https://www.youtube.com/watch?v=SzCgvTRrWGg (last accessed 28 November 2017).
64. Available at https://www.youtube.com/watch?v=iXZbuHALkvM (last accessed 27 August 2017).
65. See https://نهاية-العالم.com/%D9%8A%D8%AD%D8%B3%D8%B1-%D8%A7%D9%84%D9%81%D8%B1%D8%A7%D8%AA-%D8%B9%D9%86-%D8%AC%D8%A8%D9%84-%D9%85%D9%86-%D8%B0%D9%87%D8%A8/ (last accessed 28 October 2017).
66. Available at http://www.dotmsr.com/details/%D8%A8%D8%B9%D8%AF-%D8%B0%D9%87%D8%A8-%D8%A7%D9%84%D9%81%D8%B1%D8%A7%D8%AA-%D9%87%D9%84-%D9%8A%D9%85%D9%87%D8%AF-%D8%AF%D8%A7%D8%B9%D8%B4-%D9%84%D8%B8%D9%87%D9%88%D8%B1-%D8%A7%D9%

84%D9%85%D9%87%D8%AF%D9%8A (last accessed 28 October 2017).

67. Juergensmeyer, *Terror in the Mind of God*, p. 155.
68. Smith and Haddad, *The Islamic Understanding of Death and Resurrection*, p. 67.
69. Nu^c^aym, *The Book of Tribulations*, p. 28 (no. 137).
70. *Dabiq* 7:23–4.
71. *Dabiq* 4:14.
72. *Rumiyah* 2:27.
73. *Dabiq* 7:66.
74. ^c^Abd al-Fattāḥ, *Usṭūrat Harmajidūn*, p. 14.
75. For his biography, see Qindīl and ^c^Abd al-Rabbihi, *al-Fikr al-islāmī al-jihādī al-mu^c^āṣir*, pp. 395–7.
76. *Dabiq* 4:5.
77. *Dabiq* 13:21.
78. Cook, *Studies in Muslim Apocalyptic*, p. 254.
79. Cf. Pregill, 'ISIS, Eschatology, and Exegesis'.
80. Atwan, *Islamic State*, p. 219.
81. *Dabiq* 11:16–17.
82. *Dabiq* 14:68.
83. For an example of his modernised depiction, see Ayyūb, *al-Masīḥ al-Dajjāl*.
84. For the use of development aid as an example of Dajjāl's plot, see ^c^Abd al-Ḥakīm, *La^c^batu al-mutanawwirīn*, pp. 301–2.
85. For jihadi web forums and social media sites, see, for example, Fishman, *The Master Plan*, pp. 156–8.
86. Damir-Geilsdorf and Franke, 'Narrative Reconfigurations', p. 418.
87. For various attacks on the Saudi ruling family (interchangeably called 'Āl Salūl' instead of 'Āl Su^c^ūd' or even compared to *ṭāgūt*) and local authorities, see *Dabiq* 5:27; 6:40; 9:18; 13:7–8 and elsewhere.
88. For the essential denial of such 'apocalyptic identifications', see al-Muqaddam, *Fiqh ashrāṭ al-sā^c^a*, pp. 81–5.
89. McCants, *The ISIS Apocalypse*, p. 106.
90. See http://english.ahram.org.eg/NewsContentPrint/1/0/22476/Egypt/0/Mubaraks-fall-spawns-End-of-Times-prophecies.aspx (last accessed 20 November 2017).
91. *Dabiq* 4:38–40.

92. See Juergensmeyer, *Terror in the Mind of God*, pp. 182–4.
93. See Ayyūb, *al-Masīḥ al-Dajjāl*, p. 245. Cf. Nuᶜaym, *The Book of Tribulations*, pp. 329–45.
94. See Laycock, 'Cyclops Baby of the Apocalypse?'
95. For an illustrative video, entitled 'A baby born in Israel which looks exactly like the Dajjal', see at https://www.youtube.com/watch?v=qttVCu0wn34 (last accessed 20 December 2017).
96. See Nuᶜaym, *The Book of Tribulations*, pp. 329–45.
97. See http://www.ibtimes.co.uk/isis-use-picture-cyclops-baby-recruit-fighters-apocalyptic-battle-1465323 (last accessed 20 December 2017).
98. An example, in Persian, is available at http://www.farsnews.com/newstext.php?nn=13930631000544 (last accessed 22 November 2017).
99. Damir-Geilsdorf and Franke, 'Narrative Reconfigurations', p. 419.
100. See, for example, Ayyūb, *al-Masīḥ al-Dajjāl*, pp. 241–3.
101. Nuᶜaym, *The Book of Tribulations*, p. 221.
102. For a summary of the related traditions, see, for example, ᶜAlī, *al-Burhān fī ᶜalāmāt al-Mahdī wa ākhir al-zamān*.
103. Smith and Haddad, *The Islamic Understanding of Death and Resurrection*, p. 70.
104. For the opportunistic use of this topic within Muslim discourse, see al-Muqaddam, *Fiqh ashrāṭ al-sāᶜa*, pp. 57–9.
105. *Al-Nabaᵓ* 117:8.
106. See al-ᶜArīfī, *Nihāyat al-ᶜālam*, pp. 198–203.
107. Ibid. p. 202.
108. Cook, *Contemporary Muslim Apocalyptic Literature*, pp. 145–6.
109. For a response by ISIS to those Muslims who deny the existence of the Mahdī in Sunnism, see *al-Nabaᵓ* 114:8.
110. See, for example, al-ᶜArīfī, *Nihāyat al-ᶜālam*, pp. 208–9.
111. See, especially, *al-Nabaᵓ* 120:8–9; 117:8; 114:8.
112. *Al-Nabaᵓ* 120:8.
113. *Al-Nabaᵓ* 117:8.
114. Damir-Geilsdorf and Franke, 'Narrative Reconfigurations,' p. 421.
115. *Dabiq* 1:8.
116. *Majmūᶜ tafrīghāt*, p. 134.
117. See Vergani and Bliuc, 'The evolution of the ISIS' language', pp. 7–20.
118. See, for example, *Rumiyah* 2:12–13.

119. Olidort, *Inside the Caliphate's Classroom*, pp. 8–24.
120. For a deeper insight into this subject, see Atwan, *Islamic State*; Berger, 'How ISIS Games Twitter'; Berger and Morgan, *The ISIS Twitter Census*; Günther, 'Presenting the Glossy Look of Warfare in Cyberspace'; Kovács, 'The "New Jihadists" and the Visual Turn from al-Qa^{c}ida to ISIL/ISIS/Da$^{\circ}$ish'; Maggioni and Magri, *Twitter and Jihad*; Winter, *The Virtual 'Caliphate'*.
121. For a synoptic diagram depicting ISIS propagandistic apparatus, see Winter, *The Virtual 'Caliphate'*, p. 14.
122. Olidort, *Inside the Caliphate's Classroom*, p. x.
123. Schori Liang, *Cyber Jihad*, p. 5. Cf. Fārūq, *Dā^{c}ish*, pp. 122–4.
124. Winter, *The Virtual 'Caliphate'*, pp. 28–30.
125. For an inspiring introduction to the contemporary Islamic debates about the Internet and new media, see Larsson, *Muslims and the New Media*, pp. 193–200.
126. Juergensmeyer, *Terror in the Mind of God*, p. 194.
127. Ibid. p. 198.
128. Atwan, *Islamic State*, p. 212.
129. Filiu, *Apocalypse in Islam*, pp. 180–3.
130. Ibrāhīm and al-Najjār, *Dā^{c}ish*, p. 95.
131. See http://www.motherjones.com/politics/2015/02/isis-islamic-state-baghdadi-music-jihad-nasheeds/ (last accessed 25 October 2017).
132. Atwan, *Islamic State*, p. 14.
133. *Dabiq* 4:56.
134. Petit, 'Eschatology in the ISIS Narrative', p. 16.
135. Atwan, *Islamic State*, p. 1.
136. See Hegghammer, 'The Future of Jihadism in Europe'.
137. Zelin, *The State of Global Jihad Online*, p. 15.
138. Atwan, *Islamic State*, pp. 15–16.
139. Schori Liang, *Cyber Jihad*, p. 1.
140. Musselwhite, *ISIS & Eschatology*, p. 140.
141. Berger, 'How ISIS Games Twitter'.
142. Schori Liang, *Cyber Jihad*, p. 5.
143. Atwan, *Islamic State*, p. 12.
144. Schori Liang, *Cyber Jihad*, p. 5.
145. Atwan, *Islamic State*, p. 21.
146. Alkhouri *et al.*, *Hacking for ISIS*, p. 25.

147. Atwan, *Islamic State*, p. 18.
148. Ibid. p. 25.
149. Schori Liang, *Cyber Jihad*, p. 8.
150. See *al-Naba*ʾ 127:1–12.

6

A Feeble Folk to Whom No Concern is Accorded

> As the Hour approaches, it becomes important to reflect upon the fabricated accounts of future events, as they will undoubtedly play a role in actions taken up by various deviant sects. Of these accounts is that of the 'Mahdī' of the Rāfidah who wages war against Islam and the Muslims, contrary to the just and rightly guided Mahdī of the future described in the Sunnah. The closer the Hour approaches, the more the Rāfidah fall in line with the Jews in preparation for the appearance of this awaited evil leader.
>
> – *Dabiq*[1]

> Verily, the examination of the portents of the Hour which actually belong among the transcendental divine secret has already become a permitted playground where every Tom, Dick and Harry can freely discuss the issue.
>
> – Muḥammad ibn Ismāᶜīl al-Muqaddam[2]

Perhaps unsurprisingly, ISIS's aggressive apocalypticism has already triggered countless responses all over the Muslim world.[3] Based on a broader consideration related to the very phenomenon of the 'apocalyptic response' (or, with some degree of exaggeration, the 'counter-apocalypse'), this chapter focuses primarily on Sunni reactions to ISIS End-time propaganda. As we have seen, the diverse approaches of Muslims to the apocalypse cannot easily be generalised into a single pattern and this is equally true of Muslim reactions to the ISIS apocalyptic ethos. However, while there is definitely no single Islamic response, at the same time, the existence of more general shifts of attitude in relation to the millennial agenda, traceable within current Islamic discourse, cannot simply be denied.

The Apocalypse as a Battlefield

The main point to be made from the beginning is that the very act of questioning the ISIS apocalyptic message does not automatically mean that apocalypticism is being challenged as a way of thinking. In fact, most opponents of ISIS have no intention of contesting the relevance of the suggestion that the Hour is approaching, but only the way in which it is allegedly being abused by the group's media. This fundamental point must be constantly emphasised.

For instance, the Egyptian authors Nājiḥ Ibrāhīm and Hishām al-Najjār argue that the traditions about the Last Days in Islam generally pertain to those issues that have been revealed in order to be believed (*taṣdīq*) by Muslims and definitely not in order to be fulfilled (*tanfīdh*). Therefore, any arbitrary reading of the signs of the Hour as a manual about 'what should be done' must be decisively rejected as dangerous and opportunistic, not only in the case of ISIS. Above all, it should be rejected as being non-Islamic. The return of the caliphate, which has been so skilfully predicted and utilised by ISIS propaganda, serves as a demonstrative example.[4]

Before continuing, we should briefly introduce here the phenomenon of *fiqh ashrāt al-sāʿa* (the Islamic jurisprudence that is focused on the portents of the Hour) as a broader Muslim scholarly response to the modern boom in the sales of apocalyptic bestsellers, bringing with it a plethora of nonsense and misinterpretations. The relentless condemnation of 'End-time creativity' provided by this specific 'genre' focuses mostly on the following points: all eschatological considerations should be based strictly on Islamic sources and in accordance with Islamic principles; to use the apocalypse as an opportunistic weapon in an ideological struggle is reprehensible; the same applies also to the unsubstantiated identification of particular characters with representatives of evil in apocalyptic narratives, and so on.[5]

When discussing various reactions to ISIS End-time presentations, it is first necessary to summarise certain broader overlaps that are evident in the Muslim apocalypse itself. One such overlap occurs when Muslim apocalyptic authors strive to include other religions in their own visions of the End-time, the other when their own 'scenarios' relating to apocalyptic events become part of other, non-Islamic narratives. In the former case, Muslim apocalyptic authors incorporate all humanity into their End-time speculations, not only Muslims, although non-Muslims are mostly relegated to the role of enemies who appear during the final battles and, following their defeat, are subsequently converted to Islam. However, there is a second approach, to which Abbas Amanat refers:

> The resemblance between Islamic (more Shiite) messianic prophecies and the Jewish and Christian traditions seemingly posed a theological challenge to the Shiite apocalyptists; a problem that is tackled in this messianic output by empowering the Mahdī beyond the Islamic space and as the saviour whose Advent is anticipated in all religions.[6]

With regard to the latter case, Islamic visions of the End-time have become part of the wider eschatological fictions of some non-Muslim authors, among them the Christian fundamentalist opponents of Islam, for whom eschatology is an appropriate arena where the real nature of this supposed 'religion of evil' can be truly 'unveiled'.[7] A demonstrative example of such a view can be found in Joel Richardson's book, eloquently entitled *The Islamic Antichrist: The Shocking Truth about the Real Nature of the Beast*, which presents Islam as the fulfilment of Biblical prophecy and advocates the thesis that Islam's saviour, the Mahdī, and the Antichrist, as described in the Bible, 'are actually one and the same'.[8]

Moreover, as can easily be observed on the Internet in particular, the apocalyptic and Islamophobic agendas that are currently rife and which meet each other within the works of numerous Western authors, for instance Walid Shoebat, a US-based Islamophobic activist,[9] can be interpreted as a specific trend that promotes the instrumentalisation of the apocalypse within current anti-Islamic discourse. In this noteworthy context, we should not forget that the prejudicial policies directed at Muslims in many Western countries are actually counterproductive. Capitalising on a strategy first articulated by Anwar al-ᶜAwlaqī, ISIS ultimately aims to use terrorism to provoke Western policymakers into discriminating against Muslim citizens and refugees in their entirety, hoping that such an approach 'will act as a political centrifuge that will separate a violent fringe from the bulk of Muslims'.[10]

Nevertheless, such a challenging subject is far beyond the scope of this study. The apocalypse as a continuation of the worldly struggle by 'other means' is a phenomenon that can also actually be found in sources other than the 'Jihadists versus anti-Jihadists' narrative patterns. The true nature of this issue has been accurately expressed by Richard Landes:

> The normal dynamic of apocalyptic thinking is a zero-sum game, i.e., 'I win, you lose'. One person's messiah is another's Anti-Christ. In normal time, this translates into theocratic imperialism – my religion is right because it has replaced yours, and the proof lies in my religion's political dominion.[11]

As we already know, the 'final days' perspective offers a meaningful approach not only for those who, against a backdrop that emphasises the end of days, are planning to take the fight to their earthly opponents, but in particular for those who fail in such a conflict. In any case, the idea of using millennial ammunition against its own promoters is a very understandable method that Muslims can effectively use to challenge ISIS's supporters, especially in cyberspace.[12]

Unlike the struggles of this world, success or defeat within the apocalyptic realm is never the result of the real exercise of power and strategy, but – primarily, although not exclusively – of the strength of the media appeal in relation to specific ideas and their interpretation. Moreover, various apocalyptic expectations – or, at least, loud declarations – appearing as creative renditions of earthly wishes, can be found not only among Muslim responses to the atrocities committed by ISIS, but also within the more universal framework of modern Muslim apocalyptic creativity.

Essentially, any attempt to depict one's own enemy as being on the side of metaphysical evil in an apocalyptic battlefield is nothing new, as can be demonstrated by reference to the pages of countless pamphlets written by contemporary Muslim apocalyptists, a few of whom are introduced in the following section. As Mark Juergensmeyer's research has proven, this fundamental point verifiably applies in more general terms, not only within our Islamic framework.

The apocalyptic expectations, either allegedly fulfilled or declared to be on the verge of being realised, can ultimately serve as a mighty tool in the struggle to justify one's own ambitions and the soundness of one's own conduct. This applies not only to Muslim radicals but also supports a belief in one's own sense of belonging to the powers of good in the expected battles of the final days. In a surprisingly easy way, this can transform any 'scholarly' apocalyptical scenario into a potential spiritual weapon. An expected role in any End-time drama can be further supported and reinforced by the identification of current enemies with predicted eschatological adversaries.

Speaking about the persuasiveness of apocalyptic rhetoric, we should remind ourselves here that its most effective manifestations usually contain three core components: its diagnostic, prognostic and motivational features. This point fully applies to both the ISIS millennial message and also to the group's opponents. Essentially, the diagnostic framework defines the problem and identifies those who should be held responsible for it. In our context, this is illustrated by the identification of apocalyptic portents with various aspects of the current unflattering state of Muslim societies. In addition, the prognostic framework can offer guidance, in apocalyptic terms, as to whom the reader might trust and whether or not to follow their recommendations. Finally, the motivational framework provides incentives that inspire action; in our case either to support or reject ISIS. Thus, the whole framing as a process serves to convince target audiences by using well-rehearsed arguments that appeal to scripture, authoritative interpretation and the prioritisation of action in order to elicit support and participation.[13]

Convincing audiences regarding their own role in the 'final days' agenda is definitely not an exclusively ISIS endeavour. The following interpretation will provide the reader with a completely different perspective, depicting how the activities of ISIS can easily be placed into an apocalyptic framework by their opponents. Nevertheless, the genuine strategies deployed in order to attract Muslim audiences, either opponents or supporters of ISIS, in both cases remain the same. In the fitting words of Sabine Damir-Geilsdorf and Lisa Franke:

> Through the explicit identification of 'good' and 'evil,' as well as dualistic friend and foe concepts, these narratives provide a simple orientation scheme that supports the call to action. They call for a moral-ethically defined individual reorientation on the part of Muslims, reminding them of their transnational unity or asking them directly to take up arms against the perceived enemy. Political conflicts are being declared sacral in such narratives and thus the use of force is legitimized in the binary-termed holy action.[14]

It is thus no wonder that such an opposing perception can mainly be found within the apocalyptic narratives of those Muslim factions that feel mortally threatened by ISIS, among whom Shiites and Sufis, depicted as being supporters of corrupt and hypocritical regimes,[15] take pride of place. The apocalyptic ideas of such spiritual streams are considered by ISIS propaganda to be totally heretical.[16] (The decision has been made not to discuss here denominations that are regarded as being non-Muslim not only by ISIS but also by a significant part of the *umma* (Aḥmadīya, for instance).[17]) Simply stated, it is clear that apocalyptic ammunition can never be monopolised by one single group in an attempt to suppress ideas that deviate from their own visions. Eventually, good and evil, in apocalyptic terms, always and everywhere depends on the perspective of the narrator.

Essentially, to a certain degree, the apocalyptic imagination reveals the nature of the thinker and the millennial content can often reflect their worldly worries and concerns. An effort to support one's own arguments within the apocalyptic context often results in the use of such means that are usually considered inappropriate, for example, a recourse to weak *aḥādīth* (their defence, in apocalyptic narratives, also appears in ISIS propaganda)[18] or even to forgeries.[19] If a doubtful narration depicts a future event and the event plays out exactly as recorded, then this narration will naturally be strengthened. Whether or not this narration is sound according to Islamic standards is left for the scholars to discuss. Everything that supports the argumentation is welcome.

Any assessment of the impact – or rather the contamination – of ISIS creativity on non-ISIS apocalyptic literature is hampered by the fact that we are dealing with a very fresh, as well as a totally unprecedented, issue. Therefore, it almost seems to be too soon to attempt such an appraisal. Moreover, the number of publications by Muslim authors that really reflect the End-time message of ISIS is very limited. As far as the response of Muslim books to ISIS is concerned, their main focus is on the group's extremism and brutality, as well as its takfirism, the abuse of 'the caliphate', the destruction of monuments, and so on. Its 'apocalyptic face' has attracted much less active attention, which may be interpreted in various ways. For example, in the case of the Egyptian book market, it is possible that this reaction is the result of ISIS instrumentalising End-time motifs that are already rather ubiquitous and, as such, this brings nothing new to the local reader.[20]

A glimpse into the common perception of ISIS apocalyptic rhetoric among Muslims in cyberspace can be obtained by simply typing the Arabic keywords *dāᶜish* and *ᶜalāmāt al-sāᶜa* into a search engine. Below the list of relevant occurrences, Google also suggests other related searches, in our case the following examples: Are ISIS the holders/masters of the black flag? Does ISIS belong among the signs of the End times? Is ISIS al-Sufyani?

Sunni 'Apocalypses Light'

Reflecting on the 'apocalyptic responses' to ISIS, we might profitably start with the remark that the group's placement on the side of evil in the Last-days drama has been significantly facilitated by identifying its followers (and jihadists in general) as Kharijites (*khawārij*).[21] Perhaps the most authoritative denunciation of such trends in Islam has been conveyed by ᶜAlī Jumᶜa, the former Egyptian Grand Muftī, in his five-volume work *al-Radd ᶜalā khawārij al-ᶜaṣr* (*The Response to the Kharijites of Today*), which provides a monumental rejection of all forms of current extremism.[22]

Needless to say, it is precisely this designation that appears among the most fundamental signs of the Hour. The main reason for such an accusation is their violent rebellion against Muslim rulers as well as, in Wagemakers' apt words, in 'applying *takfīr* on the basis of "mere" major sins without verbal confirmation of sinful intention, thereby – in effect – excommunicating people on the basis of minor unbelief, just like the Khawarij did'.[23]

In general, takfirism has enormous apocalyptic potential, as well as representing worldly power. In this regard, al-Zarqāwī's legacy has helped ISIS to achieve great territorial gains but, at the same time, has prevented the group from achieving global domination. As Brian Fishman reminds us, any 'Zarqawism' that limits a group's broad appeal will help it remain resilient.[24] From the perspective of the opponents of ISIS it is precisely the irrevocable schismatic nature of ISIS that allows it to be easily located in End-time templates and to be viewed as a fulfilment of previously foretold *fitan*.[25]

One of the usual apocalyptic arguments used against ISIS – the previously discussed black banners (see 'Symbolism and Imagery of the Apocalypse' in Chapter 3) – can be found at the forefront of not only countless lectures on YouTube[26] and in statements made by laymen on other social media platforms, but also in the publications of renowned Islamic scholars. The spectrum of eschatological forces of evil with which ISIS can be identified is truly manifold, as reflected on the Internet. The black banners can thus adopt different roles when viewed from a perspective different from that which ISIS propagandists employ, that is, not as a justification of the group's claims but as proof of its links with malevolent eschatological powers.

The *aḥādīth* referring to the black flags coming from the East are mostly considered as being fabricated in order to support Abbasids' claims to power but, despite all the doubts raised as to their authenticity, they are quoted throughout Muslim Internet discussions, mainly those associated with the Mahdī or with the introduction of inter-Muslim warfare.

The Internet offers a wide range of other apocalyptic references. Some opponents consider ISIS either to be *jaysh al-khasf* (an army that should, according to tradition, disappear or be swallowed up by the ground in the desert of the Arabian Peninsula)[27] or even the Dajjāl's partisans.[28] In both cases, the group's supporters are incorporated as part of the apocalyptic powers of evil.[29] To the contrary, in *al-Nabaʾ* magazine,[30] ISIS propagandists refer to the *khasf* as an event that will afflict the enemies of the Mahdī, whose vanguard they consider themselves to be.

In the search for signs of the Hour that can be used in the apocalyptic offensive against ISIS, there is a long list of suitable items, among them, for instance, the appearance of the *khawārij*, the authority of fools, the arbitrary treatment of the Qurʾān and a great amount of killing. Despite the differences in wording, most of them basically refer to three fundamental trends: an increase in violence; the decline of genuine Islamic knowledge and the deepening of rifts.

The staggering increase in violence, the common denominator of many apocalyptic signs, fits perfectly with conditions pertaining to the Last Days, a time when everything will be taken to the extreme. For the opponents of ISIS, it is precisely the existence of this group that constitutes the embodiment of the predicted extremism. Apocalyptic authors often remind us of the related increase in cruelty. In this respect, Hisham Kabbani explains that 'leaders will be engaged in widespread torture and human rights abuses to keep themselves in power . . . People will be tyrants in order to hold onto their positions . . . They will find any way and use any method or system to maintain their hold on power.'[31] Classical sources contain many similar references, including references to beheadings, which have become a certain 'hallmark' of ISIS: 'The Messenger of God said . . .: "After me, do not return to being unbelievers, cutting each other's heads off."'[32]

The decline in genuine Islamic scholarship, the second symptomatic feature, is linked to one of the most popular subjects for Muslim apocalyptists. Apocalyptic attacks on ISIS are, in this regard, considerably facilitated by the fact that ignorance and the arbitrariness of the group's leaders in religious affairs have repeatedly been documented by many Muslim scholars. Numerous *aḥādīth* offer themselves as arguments levelled against ISIS, for example: 'The Hour will not arise until the most felicitous of the people is an idiot son of an idiot.'[33]

The third item, the extension of rifts and divisions, is a favourite and recurring theme in all Muslim apocalyptic scenarios, providing convincing arguments in the hands of ISIS critics. According to medieval traditions, the Last-days *fitan* should not only juxtapose Muslims and non-Muslims but, above all, rightly led Muslims and Muslims who have been led astray. In the view of both ISIS supporters and opponents, these final *fitan* will culminate in the emergence of this group. In a predominantly general and formulaic approach, Muḥammad Ḥisān dared to be specific when he identified the appearance of al-Baghdādī with *fitnat al-iḥlās wa al-duhaymāʾ*,[34] two specific forms of *fitna*.[35] In their critical approaches to ISIS, its Muslim opponents often suggest that even the Antichrist can quote God's Scripture to suit his own purposes.

Following the outline of the thematic composition of apocalyptic responses to ISIS, a brief overview of the main critical Sunni voices will be provided. Essentially, they can be divided into three loosely specified branches: (1) the responses of authoritative scholars and institutions; (2) traditionalists' responses; and (3) Sufi responses. In addition, a variety of millennial speculations by Harun Yahya will also be presented in order to illustrate the actual diversity of current End-time disputes in Islam.

Starting with the first category, al-Azhar University, the premier Sunni institution, has repeatedly criticised ISIS, highlighting a variety of specific non-Islamic manifestations that appear in the group's statements and activities.[36] However, al-Azhar has not been able to denounce ISIS as being un-Islamic, even though the group has committed such heinous atrocities. This is an issue that has been critically tackled by many other Muslim authorities.[37] Although the theological polemics relating to such a vigilant approach to *takfīr* are beyond the scope of this chapter, as far as the End-time agenda of ISIS is concerned, the situation is considerably easier.

The group's apocalyptic self-stylisation has been resolutely condemned by Aḥmad Maᶜbad ᶜAbd al-Karīm, a member of the scientific board of the university, who stated that the ISIS End-time narratives are based on lies since there is no reliable *ḥadīth* that identifies the time remaining to this world or indeed the date of the Day of Resurrection. This is why – specifically in the spirit of apocalypse – 'those misled astray have become leaders'.[38] His speech, in which ᶜAbd al-Karīm designates ISIS as 'one of the signs of the Hour' was delivered at a congress organised by al-Azhar for its foreign scholarship holders, and eloquently entitled '*Tafnīd awhām dāᶜish fī qaḍīyat nihāyat al-ᶜālam*' ('Refusal of the delusional imagination of ISIS relating to matters concerning the End of the world').[39]

The identification of ISIS with 'the Kharijites of today', as foretold in numerous apocalyptic prophecies, has also been supported by Aḥmad ᶜUmar Hāshim, the former president of al-Azhar, who has specifically referred to the group's striking religious ignorance, one of the popular signs of the Hour.[40] In his turn, Ḥāmid Abū Ṭālib, a member of the Academy of Islamic Studies in Egypt, explained that we are indeed living in the 'age of tribulations' (*ᶜaṣr al-fitan*) that divide the *umma* and reminded readers of the Prophet's warning regarding 'those misled covering truth with deception', pointing directly at Abū Bakr al-Baghdādī.[41] Such disunity ultimately helps, in his opinion, the enemies of Islam, a point which was eloquently expressed by another apocalyptic prophecy, one stating that 'nations will soon call upon each other, just as diners call each other to eat from a bowl' and Muslims are expected to lose out because of their supposed 'love of life and the hatred of death' – which is, by the way, exactly the same argument that has been used by ISIS against its opponents.[42]

Another example of the apocalyptic weapons used against ISIS has been provided by the authors of the 'Open Letter', addressed to Abū Bakr al-Baghdādī. This theological text has been reproduced on numerous websites and can be found in various languages. Following a long account of the supposedly non-Islamic activities of ISIS, this document also contains an exegesis of a *ḥadīth* recorded by Nuᶜaym ibn Ḥammād as an appendix, considered by the authors of the letter to be an insightful prediction of ISIS's emergence. This prophecy has already inspired and encouraged a number of the group's Muslim critics, among them, for example, Abdul Aziz Suraqah, an American convert and translator from Arabic, who is well-versed in medieval Islamic traditions.[43]

The following translation of the *ḥadīth* comes from the official English version of the letter:

> When you see the black flags, remain where you are and do not move your hands or your feet. Thereafter there shall appear a feeble insignificant folk. Their hearts will be like fragments of iron. They will have the state. They will fulfil neither covenant nor agreement. They will call to the truth, but they will not be people of the truth. Their names will be parental attributions, and their aliases will be derived from towns. Their hair will be free-flowing like that of women. This situation will remain until they differ among themselves. Thereafter, God will bring forth the Truth through whomever He wills.[44]

All interpretations of this prophecy reveal almost uncanny levels of conformity in a number of key areas and this is why this particular argument so often appears in Muslim on-line debates concerning ISIS. Suraqah, for example, explains, point by point, how the mentioned references self-evidently apply to ISIS.[45] It is not only the already discussed black flags that point in this direction, but also the forgotten and weaker members of society (whose plight inspired the title of this chapter), an image that refers to the newcomers to the Syrian conflict, who were nobodies until they became famous as a result of their violence and cruelty.

The third point, that hearts will be like fragments of iron, refers to the same extreme levels of brutality. 'The State' often had an unclear meaning in the Middle Ages, when the Arabic term *dawla* referred primarily to 'dynasty'. However, currently this item takes on a different connotation because the official name of ISIS is 'al-Dawla al-islāmīya' (the Islamic State). Nonetheless, such an updated reading should always be compared with a scholarly translation, where *dawla* does not necessarily mean 'state'. David Cook, for example, translates the corresponding passage as 'their hearts like iron anvils, they are the soldiers of the turn (*dawla*) . . .'[46]

The predicted breaking of agreements should also be read literally because ISIS refuses shariah arbitration, a fact that has been repeatedly contested by Sunni scholars.[47] The sentence 'They will call to the truth, but they will not be people of the truth' thus refers to the nature of 'the *khawārij* of today' as well as to the group's loudly proclaimed ownership of truth. 'The parental attributions', together with 'aliases derived from towns', indicate the forms of names preferred by ISIS leaders and fighters, which generally follow premodern patterns and begin with 'Abū' (father) and conclude with local, ethnic or religious adjectives (*nisba*). 'Towns', in this case, should be read as toponyms in general (al-Miṣrī, al-Zarqāwī, al-Baghdādī, for example). The last item, 'free-flowing hair like that of women', a favourite among ISIS fighters, can easily be verified by a quick glance at *Dabiq* for example.[48]

According to a Muslim discussant using the nickname Skako, the given prediction taken in its entirety proves its supernatural origin since there is no other explanation for so many completely fulfilled yet improbable details. According to his reading of the mentioned *ḥadīth*,

> the most amazing part of the prophecy is this here: The hadith says literally (in Arabic) that these people are the owners of *dawla* (state) – a word which wasn't even used in the time of Muhammad because there was no concept of 'state' in that time – the word *dawla* from the prophecy was basically used verbatim as said by Muhammad although hadith collectors for generations most probably had no idea whatsoever what it meant! But, how does ISIS call itself today? Al-Dawla al Islamiya (the Islamic State). This fact is simply amazing![49]

The idea that the emergence of ISIS on the apocalyptic side of evil was prophesied 1,400 years ago has been supported not only by anonymous discussants in cyberspace but also by the Muslim authorities. For example, the aforementioned ᶜAlī Jumᶜa, in his *khuṭba* on 19 September 2014, cited that the given *ḥadīth* provides clear evidence that the emergence of ISIS was foretold by the fourth caliph, ᶜAlī. In his sermon, Jumᶜa criticised the group's arbitrary approach to Islamic heritage, documenting their total bankruptcy in terms of religious knowledge, and concluding that 'they and those of their kind are the *khawārij* of today'.[50]

Within a spiritual framework that might be loosely designated as 'traditionalist Islam',[51] the voice of Hamza Yusuf, an influential author and American Muslim convert, is one of the most respected.[52] On several occasions, Yusuf has expressed his resistance to ISIS, including in his *khuṭba* entitled 'The Crisis of ISIS – A Prophetic Prediction',[53] in which he warns of the danger of ISIS and its followers. Via YouTube, this sermon has achieved more than half a million views[54] and its author has been labelled by ISIS as one of those 'imāms of the *kufr*' who deserve to be killed.[55] This is similar to the case of Suhaib Webb, another influential Western Muslim authority with a traditionalist profile.[56]

Yusuf refers to supporters of ISIS as 'Satans' or 'people of the Devil'.[57] In his speeches, this group is identified with the apocalyptic *khawārij*. Relying on the above-mentioned *ḥadīth*, Yusuf adduces that these people recite the Qurʾān, but they do not understand it because they have not received any genuine religious education, a fact that clearly refers to the expected End-time regress of knowledge, in general, and a specific apocalyptic prophecy, in particular. Both references are often employed as a decisive argument against ISIS claims.[58]

In order to locate current affairs within an apocalyptic framework, Yusuf also points to the bloody suppression of the civic protests that took place in the south Syrian city of Darᶜā in March 2011,[59] generally considered as being the unofficial beginning of the Syrian war that was to quickly become internationalised. Yusuf discusses a problematic saying of the Prophet that relates to a *fitna* that will be introduced by the black flags: '*Satakūnu fitna fī al-Shām, awwaluhā laᶜibu ṣibyān*',[60] which – in Cook's translation – means: 'There will be a tribulation in Syria, of which the first will be child's play.'[61]

The authenticity of this *ḥadīth* is highly disputed and, moreover, Yusuf translates it in a slightly different way: 'It begins with children playing in Darᶜa.' By doing so, he stresses the reference to the particular tragedy of the local teenagers who had been tortured and executed for having written '*al-Shaᶜb yurīdu isqāṭ al-niẓām*' ('The people want the regime to fall') as graffiti on walls.[62] To summarise, the ascent of ISIS – as seen by Hamza Yusuf – must be understood as a great *fitna* that will precede the Mahdī's appearance.

Within our brief survey, Sufi 'apocalypse light' constitutes the last but not least spiritual category. For Sufi authors, whose creed has been labelled by hateful ISIS propaganda as 'one of the most important diseases by which a lot of countries are currently afflicted',[63] the very idea of waging their ideological struggle in eschatological terms is by no means a new one. Sufis have naturally incorporated eschatological images into their symbolic ways of expression and, in their spiritual perception, the afterlife and the next world are already present here on Earth, primarily as an inner experience which is, in fact, very personal and should be experienced during one's earthly existence.[64]

The irreconcilable rivalry between Sufis and Salafists constitutes one of the most dramatic aspects of today's Islamic discourse. The tireless resistance of the Sufi cleric Hisham Kabbani in the face of Wahhabism, seen as a distorted form of Islam and – as such – projected onto his visions of the approaching End, is just one of many specific examples. He claims allegiance to Ḥaqqānīya, one of the many branches arising from the important Sufi *ṭarīqa* (order, brotherhood) of Naqshbandīya, whose inclination towards Mahdism might be, at least in part, simply a reaction to Salafism.[65] The Mahdī, along with other apocalyptic issues, is one of the most frequently covered subjects in its sheikhs' speeches. This brotherhood serves as an example of the successful connection between traditional messages and modern means of communication.[66]

The main point to be emphasised here is that, within the current Sunni framework, this order is quite exceptional because of the consistent accent it places on the End-time agenda.[67] Its apocalyptic messages can actually serve various functions. By means of such a discourse, the collective identity of *ṭarīqa* members can be strengthened, which is achieved by constructing borders between 'us', who are on the right path, and the misguided 'them', including the condemned *salafīya*. Finally, visions of the End may also serve as a kind of mental support for those followers who are trapped in poor living conditions or who are not happy about the prevailing state of society.[68] Naqshbandīya apocalypticism has also been promoted by two key representatives of this order, Sheikhs Hisham Kabbani and Muḥammad Nāzim.

Although they had authored their books (mentioned below) before ISIS appeared, both were explicitly mentioned within ISIS's hateful 'manifesto' entitled 'Kill Imams of Kufr in the West',[69] in which the deceased Sheikh Nāzim was depicted as 'an extreme Jahmī Murjiʾī' (an advocate of free will) but, as the spiritual master of Kabbani, primarily was considered to be an apostate deserving of death. This call for murderous action was widely spread in the media.[70]

Being known as an ardent opponent of Salafism (in his own words, the 'Wahhabi sect'),[71] Hisham Kabbani (born 1945) ranked this sort of Islamic purism and revivalism as being among those portents of the Hour that are currently being fulfilled as part of the general destruction of Islamic pluralism. According to his book *The Approach of Armageddon?*, today's Salafists are the genuine fulfilment of prophecies about the appearance of the *khawārij*, whose most distinguishing feature, as seen and highlighted by Kabbani, will actually be their takfirism. Of course, the comparison between Wahhabites and Kharijites has had a long tradition within Sunni discourse over the last two centuries and Sheikh Kabbani was definitely not the first to utilise it. His own original contribution, however, was to change the 'deployment' of attacks against Wahhabis into a remarkably updated apocalyptic template.

> The Khawarij of today are the followers of the Wahhabi/ 'Salafi' sect. They are actively promoting the falsehood of their cult with massive propaganda campaign whether by speakers in mosques, via the Internet, on television, or through the massive distribution

> of videos, newspapers, books, magazines, and pamphlets. All the while they are suppressing and concealing the truths of mainstream classical Islamic teaching, conspiring to silence anyone who speaks against their extremism.[72]

In terms of his teaching, those Muslims who firmly adhere to the Tradition will, during the final phase of history, paradoxically be condemned because of their allegedly non-Islamic innovations. The converse is also true – that the innovators and charlatans will be praised as the protectors of the faith. Such a period, according to Kabbani, has already arrived.[73] The Wahhabi presence can also be detected in other apocalyptic signs, for example behind the prophecy regarding the destruction of Medina (deliberately called by its original pre-Islamic name, Yathrib). In Kabbani's innovative interpretation, this devastation should be read as the hasty modernisation of this city, which has recently been undertaken by the Saudi authorities, without regard for its traditional values.[74] However, Islam, as Kabbani often highlights, was perfect at the time it was revealed and this is why there is no reason to work for its 'improvement'. The supposed purification of the original spirit of Islam, so loudly proclaimed by the Wahhabis, would actually entail the destruction of genuine Islamic scholarship, that is, a reductionist misinterpretation of the Prophet's legacy.

The devastating impact of the Wahhabis has, once again, been addressed in Kabbani's creative exegesis on the 'spiritual dismantlement of the Ka^{c}ba'. The corresponding tradition narrates that the soldiers of al-Ḥabashī, an apocalyptic warrior, will capture the Ka^{c}ba and remove it stone by stone in order to throw it into the sea. Kabbani suggests this reading:

> The Ka^{c}ba is the focal point from whence Islam originated. Unfortunately, the physical structure of the building is all that remains today from that time ... The Wahhabi sect has also dismantled the ideological foundations of Islam and destroyed the Ka^{c}ba's essence, which is the authentic understanding and teaching of Islam.[75]

The previously inconceivable war in Syria had already supposedly been foretold in 1985 by Muḥammad Nāzim ᶜĀdil al-Ḥaqqānī al-Naqshbandī (1922–2014), the spiritual teacher of Hisham Kabbani. In his collected lectures *Mystical Secrets of the Last Days*, Sheikh Nāzim discusses Armageddon, the Antichrist and, above all, the coming of the Mahdī and Jesus. By Armageddon, he understands a devastating global war between the East and West, in which the East will finally be defeated. The Antichrist is, in his opinion, already physically present on the earth, albeit imprisoned on an unknown island. The alleged purpose of Armageddon is 'to separate the chaff from the wheat, since those denying the existence of the Creator and cruel or envious people will pass away. Meanwhile, genuine believers and good-doers will survive.'[76]

What actually makes Nāzim's considerations on the final war helpful to our cause are the particular geopolitical expectations depicted in his apocalyptic vision:

> The Mahdi is going to appear after 101 hindrances . . . Now only two of them are remaining . . . One of them was that the red-coloured people came to Afghanistan. They will then go to Pakistan and then to Turkey. They must come to Turkey. They will come up to Amuq near Aleppo at the west of Aleppo. The plain of Amuq will be the place of the great slaughter. So that is the first sign, Russians coming to Turkey . . . After this, World War III will come. It is impossible for the end of the world to come until the whole world will be in two big camps. It will be eastern and western military camps and there will be the greatest fighting between them.[77]

Clearly, as Nāzim foretold that the coming of the Mahdī would take place sometime in the two-year period following 1990,[78] his vision has now to be regarded as an illustrative example of failed prophecy. However, in spite of this, his chief contribution to the Sufi apocalypse has been his linkage of specific geopolitical dreams with the End-time context. In this regard, Sufis have significantly contributed to the creation of what could be figuratively called an 'ecumenical apocalypse' since they have employed broadly shared apocalyptic vocabulary in order to emphasise how Islam can be 'vital to the lives of even their non-Muslim listeners'.[79]

Another noteworthy contribution, made by a respected Islamic scholar who is sympathetic to Sufism and opposes ISIS, is that of Muḥammad al-Yaᶜqūbī (born 1963). His book *Refuting ISIS* contains many apocalyptic references and its fundamental thesis, identifying ISIS as the *khawārij*, cannot be ever fully understood without a knowledge of its End-time connotations. In his own words, 'although the historical sect of the *Khawarij* does not exist today, we have clear proofs in the Prophetic Traditions that it would re-emerge at various times throughout the centuries of Islam'.[80] It is little wonder that Yaᶜqūbī's name has also been added to the *Dabiq* list of those Muslim authorities who deserve to be killed.[81]

A separate section needs to be devoted to Harun Yahya and his endless – and exceedingly varied – creativity.[82] Harun Yahya is the pen name of Adnan Oktar (born 1956), a prominent Turkish thinker and author. The apocalypse is one of his favourite subjects, to which he has devoted a lot of his writing.[83] Along with other modern Muslim apocalyptists, Yahya does not hesitate to utilise the End-time backdrop when addressing his worldly enemies, in his particular case Darwinists, atheists, communists, and so on. Bloody war scenarios, so prevalent in other Muslim eschatological surveys, are largely absent in Yahya's works.

The Mahdī, in his view, has actually three fundamental tasks to fulfil: (1) the elimination of philosophical systems that deny the existence of God and promote atheism; (2) the intellectual struggle with superstition and hypocrisy and the introduction of a genuine moral system based on the Qurʾān; and (3) a strengthening of the whole world of Islam and the establishment of peace, safety and prosperity.[84] The Mahdī is essentially depicted as the leader of all Muslims, no matter how much additional stress is placed on welfare issues, as well as the hi-tech benefits from his empire that are, for Yahya, a never-ending source of fascination.[85]

In his predictions concerning the Mahdī's appearance, Yahya initially followed an influential Turkish Sufi thinker, Said Nursi

(1877–1960), who was specifically preoccupied with numerology and foretold that his coming would occur one hundred years after his own death, that is, in 2060. In later years, Yahya promoted his vision of a so-called 'Turkish-Islamic union',[86] in which Turkey would become the centre of an eschatological 'golden age' and Turks would turn into a Muslim vanguard, acting as leader to other nations of Islam.[87]

Yahya's considerations regarding the Mahdī underwent a number of contradictory developments, shifting from a belief that his coming was located in the remote future to the assumption that he had already appeared on the earth, to be precise, in Istanbul, the last seat of the caliphate. The date of his coming, as settled on by Yahya, was the first year of the fifteenth century of *hijra* (1979–80). The portrayal of the Mahdī, according to Yahya, reveals many similarities with the actual author. The fundamental question as to why, on one hand, he loudly rejected attempts to be identified as Saviour, while, on the other, he did everything to promote such an assumption, remains unresolved. Nevertheless, this point lost its relevance following the rise of ISIS, which was to bring about another shift in Yahya's innovative thinking regarding the apocalypse.

The merciless nature of the Syrian war has provided Yahya with many insights that can be suitably contextualised within an apocalyptic framework. The Sufyānī, for instance, has been identified with President Bashshār al-Asad. Moreover, the Dajjāl is supposedly embodied within international freemasonry, whose distinctive symbol of one eye in a triangle, according to Yahya's explication, clearly refers to 'the one-eyed master of evil'.[88] From a geographical perspective, unlike in the works of other Muslim apocalyptic authors, Istanbul and Turkey play a major role in Yahya's visions.[89] Furthermore, he was able to incorporate numerous specific localised events into his colourful End-time narratives, an example being the Iranian revolution, the Iran-Iraq war, the Soviet occupation of Afghanistan, the building of the Keban Dam (the holding back of the River Euphrates) and even the burning of a Romanian oil tanker in the Bosporus in 1979 (identified as the apocalyptic sign of a 'flare in the east').

Currently, Yahya's apocalypticism is still in the process of evolving. His most recent observation is that ISIS is so strong that the only power able to defeat it is the Mahdī.[90] Thus, his eschatological reading of contemporary affairs in Iraq and Syria not only reflects his irreconcilable resistance to ISIS, but also his strong belief in the indispensable geopolitical sense of the Mahdī's approaching appearance.

To sum up, it is perhaps true to say that nobody denies that ISIS has pushed the discursive employment of Muslim apocalypticism to a completely new level. The actual approach adopted when dealing with the group's enemies within an 'eschatological battlefield' is definitely not original. On the contrary, what appears to be completely new is the widespread utilisation of such an approach. Being a pioneer of the deployment of massive takfirism, ISIS did not hesitate to apply such effective ammunition within the End-time context.[91] Therefore, responses to the apocalyptic delusions of ISIS had to be both inventive and offensive. The above-discussed 'typology' clearly demonstrates the diversity of responses, both in relation to their starting points and strategies. It also demonstrates the enormous potential of apocalyptic argumentation in general.

Doomsday Visions of the Shiites

Our outline of the apocalyptic responses to ISIS would not be complete without mentioning, at least very briefly, Shiite End-time visions. Indeed, the militants from both Sunni and Shiite environments claim to be fighting 'beneath the gaze of an apocalyptic messiah figure'.[92] So far, we have dealt with the Shiites primarily as the main targets of hateful ISIS propaganda. However, they also have their own apocalyptic narratives, which differ considerably from Sunni patterns (see 'Key Apocalyptic Terms and Notions' in Chapter 1) – but are, in many regards, actually complementary.

Although Shiites share most of the eschatological traditions with Sunnis, the overall tone and sense of the apocalyptic drama, as well as the genuine nature of the main apocalyptic players, sound completely different. According to Abbas Amanat's insightful summary:

> While the Sunni world witnessed numerous examples of shari^{c}a-oriented Mahdism with a distinct desire to restore pristine Islam of Muhammad's time, the Shi^{c}i world regenerated messianic impulses with distinct apocalyptic features aiming at a break with the shari^{c}a and creation of a post-millennial order ... Contrary to the Sunni Mahdi, whose advent was aimed to enhance the foundations of Islam on a periodic (centennial) basis, Shi^{c}i Islam essentially strived to invoke the Imamate paradigm so as to bring about the resurrection and an end to the prevailing dispensation.[93]

The fundamental differences between the branches can be vividly demonstrated by the example of the Mahdī, as David Cook succinctly suggests:

> One should note also that the Mahdi's personal qualities in this [i.e. Shiite] version are considerably different from Sunni apocalyptic. Here he is superhuman and prophet-like (if not a prophet himself), whereas Sunni apocalyptic emphasize his humanity, his reluctance and his fallibility (and sometimes even his personal bodily defects. These are not to be found in the descriptions of the Shii Mahdi).[94]

Moreover, this character is perfectly suited to being used for political purposes and, therefore, Muslim history refers back to many Mahdī pretenders, some of whom have been quite successful. Since the Shiite messianic figure is tied to a historical (or rather semi-historical) personality, only a few Shiite Mahdī claimants are documented.

Currently, Shiite apocalyptic ideas are undergoing an enormous transformation and revival. Millennialism is gradually slipping free of the control of the religious establishment, being increasingly used by lay preachers to interpret current events and compel their followers to take action.[95] This spiritual revival goes hand in hand with a boom in apocalyptic literature. The ubiquity and tenor of these popular pamphlets also help to illuminate the changes that have taken place regarding End-time expectations in Iran, the most important Shiite state, in recent years.

The most distinctive feature of this transformation, according to David Cook, has been the shift of popular expectations away from a future-oriented, more speculative range of traditional narrative forms of millennialism (hitherto the most common apocalyptic Shiite materials) to a more imminent and practical focus that permits greater exegetical latitude. Instead of clinging to ancient sources, current apocalyptists seek to relate their pronouncements to current events.[96]

In addition to this, contemporary Shiite apocalyptic writings have undergone a significant shift as they have sought to rid themselves of the ballast of medieval rhetoric and become an attractive part of modern religious discourse. Shiite millennialist excitement has been further encouraged by the Iraq war and subsequent turbulence,[97] best illustrated by the expansion of the so-called 'Mahdī Army' of Muqtadā al-Ṣadr, an influential Iraqi cleric. Despite fighting against each other, a lot of Sunni and Shiite militants who were drawn to the battlefield were actually motivated by an identical belief – that they constituted the vanguard of the Mahdī.[98] Needless to say, both irreconcilable sides consider their enemies to be partisan forces of the Dajjāl or, at least, his forerunners.

During the same period, the crucial role in strengthening Shiite millennialism was played by the former Iranian president Maḥmūd Aḥmadīnejād whose personal involvement in the Mahdist agenda has become well known.[99] With his election in 2005, the millennialist ethos actually became a part of state propaganda[100] and occasional attempts to predict his appearance, utilising the popular cultic centre at Jamkarān, were officially supported. At a deeper level, the systematic advocacy of the Mahdī cult may be seen as a policy aimed at playing to people's frustration with the slogans of revolutionary Islam.[101] In the words of Amanat, 'propaganda, scapegoating, and volatile rhetoric are the fruits of a state-sponsored messianic venture in today's Iran'.[102]

Associating the harbingers of the End with contemporary Middle-Eastern affairs, so essential for any effective instrumentalisation of the apocalypse, has also been reinforced by two significant episodes, both reflecting the deepening abyss between Shiites and Sunnis: (1) the killing in 2006 of al-Zarqāwī, who was often identified with the Sufyānī, and (2) King ᶜAbd Allāh's accession to the Saudi throne in

August 2005.[103] The messianic boom in Iran, furthermore, has fundamentally influenced Shiite millennialism all around the world, which also applies to Ḥizbullāh, Iran's 'extended arm' in the Syrian war.[104] This Shiite militant group and political party has been fighting on the side of the al-Asad regime, adding fuel to the already-raging sectarian fire.[105] The movement's ideologues originally placed little emphasis on the revelations regarding the Mahdī. Nevertheless, this changed from approximately 2004 onwards, when a flood of books about the Mahdī began to fly off the popular presses in Beirut. These books not only sought to introduce classical End-time prophecies to a wider Muslim audience, but also provided religiously charged interpretations of contemporary events in terms of the Mahdī's imminent return.[106]

The main point to be made here is that Shiite militants in Syria have increasingly referenced classics associated with their theology, in general, and *Kitāb al-jafr*, a mystical book attributed to Imam ᶜAlī (allegedly) and containing esoteric knowledge about the future, in particular.[107] Due to the enigmatic nature of this text, current affairs in Syria can easily be interpreted in accordance with the wishes of a particular interpreter.

Ḥizbullāh's supporters can thus believe that bloodshed in Syria links to the crucial harbingers of the Mahdī's arrival. In such terms, the current ruler of Syria should be killed in war (!) in order for the country to become fully controlled by a Sunni leader who will persecute Shiites and Christians until another army from the East (i.e. from Iran through Iraq) intervenes to liberate Syria and, subsequently, Jerusalem. There, the Mahdī will pray together with Jesus, which introduces 'the scene where the earthly time comes to an end and the divine era – where justice, fairness and peace prevail – will start'.[108]

As Mona Alami in her insightful study claims, Ḥizbullāh's involvement in the Syrian war has revived the religious myth of *Kitāb al-jafr* as an effective means of explaining this conflict:

> According to Shiite interviewees, the conflict in Syria is linked to the reappearance of the Mahdi, or redeemer, which will precede the end of days . . . Hezbollah has tapped this narrative to appeal to its most

> religious backers, but at the increased risk of inflaming Lebanese Sunnis, who have become disenchanted by their traditional leadership and increasingly attracted to Salafi and jihadist voices . . .[109]

Sales of *Kitāb al-jafr* and related texts have reportedly skyrocketed in recent years.[110] There are several YouTube videos that supposedly present copies of this book that have been recovered by Sunni fighters from Syrian battlefields.[111] The noticeable flourishing of Shiite millennialism has left its mark on the minds of millions across 'the Shiite crescent' and, therefore, many Shiites from Lebanon, Iraq and Iran are drawn to the war simply because they strongly believe that it paves the way for the Mahdī. While, in this respect, a number of Sunni and Shiite clerics are privately sceptical of the religious justification for the war, only a few have dared to express such reservations in public for fear of being misinterpreted as doubters of the Islamic prophecies.[112]

Among the Shiite apocalyptic responses to ISIS, al-Mahdī's opponents, al-Sufyānī and al-Dajjāl, play a crucial role. The general position of these two malevolent characters within the Shiite setting has been depicted by David Cook as follows:

> The fact that the Sufyānī does not represent an absolute demonic evil in the same way that the Dajjāl does has probably created a need among contemporary Shiite radicals to re-focus Shiite apocalyptic discourse upon the latter. Indeed, Dajjāl stories have become loci for demonizing the West as a whole, which is routinely portrayed as the embodiment of the Antichrist. Furthermore, anti-Semitic references to the Dajjāl regularly appear today in Shiite apocalyptic literature; only a few years ago such references were non-existent.[113]

Within Shiite exegetical creativity, al-Zarqāwī was actually a type of Sufyānī, since many of the former's features bear a marked similarity to those of the latter. In Muslim tradition, the Sufyānī is characterised, above all, by his immense cruelty and he is said to come from exactly the same region of Wādī Yābis (the northern part of Jordan) as did al-Zarqāwī.

Since the period around 2004, there has also been a tendency to gloss over the classical belief in the Sufyānī's Syrian-Muslim identity and to identify him instead with the United States.[114] However, there are other interpretations, for instance, among Shiite-Iraqi militants, where the Sufyānī has even been identified with the Free Syrian Army, fighting against the al-Asad regime.[115] Previously, Shiites attempted to identify him with a number of personalities, among them Ṣaḍḍām al-Ḥusayn or even the Jordanian king, ᶜAbd Allāh II.[116] Currently, they often do the same with Abū Bakr al-Baghdādī, a fact that leads some Shiite authorities to have doubts about this 'concretisation' approach in general.[117]

To summarise, Shiite apocalyptic imagination has actually become more focused against the United States and their allies. By holding such anti-Western attitudes, Shiites have begun to approach mainstream Sunni views much more closely than was the case a few years ago. Furthermore, at least with regard to the End-time, both factions share an increasing penchant for conspiracy, also including speculation about the 'hidden truth' behind current Middle Eastern conflicts.

Needless to say, the very genesis of ISIS and its bloody mission fit perfectly with such speculation. Moreover, by simply comparing particular predictions based on *Kitāb al-jafr* with events leading up to the current situation,[118] it is easy to see that those who believe in the book have grown more confident in relation to its veracity. This is because Syria has truly witnessed a greater degree of bloodshed that anybody ever expected, whether Muslim scholars or Western analysts. Shiite apocalyptic visions thus seem to be in the process of being gradually fulfilled.

Notes

1. *Dabiq* 11:16.
2. Al-Muqaddam, *Fiqh ashrāṭ al-sāᶜa*, p. 7.
3. Some parts of this section have been published in the *Central European Journal for Contemporary Religion*, 2: 1 (2018). Thanks to both anonymous reviewers for their helpful feedback.
4. Ibrāhīm and al-Najjār, *Dāᶜish*, pp. 90–3.
5. Al-Muqaddam, *Fiqh ashrāṭ al-sāᶜa*, pp. 6–15.

6. Amanat, *Apocalyptic Islam*, p. 234.
7. See Ayyūb, *al-Masīḥ al-Dajjāl*, pp. 5–12.
8. Richardson, *The Islamic Antichrist*, book cover.
9. See, for example, http://shoebat.com/2017/02/26/the-muslim-antichrist-is-rising-up-major-muslim-leaders-are-declaring-the-coming-of-a-divine-leader-who-will-lead-an-islamic-empire-the-islamic-antichrist-will-declare-himself-to-be-god-and-war-agai/ (last accessed 25 May 2017).
10. Fishman, *The Master Plan*, p. 258.
11. Landes, 'Jihad, Apocalypse, and Anti-Semitism'.
12. A demonstrative example, eloquently entitled *Wahhabism Unveiled: Breaking the Horns of Satan*, is available at https://hornofsatan.wordpress.com/about/ (last accessed 20 December 2017).
13. Hamid, *Sufis, Salafis and Islamists*, p. 94.
14. Damir-Geilsdorf and Franke, 'Narrative Reconfigurations', p. 433.
15. *Dabiq* 7:66.
16. *Al-Nabaʾ* 120:8.
17. See https://www.youtube.com/watch?v=Nv6pyYoXoqo (last accessed 20 December 2017).
18. See *al-Nabaʾ* 107:8.
19. For an uncompromising criticism of such opportunism, see al-Muqaddam, *Fiqh ashrāṭ al-sāʿa*, pp. 163–6.
20. Such an assessment is based on countless discussions with local booksellers, second-hand bookshop keepers, and so on, conducted during my last stay in Egypt in March 2018.
21. For this term among jihadists, see Qindīl and ʿAbd al-Rabbihi, *al-Fikr al-islāmī al-jihādī al-muʿāṣir*, pp. 352–4.
22. See Fārūq, *Dāʿish*, pp. 356–7.
23. Wagemakers, *Salafism in Jordan*, p. 196.
24. Fishman, *The Master Plan*, p. 248.
25. Cf. al-ʿArīfī, *Nihāyat al-ʿālam*, pp. 48–51.
26. See, for example, https://www.youtube.com/watch?v=0bqxN84ls6s (last accessed 25 September 2017).
27. See Nuʿaym, *The Book of Tribulations*, pp. 378–88.
28. Such claims can be found, for example, at http://mlahim.firstgoo.com/t889-topic (last accessed 25 May 2017).
29. For three particular examples of presentations on the Internet claim-

ing that ISIS are partisans of Dajjāl, see https://www.youtube.com/watch?v=g6Cx_k3r4VY, https://www.youtube.com/watch?v=6vkK7-FAiOk and http://www.ahram.org.eg/News/41352/86/335069/%D9%85%D8%B1%D8%A7%D9%8A%D8%A7/%D8%AE%D8%B1%D9%88%D8%AC-%D8%A7%D9%84%D9%85%D8%B3%D9%8A%D8%AD-%D8%A7%D9%84%D8%AF%D8%AC%D8%A7%D9%84-%D9%85%D9%86-%D9%85%D8%AA%D8%A7%D9%87%D8%A9-%D8%AF%D8%A7%D8%B9%D8%B4.aspx (all three last accessed 28 September 2017).

30. Cf. *al-Nabaʾ* 114:8.
31. Kabbani, *The Approach of Armageddon?*, pp. 119–20.
32. Nuʿaym, *The Book of Tribulations*, p. 89 (no. 434).
33. Ibid. p. 102 (no. 501).
34. See at www.youtube.com/watch?v=4CqI4R5AVos (last accessed 30 September 2017).
35. See al-ʿArīfī, *Nihāyat al-ʿālam*, pp. 144–6.
36. For more details, see Fārūq, *Dāʿish*, pp. 351–62.
37. Cf. Gabra, *The Ideological Extremism of Al-Azhar*.
38. Fārūq, *Dāʿish*, p. 359.
39. Available at http://www.youm7.com/story/2015/5/14/%D8%B9%D8%B6%D9%88-%D8%A8%D9%80-%D9%83%D8%A8%D8%A7%D8%B1-%D8%A7%D9%84%D8%B9%D9%84%D9%85%D8%A7%D8%A1-%D9%84%D8%A7-%D9%8A%D9%88%D8%AC%D8%AF-%D8%AD%D8%AF%D9%8A%D8%AB-%D9%8A%D8%AD%D8%AF%D8%AF-%D9%86%D9%87%D8%A7%D9%8A%D8%A9-%D8%A7%D9%84%D8%B9%D8%A7%D9%84%D9%85/2181801 (last accessed 29 September 2017).
40. See Fārūq, *Dāʿish*, pp. 354–5.
41. Ibid. pp. 359–60.
42. *Rumiyah* 8:20–1.
43. See https://splendidpearls.org/2014/07/04/isis-and-the-end-of-times/ (last accessed 29 July 2017).
44. 'Open Letter', p. 17.
45. Suraqah, 'ISIS and the End of Times'.
46. Nuʿaym, *The Book of Tribulations*, p. 107 (no. 520).
47. Cf. 'Open Letter'.
48. See *Dabiq* 4:34; 5:7, 15; 6:24 and elsewhere.

49. Available at http://www.nairaland.com/2981478/prophet-muhammad-prophecy-isis (last accessed 29 September 2017).
50. Available at https://www.almesryoon.com/story/559453/%D8%B9%D9%84%D9%8A-%D8%A8%D9%86-%D8%A3%D8%A8%D9%8A-%D8%B7%D8%A7%D9%84%D8%A8-%D8%AD%D8%B0%D8%B1-%D9%85%D9%86-%D8%AF%D8%A7%D8%B9%D8%B4-%D9%85%D9%86%D8%B0-1400-%D8%B9%D8%A7%D9%85 (last accessed 28 September 2017).
51. By 'traditionalist Islam' I mean here, primarily, the various contemporary responses to reductionist and purist tendencies in Islam, represented mostly by Salafists, who promote a return to the pluralism and spiritual multiplicity of the classical Islamic heritage.
52. For more information about him, see Hamid, *Sufis, Salafis and Islamists*, pp. 78–81.
53. Yusuf, 'The Crisis of ISIS'.
54. See https://www.youtube.com/watch?v=hJo4B-yaxfk (last accessed 29 September 2017).
55. *Dabiq* 14:13–14.
56. His webpages are available at http://www.suhaibwebb.com (last accessed 29 September 2017).
57. Yusuf, 'The Crisis of ISIS'.
58. Damir-Geilsdorf and Franke, 'Narrative Reconfigurations', p. 426.
59. See http://content.time.com/time/world/article/0,8599,2076778,00.html (last accessed 25 July 2017).
60. Yusuf, 'The Crisis of ISIS'.
61. Nuᶜaym, *The Book of Tribulations*, p. 191 (no. 944).
62. Cf. Karouny, 'Apocalyptic prophecies'.
63. *Al-Nabaʾ* 58:8.
64. Ostřanský, 'The Sufi Journey to the Next World', p. 499.
65. Furnish, *Ten Years' Captivation with the Mahdi's Camps*, p. 203.
66. Křížek, 'Millennialism in Sufi Perspective', p. 184.
67. Damrel, 'A Sufi Apocalypse', p. 1.
68. Křížek, 'Millennialism in Sufi Perspective', p. 192.
69. *Dabiq* 14:8–17.
70. See, for example, http://www.freep.com/story/news/local/michigan/2016/04/14/fbi-isis-threatens-muslim-leader-michigan-others/83033248/ (last accessed 29 September 2017).

71. Kabbani, *The Approach of Armageddon?*, pp. 160–1.
72. Ibid. pp. 163–4.
73. Ibid. p. 168.
74. Ibid. p. 171.
75. Ibid. p. 249.
76. Nazim, *Mystical Secrets of the Last Days*, p. 53.
77. Ibid. pp. 126–7.
78. Ibid. p. 127.
79. Damrel, 'A Sufi Apocalypse', p. 1.
80. Al-Yaqoubi, *Refuting ISIS*, p. 4.
81. *Dabiq* 14:14–15.
82. See Solberg, *The Mahdi Wears Armani*, pp. 145–84.
83. Ibid. pp. 152–3.
84. Yahya, *The End Times and Hazrat Mahdi (as)*, pp. 35–6.
85. Yahya, *The Golden Age*, pp. 28–45.
86. Solberg, *The Mahdi Wears Armani*, pp. 164–8.
87. Yahya, *The Prophet Jesus (as), Hazrat Mahdi (as) and the Islamic Union*, pp. 35–8.
88. For an impressive overview of Yahya's apocalyptic reading of the current Middle-Eastern conflicts, see http://www.harunyahya.com/en/Articles/195270/our-prophet-(saas)-foretold-the (last accessed 1 May 2017).
89. Cf. 'Interview with Harun Yahya' in Richardson, *The Islamic Antichrist*, pp. 252–4.
90. Damir-Geilsdorf and Franke, 'Narrative Reconfigurations', p. 422.
91. For Sunni responses to takfirism, see Fārūq, *Dāᶜish*, pp. 373–6.
92. See https://www.washingtontimes.com/news/2015/jan/5/apocalypse-prophecies-drive-islamic-state-strategy/ (last accessed 22 November 2017).
93. Amanat, *Apocalyptic Islam*, pp. 41, 49.
94. Cook, *Studies in Muslim Apocalyptic*, p. 226.
95. Cook, 'Messianism in the Shiite Crescent', p. 95.
96. Ibid. p. 98.
97. Cf. Pew Research Center, *The World's Muslims*, pp. 65–6.
98. McCants, *The ISIS Apocalypse*, p. 107.
99. Hitchcock, *The Apocalypse of Ahmadinejad*. See also Amanat, *Apocalyptic Islam*, pp. 239–44.

100. To gain a deeper understanding of his millennial beliefs, see the transcript of his speech at the 'World Without Zionism' conference in Tehran, in Hitchcock, *The Apocalypse of Ahmadinejad*, pp. 145–51. For his notorious speech at the United Nations, clearly expressing the wish to hasten the Mahdī's appearance, see Cook, 'Messianism in the Shiite Crescent', pp. 99–100.
101. Amanat, *Apocalyptic Islam*, p. 245.
102. Ibid. p. 250.
103. Filiu, *Apocalypse in Islam*, p. 156.
104. See Alami, 'Minding the Home Front'.
105. Atwan, *Islamic State*, p. 215.
106. Cook, 'Messianism in the Shiite Crescent', pp. 96–7.
107. For Sunni criticism of this belief, see al-Muqaddam, *Fiqh ashrāṭ al-sāᶜa*, p. 176.
108. See https://www.al-monitor.com/pulse/originals/2013/09/hezbollah-nasrallah-shiite-doctrine-syria-conflict.html (last accessed 22 November 2017).
109. Alami, 'Minding the Home Front,' pp. 6–7.
110. Petit, 'Eschatology in the ISIS Narrative', p. 20.
111. See, for example, https://www.youtube.com/watch?v=jUOKzepVy4U (last accessed 22 November 2017).
112. Karouny, 'Apocalyptic prophecies'.
113. Cook, 'Messianism in the Shiite Crescent', p. 95.
114. Cook, 'Messianism in the Shiite Crescent', pp. 93–4.
115. McCants, *The ISIS Apocalypse*, p. 108.
116. Some related exegetical speculations are available, for example, at http://seyedkhorasani.parsiblog.com/category/%D8%B3%D9%81%D9%8A%D8%A7%D9%86%D9%8A/ (last accessed 23 November 2017).
117. For a related speech of Ḥasan Naṣr Allāh, see http://seyedkhorasani.parsiblog.com/category/%D8%B3%D9%81%D9%8A%D8%A7%D9%86%D9%8A/ (last accessed 23 November 2017).
118. There are many lectures on YouTube about geopolitics as viewed through the lens of *Kitāb al-jafr*. See, for example, https://www.youtube.com/watch?v=haWCzrfldog (last accessed 28 November 2017).

7

The Hour as Goal and Vehicle: A Summary of ISIS Apocalypticism

A billion Muslims are at least attracted to an Islamic millennial scenario in which they take over the world. The vast majority is not yet apocalyptic, but it is certainly possible that both Arabs and Muslims worldwide could get swept up in a fever of apocalyptic hope and violence . . . The West cannot afford to dismiss these fantasies because we consider them as unrealistic. We have to listen to what the Jihadists say, and especially, what they say to each other . . .

– Richard Landes[1]

The key to delegitimizing Salafi-jihadists is politics, not religion and theology. Although ISIS promises deliverance and salvation through the resurrection of the caliphate, the group's religious ideology is important inasmuch as it allows ISIS to exploit a poisonous political and social environment, and to offer an alternative model (the Islamic State) to secular political authoritarianism. Syrians and Iraqis would not have embraced ISIS's Islamist ideology if their legitimate political and social grievances had been addressed.

– Fawaz Gerges[2]

You will see nothing in this world but trial and tribulation, and matters will only get worse.

– Nuᶜaym ibn Ḥammād[3]

Within the current Muslim tide of millennialism, further encouraged by the persistent state of unrest across the Middle East, ISIS appears to have by far the most developed apocalyptic rhetoric and self-presentation techniques. However, these jihadists' opportunistic employment of End-time visions is definitely not unique. With ISIS having its own spiritual 'forebears', at least within the Islamist environment, it is easy for the group's sinister legacy to spawn, with a high degree of probability, both successors and imitators.

As far as the attitudes of ISIS towards the apocalypse are concerned, we must avoid almost all obvious socio-political factors that usually help scholars to understand millennial movements at their archetypal level. Neither the strong interpersonal relationship between a charismatic leader and a relatively small cult of followers, nor the alienation of a group from the dynamic sector of society is in existence – the features characteristic of various millennialist offshoots throughout the history of humanity are not to be found. In this regard, ISIS is indeed different.

As regards their original contribution, ISIS propagandists, feeding on the sense of the End, have incorporated preexisting mainstream apocalyptic narratives into their own message. In this, they are definitely not inventors, but are simply users. ISIS promotes a millennial ethos and, at the same time, is extremely violent. However, mainstream theories related to millennial violence can hardly be applied to this organisation.[4] Essentially, ISIS has constructed its apocalyptic image as part of an overarching logic that is the so-called 'cosmic wars', highlighting the unavoidable approach of the end for this degenerated and chaotic world. And it is precisely this merciless diagnosis of the present condition that seems to be gaining ground among Muslim radicals worldwide.

Based on such metaphysical foundations, it is clear that even if the group is defeated in military terms, its message can survive all around the world. Born of a perfect storm of historical circumstances, ISIS has put down its spiritual roots, ones that will not easily be pulled up.[5] Regarding its innovative propaganda, we should question whether we are still dealing with an extreme example of radicalised Islam or whether we are rather witnessing the Islamisation of extreme radicalism. Whatever the scenario, it is clear that ISIS has become a global phenomenon and should be treated as such. Neither can the fact that ISIS has already redrawn numerous borders, both physical and imaginary, be questioned. It is the massive and systematic deployment of the apocalypse in the group's propaganda that constitutes the most distinguishable and revolutionary feature of ISIS.

Essentially, the apocalypticism of this propaganda has one common denominator: that the supposed fulfilment of any one specific sign of the Hour will prove the truthfulness of the group's millennial worldview in its entirety. ISIS propagandists thus feel absolutely no need to provide a comprehensive argument advocating its apocalyptic creed, since the alleged veracity of one partial prophecy can simply be used to confirm the validity of the aggregate. Furthermore, this can be presented as a reflection of God's will, something that cannot be anything other than perfect. It is for this reason that what might appear to be, at least from a short-term perspective, failure – the current situation – can ultimately be seen and interpreted as a mere wobble on what will prove to be a long and triumphant journey, and as an insignificant part of the great Divine Plan, which will inevitably lead to a happy ending in the form of peace, justice and redemption.[6] Needless to say, the happy end for the orthodox will mean disaster for the unbeliever. From such a perspective, impartiality is not possible.

The logic of such an approach is inexorable: the more the End-time narratives unfold, the more extreme, brutal and hectic they become. The black-and-white contours of the Armageddon drama simply exclude any 'grey zones'.[7] This is because compromise belongs to the application of common politics, and definitely not to the arsenal of an apocalyptically self-professed group. There is no doubt that it is precisely this transcendent dualism of good and evil that provides the most effective psychological motivation for ISIS supporters, or at least for some of them. Personal engagement in such a transpersonal eschatological clash easily overcomes all worldly troubles and can actually provide a sense of life for the individual. The present societal and geopolitical situation in the Middle East, particularly marked by the decimation of long decades of stability and an increase in violent sectarianism, places a mighty tool into the hands of those who are busy recruiting soldiers to fight the forces of the Antichrist.

ISIS's apocalyptic self-presentation can also be seen through the lens of a protest movement and, as such, it has its own specific means of expression and target audience. Accordingly, the young and ardent Muslim radicals who earlier and eagerly heeded the call to fight against corrupt Middle-Eastern regimes can today easily accept the 'apocalyptic challenge', whose actual novelty balances its palpable urgency. Despite its total irrationality, such a message has the capacity to provide what other motivational forces lack: a believable interpretation of the current world, together with a believable justification for their own attitudes and activities.

As we have seen throughout this book, many uncertainties relating to ISIS apocalypticism remain. However, one fundamental point is now certain: Muslim apocalyptic creativity after ISIS will never be the same again. Among other things, this group has significantly helped to fortify the anti-Jewish and anti-Zionist ethos that is so symptomatic of modern Muslim apocalyptic thought.

Evaluating its actual impact, we can state in general that the End-time appeal of ISIS propaganda has certainly been higher than the group's opponents would admit, but, at the same time, substantially lower than its promoters would wish. The group's fantastically timed apocalyptic self-presentation has, in fact, no adequate modern precedent. Simply put, ISIS has introduced a new and viable pattern of how to deal with the 'End-time agenda'.

The preceding interpretation can be summarized by several fundamental points:

(1) **The so-far obscure real motivation of ISIS leaders.** We actually do not know whether ISIS leaders really believe in the approaching Hour or whether they have instead pragmatically instrumentalised this great theme of current Muslim discourse. There are influential voices questioning the sincerity of the ISIS apocalyptic self-presentation in general, among them, for exam-

ple, the experts of the Quilliam Foundation. According to their thorough analysis of the genuine ideological roots of ISIS, 'mis-categorizing it as an apocalyptic cult hellbent on precipitating the end of the world shrouds its actual ideology and goals in mystery while making it seem much more attractive to potential sympathizers'.[8] Whatever the case, ISIS propaganda has been happy to use apocalyptic expectations as a key part of its global appeal. An often-quoted episode from the struggle in northern Syria vividly illustrates such a claim: 'If you think all these mujāhidīn came from across the world to fight Assad, you're mistaken. They are all here as promised by the Prophet. This is the war he promised – it is the Grand Battle,' a Sunni Muslim explained to a Reuters journalist. Undoubtedly, making an appeal to apocalyptic expectations is an important part of ISIS's modus operandi and goading the West into a final battle is a critical component of such a scenario.[9] Moreover, labelling ISIS as 'a non-rational actor' implies that the group's followers are crazy – which they are not. They are entirely rational, once you accept their eschatological premise, which, according to the Pew Research Center data, hundreds of millions of Muslims actually do.[10]

(2) **The rendition of the so-called 'tamed apocalypse' as an effective step towards the sustainability of the apocalyptic ethos.** The decisive shift from the unrestrained millennialism of ISIS's precursors (namely Abū Ayyūb al-Miṣrī's ethos) towards the 'tamed apocalypse' of the later official propaganda of this group has helped in finding a solution to the eternal millennialist question as to how apocalyptic motivation can be sustained in the longer term. However, we should not misrepresent the term 'tamed' as meaning something less dangerous since, in this case, the opposite is actually true. Unlike the unrestrained and spontaneous surge of millennialism, this kind of 'domesticised apocalypse' can be thoughtfully manipulated and – as such – it is definitely not a harmless phenomenon. Although the group's current leadership has avoided its predecessors' incautious prognostications relating to End-time issues, the very idea of the

apocalypse has been no less powerful in animating their doctrines, as well as their powerful recruitment strategy. The Hour being depicted as relatively near but definitely not ultimately within reach constitutes a credo that might be easily experienced but never truly verified. In the case of ISIS, we can indeed speak about a certain 'apocalyptic mutation of global jihadism'.[11] Essentially, the ISIS propaganda apparatus shares a broader Salafist vision of history, one in which there will be a period of ignorance, followed by an Islamic epoch, one which will initially bring about progress but then stagnation and bankruptcy, again leading to a state of ignorance. Muslims can only emerge through following three major steps: the acceptance of a faith (Salafism), resettlement (*hijra*) and finally *jihād*, resulting, according to the ISIS interpretation, in an eschatological clash between good and evil. In fact, all the group's propaganda focuses on these specific stages and their apocalyptic manifestation.[12]

(3) **The 'state-building' nature of apocalypticism.** Such a designation truly sounds like an oxymoron. However, ISIS's apocalypticism has proven itself to be an effective tool in the process of legitimising the group's existence (as well as with regard to its claims about the caliphate), let alone in relation to its determination to conquer. This is because a completely new form of Muslim apocalyptic obsession can be observed in the case of ISIS. From a traditional viewpoint, apocalypticism is almost exclusively regarded as a potential source of unrest and disturbance; the 'state-building apocalypse', thoughtfully developed by ISIS, has had precisely the opposite effect. As we have seen, apocalyptic narratives need to not be future-oriented, pondering over the length of time remaining, since a focus on interpreting current affairs is enough to prove the rightness of the group's mission in its entirety. With such an approach, it is simply not possible for a prophecy to 'fail'. The work of ISIS apocalyptists has been considerably facilitated by the fact that the early Muslim End-time prophecies arose as a result of sectarian conflicts waged in today's Syria and, as such, they resonate powerfully with the

current spate of sectarian fighting there. Moreover, depicting its opponents through recourse to derogative terms and portraying the struggle for hegemony as a metaphysical clash between good and evil has allowed the group to further deepen the sectarian strife and hatred, something which has contributed to its success since the beginning of 2014. The fundamental notion of the vanguard of 'Strangers' who are willing to use every means necessary to accomplish their eschatological mission has become a decisive feature in the above-discussed attempt to shift the apocalyptic ethos onto a more 'practical' level.

(4) **The most traditional content versus the most advanced forms.** As we have already realised, ISIS completely avoided taking the step that is so symptomatic of most modern Muslim apocalyptists: ISIS apocalyptic message broadcasters never succumbed to the temptation to draw on various non-Islamic segments and inspirations in order to complement and confirm their overall End-time visions. In this respect, ISIS was determined to proceed in the opposite direction when compared with the vast majority of modern Muslim apocalyptic authors, who tend to be modernists in relation to their narratives and conservatives in terms of their self-presentation (or marketing), particularly in cyberspace. To sum up, ISIS End-time visions firmly adhere to supposedly genuine Islamic sources and, simultaneously, they denounce any non-Islamic borrowings, even if they might be useful in further affirming the group's message. Essentially, the ISIS propaganda machine employs the most advanced methods when it comes to its use of visual representation, symbolism and language, and, above all, the media of choice.

(5) **Mastery of 'apocalyptical marketing'.** The language and visual imagery employed in the ISIS apocalypse vividly demonstrate how this group has mastered another important discipline, marketing.[13] This is because apocalypticism plays such a fundamental role in its recruitment strategy. Unlike the group's jihadist predecessors, ISIS has been truly able 'to sell its apocalypse' worldwide, primarily due to the group's command of new media and social

networks. In the case of ISIS, it is thus possible to observe live a phenomenon about which scholars of religious studies could only, until quite recently, theorise. Basically, jihadist Internet propaganda has become even more dangerous because, today, this main media vehicle provides an extremely effective means of delivering ideological, tactical and operational training of the kind that former jihadists had to cover in remote Afghan training camps. On the other hand, the various ISIS activities in cyberspace have brought about not only anxiety, but also a degree of reassurance since, despite the massive temptation posed by the group, ISIS still remains unacceptable to the vast majority of Muslims all over the world.

The previously elaborated 'apocalyptic arsenal' (see 'To Rome' in Chapter 4) so skilfully utilised by ISIS propagandists can hardly be suspected of being a spontaneous manifestation of its creators' individual imaginations. On the contrary, their narrative techniques and approaches to the 'End-times agenda' actually reveal considered and elaborated methods on how to safely avoid the pitfalls of 'overheated' (or, in more scientific terminology, 'unrestrained') millennialism, emotionally attached to a vision of a very close End.

To summarise the main features of this arsenal, we should initially emphasise that ISIS apocalypticism, as we have already seen, is focused more on the present and the past than on the future, as might be expected with any form of apocalypticism. Regardless of the simple fact that any speculation related to the past or the present is always 'safer' than if it were related to the future (since the former approach can never fail), in doing so ISIS propagandists ultimately support the already mentioned 'state-building nature' of their apocalyptic ethos, which facilitates, either deliberately or as a mere by-product, the process of legitimising the group, together with its controversial activities and ambitious plans.

Practically speaking, this fundamental point might be convincingly illustrated through reference to all aspects of the group's apocalyptic output. In this respect, a closer investigation of ISIS media production leads us to the notion of a certain 'apocalyptic methodology', which to some degree might actually be simply an exaggerated description of a set of approaches and narrative techniques that are symptomatic of this type of writing. As we have seen by way of an example in *Dabiq* magazine, this peculiar 'methodology' essentially comprises four pivotal tendencies that are, furthermore, mutually interwoven. In fact, all those elements, indispensable for the creation of the ISIS apocalyptic message, can reliably provide the reader with a meaningful and easily believable perspective on how to interpret contemporary world events and, above all, on how to effectively justify the existence of ISIS and its rage.

The first of them, the notion of all-encompassing decline, is essential for any apocalyptic scenario, regardless of its religious and historic milieu. This is because all generally known manifestations of decline and corruption within the Muslim environment are so succinctly exemplified through a scattered set of portents of the End, poetically referred to as 'the lesser signs of the Hour'. These can always and everywhere be easily identified and their persuasiveness thus appears to be incontestable. In the specific case of ISIS, the ubiquitous decline ultimately helps to highlight the exceptionality of the group, which is presented as being not responsible for its horrendous manifestations and thus having the right to judge but not to be judged. Here, we can simply refer to one of many possible specific examples that might exemplify one crucial rule: relentless attacks against 'corrupt and malevolent so-called Islamic scholars' are among the most popular themes of ISIS propaganda, providing a dark backdrop of moral and intellectual bankruptcy, against which the supposedly exceptional qualities of ISIS scholars come to the fore.

Universal decline is closely interconnected with a sharpening of current contradictions and conflicts, which represent the second factor in our 'apocalyptic methodology', with the Muslim apocalypse being easily recognisable and identifiable through reference to contemporary word affairs. The general apocalyptic rule says: the closer the End, the more extensive all existing contradictions will become. A major part of ISIS End-time narratives focuses precisely on the separation of the group from the rest of the world prior to the Hour by sticking as closely as possible to a supposedly faithful understanding of the Tradition. The shades of grey are expected to disappear completely in a world where black and white will be the only possible options. In this future world, as follows from the otherwise cautious and insufficiently concrete apocalyptic depictions appearing in ISIS propaganda, forgiveness will be considered to be a sin and irreconcilability a virtue. There is no doubt that the group's propaganda apparatus actually does its best to 'separate the wheat from the chaff'. As part of their ideological response to the alleged misleading of the vast majority of Muslims, the leaders of ISIS have even dusted off the most terrifying weapon of ancient inter-Muslim clashes, the accusation of disbelief (*takfīr*), which has become their spectral hallmark.

While both of the previously mentioned factors help to describe this world, from a general perspective, as a cheerless place condemned to a future of near extinction, the third – according to our brief survey, designated as being 'the idea of' an 'imaginary return to the very roots of Islam' – on the contrary, can bring about a degree of consolation, thus offering a spark of hope in an otherwise dark cloud of expectation. As we have repeatedly observed, it is precisely this concept that plays a crucial role in the jihadist recruitment strategy, because ISIS propagandists strive to describe their own group as a living embodiment of the eternal Muslim dream of a perfect Islamic society.

At the same time, ISIS ideologues, together with many modern Islamist thinkers, have come to the conclusion that some of the forms of behaviour and manners of an important section of Muslims (including, for example, the traditional way of conducting funerals or commemorating venerated figures among Sufis) strikingly resemble non-Muslim practices from the period of *jāhilīya*. In addition, this point strengthens the idea of a return to the beginning. It is not necessary to elaborate further that it is precisely this point that has already attracted countless Muslim supporters, enthused by the impassioned stories from a small island of goodness (faith, truth) in an ocean of evil (disbelief, lies). On the pages of the group's electronic media output, those supporters are indeed indirectly, yet in a sufficiently clear manner, identified with the early Muslims, the Prophet's Companions (*ṣaḥāba*), who lived during a period that is generally viewed as being a golden age of Islam. And what might provide stronger encouragement for frustrated individuals all over the Muslim world than to be compared favourably to such a group?!

Finally, the fourth very powerful tool, without which the ISIS apocalypse would not be as attractive and convincing in the eyes of its sympathisers, is conspiracy. This is because conspiracy thinking provides an effective and reliable cement to a diverse set of otherwise incoherent narratives and fragmented concepts and, above all, convincingly explains that which would otherwise be hard to explain. In the case of ISIS, it is, for example, a question of how and why the 'world of Islam' has deteriorated from the loudly celebrated perfection of its illustrious beginnings to the unfavourable present, frequently criticised by Muslim intellectuals as they drown in never-ending bouts of nostalgia. Meanwhile, since the conscientious search for an appropriate answer would require extensive knowledge as well as considerable intellectual capacity, contemporary radicals offer an immediate and unsophisticated solution – that the cause lies in a conspiracy against Muslims, led by Jews, Shiites and their allies.

Essentially, conspiracy is not only the answer but is, first and foremost, a tool that has a remarkable capacity to transmute failure into success. Sometimes, conspiracy can be found in a totally unexpected context: for example, within ISIS fabrications related to the establishment of the group's own currency, backed by gold, as a replacement for the Syrian pound, Iraqi dinar, US dollar, and so on. At that time, the group's propaganda generally denounced all currencies not backed by gold as a manifestation of the 'Jewish conspiracy'.[14] So, as we can see from numerous examples, ISIS has actively made use of conspiracy theories while, at the same time, presenting itself as a victim of conspiracy.

In the specific case of ISIS propaganda, conspiracy can help to effectively justify various particular deviations of the group's messages from mainstream Muslim thought, which also applies to the group's intensified hatred of Shiites. In order to permanently maintain such an extreme level, mere criticism and a denouncement of their supposedly heretical creed and deviant practices is not sufficient, and therefore a stronger weapon must be employed. Only a very creative form of conspiracy theory has the capacity to actually present Shiites not only as heretics (*zanādiqa*), or even infidels (*kuffār*), but primarily as the most dangerous enemies (since they are internal ones) of a 'genuinely pure Islam'. Consequently, also promoted by ISIS propaganda, reference is made to their role as an 'extended hand of the Jews',[15] with their malevolence being manifested by the presentation of a long list of tragic episodes, loosely framing the centuries of problematical coexistence that involve both the main branches of Islam.

This point can be clearly exemplified by the fall of Baghdad in 1258, which represents a milestone in the decay of the *dār al-islām*, ascribed by ISIS to a perfidious Shiite vizier.[16] The organic incorporation of anti-Shiite motifs into ISIS apocalyptic narratives has been considerably facilitated by the alleged striking similarity between the Sunni portraits of the Antichrist and the Shiite depictions of the Redeemer, the Mahdī. It is precisely this kind of eschatological comparison that is one of the most popular themes of ISIS electronic media output. Although the group has officially rejected conspiracy as a specific form of *shirk* (the violation of the absolute unity and uniqueness of God by positioning somebody or something on His level),[17] in common practice, various forms of anti-Islamic plots, meandering over the course of Islamic history, are to be frequently found in its media productions.

As already mentioned, while the degree of sincerity among the promoters of the ISIS apocalyptic message is indeed obscure, there is no reason to question their belief that they belong on the eschatological side of good. Of course, nobody can know the true depth of their faith, but we should not suppose that their belief is less intense just because of their poor education.

To summarise this issue, when we are speaking about the apocalypticism of ISIS, we are actually addressing not only the teaching, the comprehensive doctrine, but rather a complex approach to the world, a lifestyle, a certain 'spiritual anchorage', also including elaborated discursive techniques, which, in Jamel Velji's apt expression, have the capacity 'to restructure the premises of terrestrial authority'.[18]

There is no doubt that, to a significant degree, the attractiveness of apocalypticism – including the ISIS version – is not just the result of its spiritual content (its ideas, concepts, narratives, and so on) but of its presentation (its aesthetics, style and look). In this regard, apocalypticism can be seen and assessed as part of the idiosyncratic 'jihadi culture', briefly defined as 'products and practices that do something other than fill the basic military needs of jihadi group',[19] to which a pioneering collective monograph of the same name was recently devoted.

Once again, we should emphasise here that apocalypticism can never be reduced to its textual or ideological dimension. To the contrary, it is much more than a closed set of concepts, also including other fundamental, yet much less graspable, dimensions and manifestations, such as rhetoric, ethos, aesthetical qualities and so on. In this respect, Thomas Hegghammer has aptly summarised that:

> what scholars have tended to refer to as 'ideology' is really two different things: doctrine and aesthetics. Many academics today would say that jihadi poetry and hymns belong to the realm of ideology, for which we already have a lively research program. However, the literature on jihadism has mostly treated ideology as synonymous with doctrine, that is a set of ideas transmitted through language and internalized through cognition . . .[20]

So apocalypticism, from such a fitting perspective, can be viewed as part of the jihadists' distinctive aesthetic universe. Nevertheless, within this book, we have been mainly concerned (with the small exception of the section on 'Symbolism and Imagery of the Apocalypse' in Chapter 3) with the textual and ideological dimensions of ISIS apocalyptic self-presentation. This has primarily been a practical decision, because a wider approach would have left us to deal with an unmanageable number of sources and we would have had to sacrifice a lot of depth in favour of breadth. However, despite chiefly dealing here with 'apocalypticism in the narrow sense', we should be well aware of its broader understanding, research into which can undoubtedly offer new and creative ways by which to address the puzzle of contemporary jihadist End-time dreams.

As part of these concluding considerations, we should also note that a complex assessment of ISIS apocalypticism can lead us to a variety of completely different 'diagnoses' in accordance with the employed concepts and terminologies used within a religious studies framework. Simply stated, any attempt to properly evaluate the genuine role of ISIS 'End-time self-presentations' will largely depend on the accepted definitions of apocalypticism and millennialism, which is an arena – as discussed in Chapter 1 – where renowned scholars have not yet been able to reach a consensus.

Ultimately, it does not matter whether we are speaking in concert with Richard Landes about the 'millennialism of global jihadism' or together with Catherine Wessinger about 'managed millennialism' (which is a scholarly equivalent of our phrase 'tamed apocalypse'). In either case, one substantial finding seems to be unquestionable: the real significance and visibility of apocalypticism for ISIS has been significantly reinforced by the group's lack of ideas. Fawaz Gerges refers to this issue in the following way:

> Despite ISIS's impressive military prowess and achievements, it suffers from a structural defect: the absence of a positive blueprint for governance and a debilitating vacuum of ideas. Beyond ideological and moral rhetoric, the organization has not offered the Sunni communities in Iraq and Syria a positive program of action or a positive vision of governance . . . This fundamental defect is common to all Salafi-jihadists who prioritize warfare over welfare. They obsess over physical and military power, disregarding soft power and political theory as an infringement on and violation of shariah or Qurʾanic law . . . Much like it was for Al Qaeda before it, the world according to ISIS is characterized by a perpetual war against real and imagined enemies. Society is in constant mobilization, on a permanent war footing, to fend off enemies who lurk everywhere and hatch conspiracies against the Islamic State.[21]

Needless to say, what Fawaz Gerges refers to as vulnerability can also be interpreted from a totally opposite perspective, that is, as a strategic advantage. This is because the lack of ideas actually allows a potential supporter to bring their own worldview (or, more accurately, an Islamist ideology) and insert it into the standard template that is the black-and-white reality of an irreconcilably divided world, thus addressing the prospect of near extinction.

This very symptomatic 'vacuum of ideas' has also been identified by other respected experts writing about ISIS, among them Brian Fishman who, in his excellent book *The Master Plan*, has resolutely refused, in the specific case of ISIS, to speak about a comprehensive message or a coherent ideology, rather choosing to describe the group's really poor spiritual equipment as 'a dystopian cultural movement wrapped around a core set of ideological principles'.[22]

However, if, after all, a number of innovative contributions have been made by ISIS to the current Islamist environment, whether in areas of thought or practice, they are all related to the apocalypse to a greater or lesser extent. This is also the case with regard to the mastering of the art of making enemies, so symptomatic of ISIS policy everywhere and in all situations, as well as the group's irreconcilability and its total lack of commitment to a sense of compromise, and with its obsession with physical power and warfare, and so on. But let us pass the floor, once again, to Fawaz Gerges:

> With ISIS, there are no blurred lines or grey areas, only followers and enemies: you either pledge allegiance to Baghdadi and his ideology or are labelled an enemy who could be killed. There is no neutral stance between good and evil; passivity is seen as apostasy. This binary black-and-white worldview pitted the organization against the world, including the godfathers of Salafi-jihadist thought.[23]

Essentially, any reflective evaluation of the apocalyptic contribution of ISIS would reveal that the popularity of apocalypticism in the Muslim environment in general, and its ISIS version in particular, depends not only on its presentation (as mentioned above: not only the ideas, but also the style) but, above all, on the state of mind of the readers, something that will always be highly dependent on the prevailing situation in Muslim countries and their status within a globalising world that is full of uncertainties. Under such circumstances, any kind of prognosis would indeed be precarious and, therefore, we can conclude this section by reference to a favoured phrase of the Muslim scholars, one that traditionally expresses their uncertainty and humility: *Allāhu a^c^lam* (God knows better).

When faced with the sinister temptations of ISIS indoctrination, it is definitely not an easy task to identify what should be done. Unfortunately, given the current security situation, the spread of Islamism represents a real threat to the entire world,[24] a truth that undeniably also applies to the 'apocalyptic mutation' of global jihadism. Numerous terrorist attacks in recent years have irrefutably proven that jihadist propaganda has a real potential to radicalise potential attackers. The role of eschatological content in this process of radicalisation has to be soberly assessed, but definitely should not be underestimated or even marginalised. This is because the apocalypse, for today's Muslim radicals, has the capacity to provide a certain spiritual 'enrichment' to their ideology, as well as a specific remedy for their earthly frustrations.

Moreover, framing your fight from an 'eschatological perspective', so vigorously pursued in ISIS propaganda, has already been adopted as a strategy by its enemies, and in this way both parties reinforce each other in the spreading of the apocalyptic ethos that further fuels their worldly conflicts. In this regard, any effective counterbalance to ISIS, as Abdel Bari Atwan has correctly suggested, 'would have to be rallied behind another powerful Islamic figure or popular movement'[25]. The best way to defeat this group rests not with denying the role of Islam in the 'Islamic State', but rather in rejecting the specific interpretation of Islam promoted by ISIS propaganda in general.

In turn, the ISIS apocalypse in particular cannot be counterbalanced by a mere rejection of Muslim apocalypticism as such. In the current restless atmosphere that exists all over the Muslim world, such a step is hardly conceivable. The ISIS version of the Final-days events needs to be overcome by another 'friendlier' or 'softer' manifestation ('counter-apocalypse'), for which we earlier applied the metaphorical designation 'apocalypse light'. In doing so, the apocalypticism espoused by ISIS would not be denounced for being 'apocalyptic' but would rather be targeted – 'in apocalyptic terms' – for being a misleading interpretation within a generally respected Muslim eschatological framework.

The specific 'apocalyptic responses' to ISIS mentioned earlier might allow us to identify a number of viable patterns. The development of a convincing and generally acceptable Last Days scenario, devoid of a strong anti-Western or anti-Jewish ethos and a reliance on conspiracy theories, one that ultimately offers hope to Muslims rather than the prospect of a continuation of sectarianism, retaliation and bloodshed, would be the best weapon to adopt in the fight against the frightening End-time nightmare promulgated in ISIS propaganda.

The actual potential for non-Muslims to influence this intra-Muslim dialogue are very limited. While it is true that they can seek to encourage those Muslim forces considered to be 'more progressive', such support from the West can easily undermine the position of those it seeks to encourage in the eyes of an important section of Muslim society. Furthermore, effective questioning of the ISIS 'End-time agenda' has been made more difficult by the simple fact that the group's apocalyptic reading of reality can neither be denied, nor verified. ISIS propagandists have indeed learned their lesson from the mistakes made by their predecessors, and thus they have become extremely careful as regards any verifiable statements relating to the near future.

As far as the actual nature of the apocalyptic appeal of ISIS is concerned, the opinion of the author of this book is that its attraction largely results not from the religious content itself but, above all, from its psychological impact, since the apocalyptic narratives provide a very simple orientation by adopting the clear-cut dualistic identification of good and evil. The key to understanding their success thus lies primarily in the desire of the human psyche to overcome all earthly troubles and suffering by joining the transpersonal eschatological struggle between good and evil – not in the specific attractiveness of the Islamic apocalyptic visions themselves.

Of course, it is not known whether ISIS propagandists are really aware of this fundamental point, we can only guess. Nevertheless, in their message to the world, the emotions – as an important mobilising factor – are deliberately deployed in a quite strategic manner.[26] The theological subtleties related to the Islamic apocalypse never actually reach the common Muslim audience – in contrast to the group's black-and-white vision of an irrevocably divided world that is approaching its inevitable end.

Currently, it is clear that ISIS has failed to achieve its objective of creating a globe-spanning caliphate. However, even in failure ISIS has the capacity to kill large numbers of people. Reluctantly, we have to admit that there is no effective and proactive response to the ISIS message and that the situation may get even worse due to the misjudged reaction of the West towards Muslims in general. Unfortunately, ISIS may thus continue to be attractive to those who live in an increasingly Islamophobic Europe or an unstable and visionless Middle East.

Only time will reveal the true strength of the ISIS appeal – whether its lure can be maintained without the military success of its promoter. Essentially, ISIS sought to create an over-reaction on the part of non-Muslims and for them to direct their hatred against all Muslims, hoping that this might ultimately lead to a world that is intrinsically divided into two adversarial camps, with 'no grey in-between', precisely in accordance with the group's gloomy strategic dreams. Needless to say, the West must resist such a scenario.[27]

I would hypothesise that ISIS propaganda substantially meets the characteristics associated with the notion of 'cosmic wars' since it really imparts 'a sense of importance and destiny to men who find the modern world to be stifling, chaotic, and dangerously out of control'.[28] These wars, in the words of Mark Juergensmeyer,

> identify the enemy, the imputed source of their personal and political failures; they exonerate these would-be soldiers from any responsibility for failures by casting them as victims; they give them a sense of their own potential for power; and they arm them with the moral justification, the social support, and the military equipment to engage in battle both figuratively and literally.[29]

As far as we know, the black-and-white contours of the End-Time drama actually offer an unsophisticated sense of life to otherwise uprooted young Muslims, not only those who live in the West. Nevertheless, any meaningful assessment of the actual role of millennialism as a motivational factor in encouraging deprived jihadists to join ISIS lies far beyond the scope of this study. In this currently unfolding narrative, a lot of work still remains to be done.

Regardless of the diverging opinions expressed by experts with regard to the future of the ISIS phenomenon, for the time being at least, one point seems to be fairly clear: next-generation scholars will consider the emergence of ISIS as a turning point in the development of Muslim apocalypticism and millennialism.

[While preparing this book for publication, the military defeat of ISIS has been completed. Nevertheless, the group continues to disseminate its apocalyptic propaganda.[30] The end of the ISIS story has yet to be written...]

Notes

1. Landes, 'Jihad, Apocalypse, and Anti-Semitism'.
2. Gerges, *ISIS*, pp. 290–1.
3. Nuᶜaym, *The Book of Tribulations*, p. 4 (no. 13).
4. Petit, 'Eschatology in the ISIS Narrative', p. 23.
5. Atwan, *Islamic State*, p. 211.
6. Cf. a speech of Abū Bakr al-Baghdādī, delivered in the period of failures, in *al-Nabaʾ* 99:8–11.
7. Cf. *Dabiq* 7:66.
8. See https://www.albawaba.com/news/isis-bible-was-just-translated-and-its-brutally-pragmatic-1132408 (last accessed 25 February 2019). See also al-Ansari and Hasan, *Tackling Terror: A Response to Takfiri Terrorist Theology*.
9. See Stern, 'ISIS's Apocalyptic Vision'.
10. Furnish, *Ten Years' Captivation with the Mahdi's Camps*, p. 33.
11. Filiu, *Apocalypse in Islam*, p. 193.
12. Atwan, *Islamic State*, p. xii.
13. For social mechanisms used in the dissemination of the ISIS apocalyptic

ethos, see Berger, 'The Metronome of Apocalyptic Time', pp. 61–9. Cf. also Shandab, *Munāẓara maʿa ʿaql dāʿish*, pp. 117–50.

14. See, for example, https://archive.org/details/TheRiseOfTheKhilafahReturnOfTheGoldDinar_201509 (last accessed 12 September 2018).
15. See, for example, *Dabiq* 13:32–45.
16. Cf. al-Zarqāwī, *Kalimāt muḍīʿa*, p. 237.
17. See *Dabiq* 9:14–19.
18. Velji, *An Apocalyptic History*, p. 105.
19. Hegghammer (ed.), *Jihadi Culture*, p. 5.
20. Ibid. p. 2.
21. Gerges, *ISIS*, pp. 279–80.
22. Fishman, *The Master Plan*, p. x.
23. Gerges, *ISIS*, p. 284.
24. See Hegghammer, 'The Future of Jihadism in Europe'.
25. Atwan, *Islamic State*, p. 221.
26. Vergani and Bliuc, 'The evolution of the ISIS' language', p. 7.
27. Cf. Rapoport, 'The Islamic State Wants the West to Over-React and Hasten Apocalypse'.
28. Juergensmeyer, *Terror in the Mind of God*, p. 190.
29. Ibid. p. 190.
30. See, for example, *al-Nabaʾ* 170:9, from February 2019.

Appendix 1
A Brief Glossary of Muslim Apocalyptic and Eschatological Vocabulary

- *al-ākhira*, the Next World.
- *ᶜalāmāt al-sāᶜa*, the signs of the Hour (also *ashrāṭ al-sāᶜa*). The general designation intended for the apocalyptic portents foreshadowing the End of the world according to the Muslim tradition.
- *ᶜalāmāt al-sāᶜa al-kubrā*, the greater signs of the Hour. The sequence of clashes between the powers of good and evil, based either on cursory Qurᵓānic references or prophetic *aḥādīth*.
- *ᶜalāmāt al-sāᶜa al-ṣughrā*, the lesser signs of the Hour. The set of apocalyptic events and tendencies, preordained to foreshadow the coming of the Mahdī. Most of them refer to various manifestations of corruption and decline in either societal or religious terms.
- *al-Aᶜmāq*, a belt of valleys in northern Syria; a frequently fought-over area of land lying between two warring empires during the first centuries of Islam.
- *ashrāṭ al-sāᶜa*, another designation for the signs of the Hour, mostly preferred by Shiites.
- *barzakh*, an Arabic word of Persian origin generally referring to a barrier, separation, etc. Within the eschatological framework, the *barzakh* is viewed as the place between hell and heaven where the soul resides after death (*mawt*), awaiting the Day of Resurrection.
- *Dābba*, the short form of the 'Beast of the Earth' (*dābbat al-arḍ*),

an apocalyptic animal which appears in a vague Qurʾānic verse (27:82) and whose only assignment is to distinguish between believers and unbelievers after the sun rises in the west.

- *Dabiq*, the title of the key propaganda journal published by ISIS.
- *Dābiq*, a locality in northern Syria where the great apocalyptic battle is predicted to take place.
- *al-Dajjāl*, the Islamic Antichrist. The short form of the name *al-Masīḥ al-dajjāl* ('false Messiah'). The chief representative of evil in the Muslim apocalypse. Throughout this book, both terms, *Dajjāl* and Antichrist, are used interchangeably.
- *al-dunyā*, this temporal world; generally used in contrast to the Next World (*al-ākhira*).
- *al-fitan wa al-malāḥim*, literally 'tribulations and struggles', a favourite title of medieval Muslim apocalyptic writings and, in a broader sense, a designation of this entire genre.
- *fitna* (pl. *fitan*), an apocalyptic tribulation. In Arabic, *fitna* has a number of meanings. The original connotation was 'to purify gold and silver by smelting them'. In the apocalyptic context, a wide variety of connotations of this word cover the various tribulations and temptations that will test people in preparation for the Next Word, as well as describing the various splits that will lead to fratricidal fighting among Muslims.
- *al-ghurabāʾ*, 'the Strangers'. One of the most powerful topics within ISIS propaganda, generally referring to those people who have abandoned their own country and made a journey (*hijra*) in order to settle in ISIS territory. According to a *ḥadīth*, Muslims are called upon to be strangers among the people around them and Salafists apply this term to themselves in order to explain and justify their being totally different from others.
- *al-Ḥabashī*, the Abyssinian. An apocalyptic figure whose destructive campaign will reach Mecca and in a battle with whom Jesus will die.
- *harj* (or *haraj*), an enigmatic neologism used by Muḥammad, referring to a lot of killing.

- *Harmajidūn*, Armageddon. Within modern Muslim apocalyptic literature, this lexical borrowing is often used synonymously with the medieval designation *al-malḥama al-kubrā*.
- *hijra*, resettlement. In our context, resettlement in the area under ISIS control.
- *ᶜĪsā*, Jesus (both names are used interchangeably here). The representative of good in the Islamic apocalypse. What should be stressed here is the fact that the Muslim perception of Jesus, including his second coming, fundamentally differs from the Christian perspective.
- *Isrāfīl*, Rafael, the angel in the Islamic tradition responsible for blowing the trumpet (*ṣūr*) that will announce the time of the Hour.
- *jāhilīya*, the pre-Islamic period, generally seen as an age of ignorance and barbarism. In modern Muslim apocalypticism, it is often compared with the present state of decline.
- *janna*, garden. The most often-used Arabic term for paradise, also referred to as *ᶜadan* or *firdaws*.
- *khasf*, being swallowed up by the Earth, appearing among the final phase of apocalyptic signs.
- *khawārij*, Kharijites or rebels. *Khawārij* can be understood as a specific strand within Islam, originating from the section of Caliph ᶜAlī's followers who left his army (657). However, it can also be viewed as a general designation for rebels or sectarians, often appearing in Muslim apocalyptic prophecies.
- *al-Mahdī*, a Muslim redeemer (in Arabic, 'rightly guided one') whose rule is prophesied as being a natural link between the lesser signs of the Hour (as an 'apocalyptic overture') and the greater signs. It is believed that the Mahdī will unite all the world under the rule of Islam.
- *malḥama* (pl. *malāḥim*), a fierce apocalyptic battle or war prior to the coming of the Mahdī.
- *al-malḥama al-kubrā*, a great apocalyptic war, a Muslim Armageddon (also *Harmajidūn*).
- *al-Masīḥ*, Messiah, the common name given in Arabic to ᶜĪsā ibn Mariam ('Muslim Jesus').

- *nār*, fire. The most frequently used Arabic designation for hell, also referred to as *jahannam*.
- *al-Qaḥṭānī*, originally the South Arabian messianic figure who is inconsistently perceived.
- *Qusṭanṭīnīya*, Constantinople. In this form, the city appears as an apocalyptic dream destination of early Muslims, whose conquest will foreshadow the coming of the Antichrist.
- *rāfiḍa*, Shiites in ISIS terminology; literally, 'those who refuse'. In general, a derogatory term used by Sunnis against Shiites because the latter rejected the legitimacy of the first three caliphs to succeed the Prophet Muḥammad.
- *Rumīya*, Rome, appearing in this form in a number of apocalyptic prophecies as a symbol of the far-reaching success of Muslim armies prior to the coming of the Mahdī.
- *al-sāᶜa*, the Hour. The most frequently used Arabic name for the End of this world (*dunyā*).
- *Shayṭān*, Satan. It can also refer generally to all evil forces under the leadership of the arch-devil, known as Iblīs.
- *al-Ṣufyānī*, an apocalyptic character of ambiguous nature, originally a Syrian messianic figure. Additionally, in the Shiite tradition, he is mostly depicted as an ally of the Devil. Some Sunni sources even consider him to be a forerunner of the Mahdī.
- *Ṭāghūt*, a Qurᵓānic proper name and also the generic word for an idol. ISIS broadly applies this term to 'tyrannical idolaters', i.e. the leaders of Muslim-majority states who are accused of the repression of Islamists and the refusal to apply Islamic law in its entirety.
- *ᶜulamāᵓ* (singular *ᶜālim*), literally 'the learned ones', the Islamic scholars. In the apocalyptic framework, their alleged decline pertains to multiple portents of the End.
- *umma*, the community of Muslims. In the apocalyptic context, the *umma* is subjected to continuous tribulation and its cohesiveness is tested and tempted by never-ending *fitan*.
- *Yahūd*, Jews. They are presented as the apocalyptic allies of *Dajjāl* and the enemies of Muslims.
- *Yājūj wa Mājūj*, Gog and Magog (both pairs of names are used inter-

changeably). The apocalyptic tribes whose invasion of the world constitutes one of the greater signs of the Hour.

- *al-Yamanī*, a pre-messianic figure in Shiite eschatology, a figure who is prophesied to appear to the people to guide them along the right path prior to the coming of the Mahdī. He also appears in the Sunni context. However, his role is the subject of many disputes.
- *Yawm al-qiyāma*, the Day of Resurrection

Appendix 2
A Comprehensive Chronological Overview of the ISIS Phenomenon

1999	al-Zarqāwī founds Jamāᶜat al-tawhīd wa-l-jihād, a predecessor of ISIS
2001	the September 11 attacks
2003	the US invasion of Iraq
Feb.–Dec. 2004	Abū Bakr al-Baghdādī arrested and imprisoned in an American prison, Camp Bucca
2004	al-Zarqāwī renames his organisation al-Qāᶜida in Iraq (AQI)
2006	the execution of Ṣaddām Ḥusayn
2006	al-Zarqāwī killed
2006	the Islamic State in Iraq (ISI) is proclaimed by Abū Ayyūb al-Miṣrī, an ardent supporter of the apocalyptic ethos disseminated by this group
2007	ISI decides to adopt its famous black flag, referring to its millennial message
2010	Abū Ayyūb al-Miṣrī and Abū ᶜUmar al-Baghdādī killed in an air raid
2010/11	the beginning of the so-called Arab Spring
2011	Usāma bin Lādin killed
2011/12	the US withdrawal from Iraq

2013	the group is renamed as the Islamic State in Iraq and Levant/al-Shām (ISIL/ISIS)
4 Jan. 2014	ISIS conquers al-Fallūja
14 Jan. 2014	ISIS occupies al-Raqqa in Syria
3 Apr. 2014	al-Qāᶜida breaks its ties with ISIS
10 Jun. 2014	ISIS occupies Mosul
29 Jun. 2014	Abū Bakr al-Baghdādī declares a caliphate at the Great Mosque of al-Nūrī
5 Jul. 2014	the first issue of *Dabiq* magazine ('The Return of Khilafah') is published
7 Aug. 2014	President Obama approves air strikes against ISIS
19 Aug. 2014	ISIS beheads the US journalist James Foley
Aug. 2014	ISIS occupies the Sinjār Mountains and commences the genocide of the Yezidis
10 Sep. 2014	the third issue of *Dabiq* ('A Call to *Hijra*') is published
22 Sep. 2014	a spokesperson for ISIS calls for attacks to be made against citizens of the USA and its allies
Oct. 2014	ISIS spreads its activities to Libya
9 Nov. 2014	ISIS lays siege to Kobani (ᶜAin al-ᶜArab)
16 Nov. 2014	ISIS releases a video filmed in Dābiq, which contains an apocalyptic warning to the US-led coalition delivered by the British militant Mohammed Emwazi
2015	the beginning of the European migration crisis
3 Jan. 2015	ISIS burns alive the Jordanian pilot Muᶜādh al-Kasāsba
7 Jan. 2015	an armed attack against the editorial office of the *Charlie Hebdo* magazine
12 Feb. 2015	the seventh issue of *Dabiq* ('From Hypocrisy to Apostasy: The Extinction of the Grayzone') is published
11 May 2015	ISIS conquers Palmyra
30 Sep. 2015	Russia commences air strikes in Syria
19 Jan. 2016	the thirteenth issue of *Dabiq* ('The Rafidah from Ibn Saba' to the Dajjal') is published

26 Jun. 2016	the Iraqi army, supported by US forces, conquers al-Fallūja
31 Jul. 2016	the fifteenth, and final, issue of *Dabiq* ('Break the Cross') is published
30 Aug. 2016	Abū Muḥammad al-ᶜAdnānī, chief propagandist of ISIS, killed
5 Sep. 2016	the first issue of *Rumiyah* magazine, replacing *Dabiq*, is published
16 Oct. 2016	Dābiq is seized by Syrian rebels, supported by the Turkish army
17 Oct. 2016	the launch of the campaign against Mosul
31 May 2017	Turkī Binᶜalī, the self-proclaimed 'Grand Muftī' of ISIS, is killed in an air strike
21 Jun. 2017	the destruction of the al-Nūrī mosque in Mosul, where the birth of ISIS was officially declared
9 Dec. 2017	the Iraqi prime minister, Haidar al-Abādī, declares victory over ISIS

Appendix 3
An ISIS 'Apocalyptic Reader'

Due to the extraordinary amount of material which could be classified as 'ISIS End-Time rhetoric and propaganda', the following section provides only a tiny taster, a minute fraction of the vast sea of sources, actually comprising a very heterogeneous set of items. What has been chosen from both the group's English-language propaganda and, only very briefly, the Arabic-language works of its spiritual inspirers and forerunners (in my own translation) Abū Muṣᶜab al-Sūrī and Abū Muṣᶜab al-Zarqāwī, is intended, above all, to suitably supplement the previous theoretical interpretation. The emphasis has been placed on a selection of excerpts that vividly illustrate some of the discussed themes and motifs that constitute the ISIS 'apocalyptic arsenal'. The selected excerpts from both *Dabiq* and *Rumiyah* are left unadjusted, including specific Arabic phrases, religious formulas, and so on.

Excerpts from *Dabiq* Magazine

No. 1, pp. 4–5: As for the name of the magazine, it is taken from the area named Dabiq in the northern countryside of Halab (Aleppo) in Sham. This place was mentioned in a hadith describing some of the events of the Malahim (what is sometimes referred to as Armageddon in English). One of the greatest battles between Muslims and crusaders will take place near Dabiq.

Abu Hurayrah reported that Allah's Messenger said, "The Hour will not be established until the Romans land at al-Aʾmaq or Dabiq (two places near each other in the northern countryside of Halab). Then, an army of the best people on the earth at that time from al-Madinah will leave to engage them.

When they line up in ranks, the Romans will say, 'Leave us and those who were taken as prisoners from amongst us so we can fight them.' The Muslims will say, 'Nay, by Allah, we will not abandon our brothers to you.' So, they will fight them.

Then one third of them will flee; Allah will never forgive them. One third will be killed; they will be the best martyrs with Allah. And one third will conquer them; they will never be afflicted with fitnah. Then they will conquer Constantinople.

While they are dividing up the war booty, having hung their swords on olive trees, Shaytan [Satan] will shout, 'The [false] Messiah has followed after your families [who were left behind.]' So, they will leave [for their families], but Shaytan's claim is false.

When they arrive at Sham, he comes out. Then, while they are preparing for battle and completing their ranks, prayers are called. So, ʿIsa Ibn Maryam will descend and lead them.

When the enemy of Allah sees him, he will melt as salt melts in water. If he were to leave him, he would melt until he perished, but he kills him with his own hand, and then shows them his blood upon his spear" [Sahih Muslim].

Shaykh Abu Musʾab az-Zarqawi (rahimahullah) [may God have mercy upon him] anticipated the expansion of the blessed jihad from Iraq to Sham and linked it to this hadith, saying, "The spark has been lit here in Iraq, and its heat will continue to intensify – by Allah's permission – until it burns the crusader armies in Dabiq" [Ayna Ahlul-Muruʾat].[1]

According to the hadith, the area will play an historic role in the battles leading up to the conquests of Constantinople, followed by Rome. Presently, Dabiq is under the control of the crusader backed

[1] For the context of this famous quotation, see the last excerpt in this appendix.

sahwat [moderate Islamists], close to the frontline between them and the Khilafah. May Allah purify Dabiq from the treachery of the sahwah and raise the flag of the Khilafah over its land . . .

No. 4, pp. 35–6: From certain conviction and optimism based upon husnudh-dhann billāh [having good expectations of God], fiqh of the fitan and malāhim, and living tawhīd and jihād, are the words of the Islamic State leaders – Abū Mus°ab az-Zarqāwī, Abū Hamzah al-Muhājir, and Abū ᶜUmar al-Baghdādī – may Allah accept them all. They knew that the efforts of the mujahidin in Iraq would lead to the Malhamah – whenever it occurred . . .

Abū Hamzah al-Muhājir (rahimahullāh) said, "As for you O knights of tawhid [belief in the oneness of God], monks of the night, lions of the jungle, may Allah reward you on behalf of us and the Muslims with every good. For I have seen war and its men, and I testify by Allah, I testify by Allah that our ummah in the land of the two grand rivers (Iraq) did not skimp on bestowing its best sons and most truthful nobles upon us. For my eyes have not seen anyone like them, nor have I heard of anyone like them except for the first leading group of Muslims (the Sahābah). So I testify that they are the most truthful of people in speech, the most faithful to their promises, the most firm of men, and the strongest in obeying Allah. I do not doubt for a moment – and Allah knows such – that we are the army that will pass on the banner to the slave of Allah the Mahdī. If the first of us is killed, then the last of us will pass it on to him" [Sayuhzamul-Jam°u Wa Yuwallūnad-Dubur].

Abū ᶜUmar al-Baghdādī (rahimahullāh) said, "The Iraqi Jihād brought back life to jihādī regions which had weakened a bit after their strength. It also prepared the path for attacking the Jewish State and retaking Baytul-Maqdis [Jerusalem]. It is as if I stand before the ᶜasā°ib (bands) of Iraq that leave from here to give support to the Mahdī whilst he holds on to the curtains of the Ka°bah" [Hasād as-Sinīn].

No. 4, p. 37: Shaykh Abū Muhammad al-ʾAdnānī ash-Shāmī (hafidhahullāh) [may God protect him] said, "O soldiers of the Islamic State, be ready for the final campaign of the crusaders. Yes, by Allah's will, it will be the final one. Thereafter, we will raid them by Allah's permission and they will not raid us" [Indeed Your Lord Is Ever Watchful].

And he said, "And so we promise you (crusaders) by Allah's permission that this campaign will be your final campaign. It will be broken and defeated, just as all your previous campaigns were broken and defeated, except that this time we will raid you thereafter, and you will never raid us. We will conquer your Rome, break your crosses, and enslave your women, by the permission of Allah, the Exalted. This is His promise to us; He is glorified and He does not fail in His promise. If we do not reach that time, then our children and grandchildren will reach it, and they will sell your sons as slaves at the slave market" [Indeed Your Lord Is Ever Watchful].

And he said, "Therefore Allah will give you (soldiers of the Islamic State) victory. Indeed, Allah will give you victory. By Allah, Allah will give you victory. So, guarantee for us two matters, and we will guarantee you by Allah's permission constant victory and consolidation. First, do not oppress anyone nor be content with oppression by being silent about it and not raising the matter to those in authority. Second, do not become conceited or arrogant. This is what we fear from you and fear for you" [Indeed Your Lord Is Ever Watchful].

And he said, "O Allah, make it their last crusader campaign, so that we raid them and they do not raid us" [Indeed Your Lord Is Ever Watchful].

He expresses without any doubt that if the mujahidin hold on to their covenant with their Lord while relying upon Him alone, then this weak, pitiful, and abortive crusade will be the final one encompassing the eventual truce and crusader treachery leading up to al-Malhamah al-Kubrā [the greatest battle], and Allah knows best.

No. 7, p. 66: As the world progresses towards al-Malhamah al-Kubrā, the option to stand on the sidelines as a mere observer is being lost. As those with hearts diseased by hypocrisy and bidᵓah [heretical innovation] are driven towards the camp of kufr, those with a mustard seed of sincerity and Sunnah are driven towards the camp of īmān [belief].

Muslims in the crusader countries will find themselves driven to abandon their homes for a place to live in the Khilāfah, as the crusaders increase persecution against Muslims living in Western lands so as to force them into a tolerable sect of apostasy in the name of "Islam" before forcing them into blatant Christianity and democracy.

Muslims in the lands ruled by the apostate tawāghīt will find themselves driven to the wilāyāt [provinces] of the Islamic State, as the tawāghīt increase their imprisonment of any Muslim they think might have a mustard seed of jealousy for his religion, or lead them to apostatize by working as agents, soldiers, and puppets serving the banner of the tāghūt.

Mujāhidīn in the lands of jihād will find themselves driven to join the ranks of the Khilāfah, or forced to wage war against it on the side of those willing to cooperate with the munāfiqīn [hypocrites] and murtaddīn against the Khilāfah. If they do not execute these treacherous orders, they will be considered khawārij by their leaders and face the sword of "independent" courts infiltrated by the Sufis, the Ikhwān [Muslim Brothers], and the Salūlī sects [Saudis].

Eventually, the grayzone will become extinct and there will be no place for grayish calls and movements. There will only be the camp of īmān versus the camp of kufr.

Then, when ᶜĪsā (ᶜalayhis-salām) [peace be upon him] descends, breaks the cross, and abolishes the jizyah [capital tax imposed on non-Muslims], there will not be any place left for the camp of kufr to exist on the Earth, not even as humbled dhimmi [protected non-Muslims] subjects living amongst the Muslims in the camp of truth . . . Thereafter, the Beast will appear and mark the hypocrites who remained as individuals hidden in the camp of truth, thereby bringing an end to hypocrisy on the individual level after the Malāhim had finished hypocrisy on the level of calls and movements . . .

No. 15, p. 13: At the same time, the camp of sincerity gathered in the Levant and Iraq and spread to other corners of the earth, reviving thereby the Caliphate, which had been absent for centuries, since the collapse of the Abbasid state. The battle between the Muslims and the Jews, between the Muslims and the Romans, and the revival of the Caliphate, were all from among the signs foretold by the Prophet through revelation. And yet, the disbeliever doubts!

Indeed, it is Allah who prepared the Earth for the bloodiest battle before the Hour, to see His slaves sweat in spilling their blood and that of His enemies. All the factors were laid down precisely. The Crusaders and the Jews in the Levant, the Rafidah in Iraq and Persia, and the Caliphate in the centre. It is the clash of encampments – "civilizations" – that many saw coming, as it is found in Allah's signs throughout history and current events.

And yet the denier claims that all this is the result of mere chaos!

Extracts from *Rumiyah* Magazine

No. 3, pp. 25–6 (*Towards the Major Malhamah of Dabiq*): The great events unfolding now in northern Sham – in Dabiq and its surroundings – are but signs of the coming malahim, inshaallah. These great events will force the Crusaders – sooner or later – to accept the terms of the Jamaʾah of the Muslims, a truce that is precedent to the Major Malhamah of Dabiq. Today, the old discords are being renewed within the ranks of the enemies of Allah. The Crusaders of the West oppose the Crusaders of the East and their murtadd allies oppose one another. The Turks oppose the Kurds, the Sahwat of Turkey oppose the Sahwat of Jordan, the Rafidah oppose the Kurds of Iraq, the Kurds of the west oppose the Kurds of the east, and the Nusayriyyah oppose the Kurds of Sham. "You think they are together, but their hearts are in disagreement. That is because they are a people who do not reason" (Al-Hashr 14).[2]

This war of attack and withdrawal occurring in Dabiq and its surrounding areas – the minor battle of Dabiq – will inevitably lead to the

[2] Qurʾān 59:14.

Major Malhamah of Dabiq, even if a withdrawal were to precede it by Allah's decree. Indeed, the Malhamah will come about after that which Allah and His Messenger have promised is materialized, including the treaty between the Muslims and the Romans followed by the Romans' betrayal that leads to the Major Malhamah of Dabiq. Thereafter, will come the certain conquest of Constantinople (and then the city of Rome).

Abu Hurayrah narrated that the Prophet said, "Have you heard of a city with one side on land and another side on the sea?" They said, "Yes, O Messenger of Allah." He said, "The Hour will not be established until seventy thousand from Bani Ishaq [or 'from Bani Isma'il'] attack it. When they reach it, they will camp, and they will not fight with any weapons or shoot any arrows. They will say, 'La ilaha illallah [There is no god but God], wallahu akbar [God is great],' and one of its two sides [or 'the side that's on the sea'] will collapse. Then they will say a second time, 'La ilaha illallah, wallahu akbar,' and its other side will collapse. Then they will say a third time, 'La ilaha illallah, wallahu akbar,' and a breach will be made for them. They will thus enter it and collect ghanimah [booty]. As they are dividing the ghanimah, a shout reaches them, saying, 'The Dajjal has emerged!' So they will leave everything and return" (Reported by Muslim).

Excerpts from *The Call of a Global Islamic Resistance* by Abū Muṣᶜab al-Sūrī

The Part about the Strangeness, the Strangers and Those who are Steadfast for the Sake of God[3]

In this Jewish American period, as it is said ... The days, in which Muslims have become the strangers among unbelievers from people of the Earth, overshadowed us. Muslims have become the strangers amid hundreds of millions of Muslims ... Those who truly observe what God has ordained and has forbidden through their religion have become the strangers amid the worshippers ... And those who call

[3] Al-Sūrī, *Daᶜwa*, p. 79.

to faith and sound belief have become the strangers amid those who truly observe God . . . And those who call to God, ordering what is right and forbidding what is wrong, have become the strangers among those believers . . . And those who call for jihad against the enemies of God and for the suppression of the assaults of unbelievers, apostates and hypocrites have become the strangest strangers.

The messenger of God, blessings of God be upon him and peace, said the truth. Look, there we are, approaching what He has foretold through His saying: 'Islam began as strange and it will return strange as it began, so glad tidings to the strangers.'

And praise be to God, the messenger of God, blessings of God be upon him and peace, verily announced that 'there will always be a group from my *umma* that will fight on the truth, triumphant against those who oppose them and the last of them will fight the Dajjāl.' And to ensure them, He, blessings of God be upon him and peace, said: 'There will always be a group from my *umma* that will be steadfast on the order of God, they will not be harmed by those who oppose them, until the order of God comes and they will be triumphant over all humankind.'

Verily, we are writing this book precisely for the sake of those strangers who are steadfast on the order of God, who will not be harmed by those people, who have abandoned them, and who will wage fighting for this religion until the order of God comes.

Truly, we are writing it in order that this firm and faithful group appears to counter, patiently and constantly, the reckless violent hurricanes of America and its allies, paying no attention to American arrogance, nor to the quantity of its allies, that will not allow them to be driven away by its servants and that will consist of those strangest strangers from humankind . . . The strangers who are steadfast on the order of God and fight on the truth here and there . . . Verily, we are writing this book just for them.

Verily, we are writing it while living thanks to God who gives us what He wants – and we ask Him for sincere devotion, steadfastness and acceptance through His mercy –, we are living meanwhile our brothers who are fighting or migrating for the sake of God are indeed in the strongest state of strangeness, siege, expulsion, killing and capture. Therefore, we supply here the provisions through which we can strengthen our number and consolidate ourselves . . . and thus we introduce glad tidings to those patient and steadfast whom we consider to be those who have proven the truth of what they have promised to God. From them are those who fulfilled their vows and passed away, and from them are also those who are still waiting and did not get changed . . . Also we introduce this book to all those who are determined to seek enrolment in the caravan of the strangers and to join those steadfast on the order of God from the following generations who, God be with them, will raise, as it is hoped, the banner of their religion. Then, every Pharaoh and every Hāmān[4] from the pharaohs of unbelievers and apostates will see . . . and all their soldiers what they were afraid of . . .

The Current Situation of Muslims[5]

The disappearance of the religion: The *umma* has almost lost most of its religious constituents and this fact becomes clear amid manifestations of the suicide of religious life and its corruption among the majority of Muslims as well as the decay of its conditions and loss of its sacrosanct things. And the most important of those things is the absence of judgment according to the Divine law. The most relevant aspects of that can be displayed as follows:[6] (1) The absence of judgment according to the Divine law in all the countries of Muslims . . .; (2) The occupation of the three Holy places of the nation of Islam . . .; (3) The corruption of the doctrine of the *tawḥīd* among most Muslims, the spread of despicable innovations and the obliteration of the Tradition . . .; (4) The spreading of immorality, disobedience and forbidden or reprehensible activities . . .

[4] Both *Fir*ᶜ*awn* (Pharaoh) and *Hāmān* (Haman) appear in the Qurʾān, embodying arrogance of power

[5] Al-Sūrī, *Da*ᶜ*wa*, p. 91.

[6] What follows in this paragraph are only the subtitles of appropriate sections.

The Strangeness of the People of Truth[7]

Due to the manifestations of the corruption of the religion and the superiority of those led astray, most of the senior-ranking people within societies of Muslims are actually the elders of the criminals coming from those leaders of politicians, businessmen, artists and spoiled people as well as those perverted who are dependent on them and whose conditions we have already introduced.

The class adhering to its religion, who command good and forbid evil, calling for change, has become strange in society. And the group of believers clinging to sound doctrine and behaviour under the obligation of the fundamentals of religion has become, moreover, strange in this pious class. And the minority of those waging jihad in the path of God, facing the enemies of God in internal and external terms for the sake of the improvement of those conditions and pushing back this misfortune has become strange in the midst of that group. And its state has become according to what the Messenger of God, praise be upon him and peace, had described and what we have already discussed within the chapter about the strangeness, the strangers and those who are steadfast for the sake of God.

In such conditions, the twentieth century of the Christian era elapsed and we have entered the twenty-first century. And you can verily find that it is as if most people are ready to follow the Antichrist. There is no other way to withdraw from them than departure . . .

An Exploration of Excerpts from the *Aḥādīth*, News and Signs Mentioned in the Events Associated with the End-time, Which Include Fierce Battles, Tribulations and Signs of the Approach of the Hour[8]

There will come a time upon you when nobody will be saved except one who calls the call of one being drowned.

[7] Al-Sūrī, *Daʿwa*, p. 100. *Al-Ḥaqq* means truth but it is also one of the so-called beautiful names of God, so *ahl al-ḥaqq* simply refers to those Muslims who are guided correctly.

[8] Al-Sūrī, *Daʿwa*, p. 1519. The following apocalyptic *aḥādīth* were selected from those

At the end of this community, there will be men riding on saddlecloths until they reach the doors of their mosques. Their women will be dressed but naked and their heads will look like the humps of emaciated camels . . .

There will come a time upon the people when they will gather in the mosques but there will be no believer among them.

Verily, God started this matter when he started with prophecy and mercy. Then it turns into a caliphate, then it turns into a sultanate and mercy, then it turns into a kingdom and mercy, then it turns into despotism . . .

Before the Hour, there will be days in which ignorance will descend and knowledge will be taken away to such a degree that a man will come to his mother and strike her with the sword of ignorance.

Neither Satan, nor the Antichrist are those of whom I am most afraid but what you should be most careful about are the misguided imams.

The Hour will not come until all the tribes make hypocrites of their masters.

There will be tribulations in my community to such a degree that a man will abandon his father and brother and the man will wander in his misfortune like an adulteress in her adultery.

The Messenger of God, praise be upon him and peace, mentioned *harj* [bloodshed] before the Hour to such a degree that a man will kill his neighbour, brother and cousin. He was asked whether they would have their rationality on that day. He said that the intellect of most people at that time would be removed . . .

I have heard the Messenger of God, praise be upon him and peace, mentioning *fitna*. I asked, 'O Messenger of God, when will it happen?'

sections of the text that have been underlined or otherwise highlighted, which may well explain their extraordinary importance for either the author or editor of the *Daᶜwa*.

He said, 'When man does not believe his table companion.'

There will come a time upon my community when readers will expand, *fuqahāʾ* [Islamic lawyers] will diminish and knowledge will be withdrawn and killing will increase . . .

Verily, from the signs of the Hour and its harbingers we believe that the number of children of adultery will increase . . .

The Hour will not come until the Qurʾān is open and time contracts . . .

The sign of the pillar of fire will appear, rising from the direction of the east. All people of the world will see it. Whoever recognizes it should prepare a meal for the year for his family.

The fourth *fitna* will take eighteen years and then disappear. And the Euphrates will uncover a mountain of gold and the community will slowly advance towards it. Then, from every nine people, seven will be killed.

When you conquer Rome, enter its great eastern church from its eastern gate, then cross seven courtyards and tear out the eighth one. And verily, there is the stick of Moses and the gospel underneath that has embellished Jerusalem.

The Hour will not come until a man from Qaḥṭān appears, leading the people with his stick.

If only one day of this world remained, God would lengthen that day till He raised up in it a man who belongs to me or my family, whose father's name is the same as my father's, who will fill the earth with equity and justice as it has been filled with oppression and tyranny until now.

An Excerpt from al-Zarqāwī's Speech Entitled *Where are the People of Knight's Virtues?*[9]

Prepare yourself for the war that has burst out. Listen closely, look sharply and watch what will happen around you! Let your hands be on triggers! A desolate desert is in front of you as well as night of gloominess and fierce tribulation. Then, you will be victorious – by Allah's permission – if you are patient and vie in patience. So, trust in God, be patient, vie in patience, move into the fighting positions and fear God! Then you might be prosperous.

The spark has been lit here in Iraq, and its heat will continue to intensify – by Allah's permission – until it burns the crusader armies in Dābiq.

O heroes of Islam in every place of the land of Iraq!

Disbelief was shooting at us from a single bow. And mountains of deception have been prepared for us, in agreement with the people of disunity and hypocrisy, in order to humiliate men, violate the credit of women, hurt human dignity, in order to raise the cross over our land and under our sky. Do not accept this temporary world in exchange for your religion! And do not incline towards the tricks by which imposters pretend to give sincere advices in order to turn you away from the martyrdom or victory . . .

[9] Al-Zarqāwī, *Kalimāt muḍīʿa*, pp. 162–3.

Appendix 4
Overview Map

A black-and-white overview map of the Middle East, including the most important toponyms related to both ISIS locations and key places of Muslim apocalyptic imagery. © Kartografie PRAHA, a. s., 2019.

Bibliography

Primary Sources

ᶜAbd al-Fattāḥ, Muḥammad, *Usṭūrat Harmajidūn: Maᶜrakat al-nihāya al-kubrā*, Cairo: Dār al-ḥayāt, 2008.

ᶜAbd al-Ḥakīm, Manṣūr, *Laᶜbat al-mutanawwirīn wa-l-niẓām al-ᶜālamī al-jadīd*, Damascus: Dār al-kitāb al-ᶜarabī, 2012.

Abū Mālik, Muḥammad, *ᶜAlāmāt al-sāᶜa al-ṣughrā wa-l-kubrā*, Alexandria: Dār al-īmān, 2002.

al-ᶜAdnānī, Abū Muḥammad, *Lan yaḍurrukum illā adhan* (audio recording), ISIS: Mu'assasat al-furqān, 2013, available at https://archive.org/details/Elfrkan-3dn_02 (last accessed 22 October 2017).

al-Albānī, Nāṣir al-Dīn, *Takhrīj aḥādīth faḍāʾil al-Shām wa al-Dimashq*, Riyadh: Maktabat al-maᶜārif, 2000.

ᶜAlī, b. Ḥusām al-Dīn, *al-Burhān fī ᶜalāmāt al-Mahdī wa ākhir al-zamān*, al-Mansūra: Dār al-ghad al-jadīd, 2003.

al-ᶜAqīda (a textbook published by ISIS; author, place of publication and the publisher not stated), available at https://azelin.files.wordpress.com/2015/10/the-islamic-state-islamic-creed.pdf (last accessed 29 July 2017).

al-ᶜArīfī, Muḥammad, *Nihāyat al-ᶜālam: Ashrāṭ al-sāᶜa al-ṣugrā wa-l-kubrā*, Riyadh: Dār al-tadmurīya, 2010.

Ayyūb, Sa^cīd, *al-Masīḥ al-Dajjāl: Qirā^ʾat siyāsīya fī uṣūl al-diyānāt al-kubrā*, Cairo: Dār al-fatḥ li-l-i^clām al-^carabī, 2007.

al-Baghdādī, Abū Bakr, *Baqīya fī al-^cIrāk wa al-Shām* (audio recording), ISIS: Mu^ʾassasat al-furqān, 2014, available at https://archive.org/details/glxglx151_yahoo (last accessed 20 October 2017).

al-Baghdādī, Abū Bakr, 'Even if the Disbelievers Despise Such', ISIS: Mu^ʾassasat al-ḥayāt, 2014, available at https://archive.org/stream/EvenIfTheDisbelieversDespiseSuch/Even%20if%20the%20Disbelievers%20Despise%20Such#page/n0/mode/1up (last accessed 21 November 2017).

al-Baghdādī, Abū Bakr, *Taghṭīya khāṣa li-l-khutba wa ṣalāt al-jum^ca fī al-jāmi^c al-kabīr bi-madīnat al-Mawṣil* (video recording), ISIS: Mu^ʾassasat al-furqān, 2014, available at https://www.liveleak.com/view?i=94b_1404575388 (last accessed 22 November 2017).

al-Baghdādī, Abū ^cUmar, *Risāla ilā ḥukkām al-bayt al-abyaḍ*, 2008, available at https://www.paldf.net/forum/showthread.php?t=318578 (last accessed 22 July 2017).

Bayūmī, Muḥammad, *^cAlāmāt yawm al-qiyāma al-ṣughrā*, al-Mansūra: Maktabat al-īmān, 1995.

Bayūmī, Muhammad, *Nubu^ʾāt al-nabī*, Cairo: Dār al-hādī, 2002.

Bin Laden, Usama (2005), *Messages to the World: The Statements of Usama bin Ladin*, ed. Bruce Lawrence, New York: Verso.

Dabiq (issues 1–15), a propagandistic magazine published by ISIS, 2014–16.

Gharīb, Abū Usāma, *Minnat al-^cAlī bi-thabāt shaykhinā Turkī al-Bin^calī*, (place of publication and publisher unknown), 2013, available at https://archive.org./download/minato.alali001/minato.alali001.pdf (last accessed 29 December 2017).

al-Ḥawālī, Safar, *Yawm al-ghaḍab*, (place and publisher not stated), 2001, available at http://www.alhawali.com/main/5898-2-1---يوم-الغضب-هل-بدأ-بانتفاضة-رجب--.html (last accessed 9 June 2017).

Ḥisān, Muḥammad, *Aḥdāth al-nihāya*, al-Manṣūra: Maktabat fayyāḍ, 2007.

Jum^ca, ^cAlī, *al-Radd ^calā khawārij al-^caṣr*, 5 vols, Cairo: Dār al-muqaṭṭam, 2016.

Kabbani, Hisham, *The Approach of Armageddon? An Islamic Perspective*, Washington, DC: Islamic Supreme Council of America, 2003.

Lari, Sayyid, *Resurrection, Judgement, and the Hereafter: Lessons on Islamic*

Doctrine, vol. III, Qom: Foundation of Islamic Cultural Propagation in the World, 2003.

*Majmū*ᶜ *tafrīghāt kalimāt al-qāda bi-dawlat al-*ᶜ*Irāq al-islāmīya*, ISI: Nukhbat al-iᶜlām al-jihādī, 2010, available at https://archive.org/download/Dwla_Nokhba/mjdawl.doc (last accessed 2 February 2018).

*Mashrū*ᶜ*īyat al-rāya fī al-islām*, ISI (location, publisher and year not stated), available at https://ctc.usma.edu/harmony-program/a-religious-essay-explaining-the-significance-of-the-banner-in-islam-original-language-2/ (last accessed 3 January 2018).

al-Muhājir, Abū Hamza, *al-Dawla al-nabawīya*, 2008, available at https://ia802605.us.archive.org/16/items/Archive-Of-Abo-Hamzah-Talks/Aldawalah-alnbaweyah_text.pdf (last accessed 29 September 2017).

Muslim, ibn al-Ḥajjāj, *Ṣaḥīḥ Muslim*, Cairo: Dār akhbār al-yawm, 2004.

*al-Naba*ᵓ (issues 1–146), an Arabic-language magazine published by ISIS, 2014–.

Naji, Abu Bakr, *The Management of Savagery: The Most Critical Stage through Which the Umma Will Pass*, trans. and comm. William McCants, Cambridge: John M. Olin Institute for Strategic Studies, 2006, available at https://azelin.files.wordpress.com/2010/08/abu-bakr-naji-the-management-of-savagery-the-most-critical-stage-through-which-the-umma-will-pass.pdf (last accessed 20 November 2017).

Nazim, Muhammad, *Mystical Secrets of the Last Days*, Chicago: Kazi Publications, 1994.

Nuᶜaym, Ibn Hammad, *The Book of Tribulations: The Syrian Muslim Apocalyptic Tradition*, trans. David Cook, Edinburgh: Edinburgh University Press, 2017.

Nuᶜaym, Ibn Ḥammād, *Kitāb al-fitan*, Cairo: Maktabat al-tawḥīd, 1991.

'Open Letter' from the Muslim authorities addressed to Abū Bakr al-Baghdādī, 2014, available at http://www.lettertobaghdadi.com/14/english-v14.pdf (last accessed 29 July 2017).

Pew Research Center, *In Nations with Significant Muslim Populations, Much Disdain for ISIS*, 2015, available at http://www.pewresearch.org/fact-tank/2015/11/17/in-nations-with-significant-muslim-populations-much-disdain-for-isis/ (last accessed 29 September 2017).

Pew Research Center, *The World's Muslims: Unity and Diversity*, 2012, available at http://www.pewforum.org/files/2012/08/the-worlds-muslims-full-report.pdf (last accessed 25 November 2017).

Al Qaᶜidy, Abu Amru, *A Course in the Art of Recruiting: A graded, practical program for recruiting via individual daᶜwa*, (location, publisher and year not stated), available at https://ia800300.us.archive.org/32/items/ACourseInTheArtOfRecruiting-RevisedJuly2010/A_Course_in_the_Art_of_Recruiting_-_Revised_July2010.pdf (last accessed 21 February 2018).

Qindīl, Muḥammad, and Aḥmad ᶜAbd al-Rabbihi (eds), *al-Fikr al-islāmī al-jihādī al-muᶜāṣir*, vol. 1, Cairo: al-Marāyā, 2016.

al-Qurṭubī, Muḥammad, *al-Tadhkira fī aḥwāl al-mawtā wa umūr al-ākhira*, Cairo: Maktabat Miṣr, 2000.

Richardson, Joel, *The Islamic Antichrist: The Shocking Truth about the Real Nature of the Beast*, Los Angeles: WND Books, 2009.

Rifᶜat, Sayyid, *Rasāʾil Juhaymān al-ᶜUtaybī qāᶜid al-muqtaḥimīn li-l-masjid al-ḥarām bi-Makka*, Cairo: Maktabat Madbūlī, 2004.

Rumiyah (issues 1–12), a propagandistic magazine published by ISIS in English, 2016–17.

al-Shahāwī, Majdī, *Aḥwāl al-qiyāma*, al-Manṣūra: Maktabat al-īmān, 1992.

al-Shahāwī, Majdī, *al-Masīḥ al-dajjāl wa Yaʾjūj wa Maʾjūj*, al-Mansūra: Maktabat al-īmān, 1993.

al-Shaᶜrāwī, Muḥammad, *Aḥdāth nihāyat al-ᶜālam*, Cairo: Dār al-tawfīqīya li-l-turāth, 2011.

al-Shaᶜrāwī, Muḥammad, *al-Dār al-ākhira*, Cairo: Dār al-tawfīqīya li-l-turāth, 2010.

al-Siyāsa al-sharᶜīya, a textbook published by ISIS, (author, place of publication, publisher and date not stated), available at https://azelin.files.wordpress.com/2015/10/the-islamic-state-sharc4abah-politics.pdf (last accessed 26 July 2017)

Suraqah, Abdul Aziz, 'ISIS and the End of Times', 2014, available at https://splendidpearls.org/2014/07/04/isis-and-the-end-of-times/ (last accessed 25 September 2017).

al-Suri, Abu Musᶜab, *The Call for a Global Islamic Resistance*, three sections taken from the book (place of publication, publisher and date not stated), available at https://ia600304.us.archive.org/27/items/TheGlobalIslamicResistanceCall/The_Global_Islamic_Resistance_Call_-_Chapter_8_sections_5_to_7_LIST_OF_TARGETS.pdf (last accessed 25 May 2017).

al-Sūrī, Abū Muṣᶜab, *Daᶜwat al-muqāwama al-islāmīya al-ᶜālamīya* (place of publication, publisher and date not stated), available at https://

ia800303.us.archive.org/25/items/Dawaaah/DAWH.pdf (last accessed 25 May 2017).

al-Suri, Abu Musᶜab, 'The Military Theory of the Global Resistance Call: Key Excerpts', in Brynjar Lia, *Architect of Global Jihad: The Life of Al Qaeda Strategist Abu Musᵓab al-Suri*, London: Hurst & Company, 2014, pp. 347–484.

Yahya, Harun, *The End Times and Hazrat Mahdi (as)*, Istanbul: Global Publishing, 2011, available at http://www.atlasofcreation.com/en/Books/972/the-End times-and-hazrat (last accessed 24 November 2017).

Yahya, Harun, *The Golden Age*, Kuala Lumpur: A. S. Noordeen, 2003, available at http://harunyahya.com/en/Books/977/The-Golden-Age?view=desktop (last accessed 25 August 2017).

Yahya, Harun, *The Prophet Jesus (as), Hazrat Mahdi (as) and the Islamic Union*, Istanbul: Global Publishing, 2012, available at http://den-e-islam.blogspot.cz/2014/06/the-prophet-jesus-as-hazrat-mahdi-as.html (last accessed 25 August 2017).

Yahya, Harun, *Signs of the Last Day: The Splitting of the Moon*, 2010, available at http://www.harunyahya.com/en/Short-documentaries/25835/Signs-of-the-last-day-The-splitting-of-the-moon (last accessed 22 November 2016).

al-Yaqoubi, Muhammad, *Refuting ISIS*, Herndon: Sacred Knowledge, 2016.

Yusuf, Hamza, 'The Crisis of ISIS: A Prophetic Prediction', Berkeley: Zaytuna College, 2014, available at https://www.youtube.com/watch?v=hJo4Byaxfk (last accessed 3 November 2017).

al-Zarqāwī, Abū Muṣᶜab, *Kalimāt muḍīᶜa: al-Kitāb al-jāmiᶜ li-khutab wa kalimāt al-shaykh al-muᶜtaz bi-dīnihi Abī Muṣᶜab al-Zarqāwī*, (place of publication not stated): Warshat ᶜamal al-burāq, 2006, available at https://ia802205.us.archive.org/7/items/Abu-Musab-Zarkawi-Speechs/AMZ-Ver1.pdf (last accessed 22 November 2017).

al-Zawāwī, Rabīᶜ, *al-Mufsidūn fī al-arḍ: Yahūd*, Alexandria: Dār al-īmān, 1998.

Secondary Sources

Alami, Mona, 'Minding the Home Front: Hezbollah in Lebanon', *Washington Institute for Near East Peace*, August 2014, available at http://www.washingtoninstitute.org/uploads/Documents/pubs/ResearchNote21_Alami.pdf (last accessed 22 November 2017).

Alkhouri, Laith, Alex Kassirer and Allison Nixon, 'Hacking for ISIS: The Emergent Cyber Threat Landscape', *Flashpoint*, April 2016, available at http://fortunascorner.com/wp-content/uploads/2016/05/Flashpoint_HackingForISIS_April2016-1.pdf (last accessed 25 May 2017).

Alvanou, Maria, 'Symbolisms of basic Islamic imagery in jihadi propaganda', *Italian Team for Security, Terroristic Issues & Managing Emergencies*, (date not stated), available at http://www.itstime.it/Approfondimenti/Symbolisms%20of%20basic%20islamic%20imagery.pdf (last accessed 20 November 2017).

Amanat, Abbas, *Apocalyptic Islam and Iranian Shiʾism*, London: I. B. Tauris, 2009.

Amanat, Abbas, *Resurrection and Renewal: The Making of the Babi Movement in Iran, 1844–1850*, New York: Cornell University, 1989.

al-Ansari, Salah, and Usama Hasan, *Tackling Terror: A Response to Takfiri Terrorist Theology*, London: The Quilliam Foundation, 2018.

Atwan, Abdel Bari, *Islamic State: The Digital Caliphate*, London: Saqi Books, 2015.

Aydin, Hilmi, *Pavilion of the Sacred Relics: Topkapi Palace Museum, Istanbul*, Clifton: Tughra Books, 2012.

Bashir, Shahzad, *Messianic Hopes and Mystical Visions: The Nurbakhshiya between Medieval and Modern Islam*, Columbia: University of South Carolina Press, 2003.

Beránek, Ondřej, and Bronislav Ostřanský, *Islámský stát: Blízký východ na konci časů* (*The Islamic State: The Middle East in the End Times*), Prague: Academia, 2016.

Beranek, Ondrej, and Pavel Tupek, *From Visiting Graves to Their Destruction: The Question of Ziyara through the Eyes of Salafis*, Crown Paper 2, Waltham: Brandeis University, 2002.

Beránek, Ondřej, and Pavel Ťupek, *The Temptation of Graves in Salafi Islam: Iconoclasm, Destruction and Idolatry*, Edinburgh: Edinburgh University Press, 2018.

Berger, John M., 'How ISIS Games Twitter', *The Atlantic*, 16 June 2014, available at www.theatlantic.com/international/archive/2014/06/isis-iraq-twitter-social-media-strategy/372856/ (last accessed 2 November 2016).

Berger, John M., 'The Metronome of Apocalyptic Time: Social Media as Carrier Wave for Millenarian Contagion', *Perspectives on Terrorism*, 9: 4 (2015), pp. 61–71.

Berger, John M., and Jonathon Morgan, *The ISIS Twitter Census: Defining and describing the population of ISIS supporters on Twitter*, Washington, DC: The Brookings Project on U.S. Relations with the Islamic World, Analysis Paper no. 20, March 2015, available at https://www.brookings.edu/wp-content/uploads/2016/06/isis_twitter_census_berger_morgan.pdf (last accessed 25 September 2017).

Bowie, Fiona (ed.), *The Coming Deliverer: Millennial Themes in World Religions*. Cardiff: University of Wales Press, 1997.

Brisard, Jean-Charles, and Damien Martinez, *Zarqawi: The New Face of al-Qaeda*, Cambridge: Polity Press, 2005.

Bunzel, Cole, *From Paper State to Caliphate: The Ideology of the Islamic State*, Washington, DC: The Brookings Project on U.S. Relations with the Islamic World, Analysis Paper No. 19, March 2015, available at https://www.brookings.edu/wp-content/uploads/2016/06/The-ideology-of-the-Islamic-State.pdf (last accessed 25 May 2017).

Byman, Daniel L., and Jennifer R. Williams, 'ISIS vs. Al Qaeda: Jihadism's global civil war,' *Brookings Institution*, 24 February 2014, available at http://www.brookings.edu/research/articles/2015/02/24-byman-williams-isis-war-with-alqaeda (last accessed 20 November 2017).

Cohn, Norman, *The Pursuit of the Millennium: Revolutionary Millenarians and Mystical Anarchists of the Middle Ages*, Oxford: Oxford University Press, 1970.

Cook, David, 'Abu Musᶜab al-Suri and Abu Musᶜab al-Zarqawi: The Apocalyptic Theorist and the Apocalyptic Practitioner', in Nadia Al-Bagdadi, David Marno and Matthias Riedl (eds), *The Apocalyptic Complex: Perspectives, Histories, Persistence*, Budapest: Central European University, forthcoming.

Cook, David, *Contemporary Muslim Apocalyptic Literature*, New York: Syracuse University Press, 2008.

Cook, David, 'Iraq as the Focus for Apocalyptic Scenarios', New York: The Combating Terrorism Center, West Point, 2008, available at https://ctc.usma.edu/posts/iraq-as-the-focus-for-apocalyptic-scenarios (last accessed 12 November 2017).

Cook, David, 'Jesus' Return in Islam: Problems and Prophecies', in Zdeněk Vojtíšek (ed.), *Millennialism: Expecting the End of the World in the Past and Present*, Prague: Dingir, 2013, pp. 169–82.

Cook, David, 'Messianism in the Shiite Crescent', in Hillel Frandkin, Husain

Haqqani, Eric Brown and Hassan Mneimneh (eds), *Current Trends in Islamist Ideology: Volume 11*, Washington, DC: Hudson Institute: Center on Islam, Democracy, and the Future of the Muslim World, 2011, pp. 91–103, available at https://www.hudson.org/content/researchattachments/attachment/1280/cook_vol11.pdf (last accessed 25 November 2017).

Cook, David, 'Paradigmatic Jihadi Movements', New York: The Combating Terrorism Center, West Point, 2006, available at https://www.ctc.usma.edu/wp-content/uploads/2010/06/Paradigmatic-Jihadi-Movements.pdf (last accessed 25 November 2017).

Cook, David, *Studies in Muslim Apocalyptic*, Princeton: The Darwin Press, 2002.

Damir-Geilsdorf, Sabine, and Lisa M. Franke, 'Narrative Reconfigurations of Islamic Eschatological Signs: The Portents of the "Hour" in Grey Literature and on the Internet', *Archiv Orientální*, 83: 3 (2015), pp. 411–37.

Damrel, David, 'A Sufi Apocalypse', *SIM Newsletter*, 1: 4 (1999), pp. 1–4, available at https://openaccess.leidenuniv.nl/bitstream/handle/1887/17326/ISIM_4_A_Sufi_Apocalypse.pdf?sequence=1 (last accessed 22 April 2017).

Edgar, Iain R., 'The Dreams of Islamic State', *Perspectives on Terrorism*, 9: 4 (2015), pp. 72–84.

Fārūq, ᶜAmr, *Dāᶜish: Sufarāʾ jahannam*, Cairo: Kunūz, 2015.

Filiu, Jean-Pierre, *Apocalypse in Islam*, trans. M. B. DeBevoise, Berkeley: University of California Press, 2011.

Fishman, Brian, *The Master Plan: ISIS, Al-Qaeda, and the Jihadi Strategy for Final Victory*, New Haven: Yale University Press, 2016.

Fromson, James, and Steven Simon, 'ISIS: The Dubious Paradise of Apocalypse Now', *IISS: The International Institute for Strategic Studies*, 2015, available at www.iiss.org/-/media/silos/survival/2015/survival-57-3/57-3-02-fromson-and-simon/57-3-02-fromson-and-simon.pdf (last accessed 17 April 2017).

Furnish, Timothy R., 'Islam', in Richard Landes (ed.), *Encyclopaedia of Millennialism and Millennial Movements*, London: Routledge, 2000, pp. 187–92.

Furnish, Timothy R., *Ten Years' Captivation with the Mahdi's Camps: Essays on Muslim Eschatology, 2005–2015*, (place of publication not stated): Timothy R. Furnish, 2015.

Gabra, Maher, *The Ideological Extremism of Al-Azhar*, Washington, DC: The Washington Institute, 2016, available at http://www.washingtoninstitute.org/policy-analysis/view/the-ideological-extremism-of-al-azhar (last accessed 25 September 2017).

Gambhir, Harleen K., *Dabiq: The Strategic Messaging of the Islamic State*, Washington, DC: Institute for the Study of War, 2014, available at http://www.understandingwar.org/sites/default/files/Dabiq%20Backgrounder_Harleen%20Final.pdf (last accessed 25 May 2017).

Gerges, Fawaz, *ISIS: A History*, Princeton: Princeton University Press, 2017.

Gorenberg, Gershom, *The End of Days: Fundamentalism and the Struggle for the Temple Mount*, Oxford: Oxford University Press, 2000.

Günther, Christoph, 'Presenting the Glossy Look of Warfare in Cyberspace: The Islamic State's Magazine *Dabiq*', *CyberOrient* 9: 1 (2015), available at www.cyberorient.net/article.do?articleId=9538 (last accessed 2 February 2017).

Guthrie, Alice, 'Decoding Daesh: Why is the new name for ISIS so hard to understand?', *Free Word*, 19 February 2015, available at https://www.freewordcentre.com/explore/daesh-isis-media-alice-guthrie (last accessed 5 April 2017).

Hamid, Sadek, *Sufis, Salafis and Islamists: The Contested Ground of British Islamic Activism*, London: I. B. Tauris, 2016.

Hegghammer, Thomas, 'The Future of Jihadism in Europe: A Pessimistic View', *Perspectives on Terrorism*, 10: 6 (2016), available at http://www.terrorismanalysts.com/pt/index.php/pot/article/view/566/html (last accessed 25 May 2017).

Hegghammer, Thomas, *Jihad in Saudi Arabia: Violence and Pan-Islamism since 1979*, Cambridge: Cambridge University Press, 2010.

Hegghammer, Thomas (ed.), *Jihadi Culture: The Art and Social Practices of Militant Islamists*, Cambridge: Cambridge University Press, 2017.

Hitchcock, Mark, *The Apocalypse of Ahmadinejad: The Revelation of Iran's Nuclear Prophet*, Colorado Springs: Multnomah Books, 2007.

Ḥusayn, Fuʾād, *al-Zarqāwī: al-Jīl al-thānī li-l-Qāʿida*, Beirut: Dār al-khayyāl, 2005.

Ibrāhīm, Nājiḥ, and Hishām al-Najjār, *Dāʿish: al-Sikkīn allatī tadhbuḥ al-islām*, Cairo: Dār al-shurūq, 2015.

Juergensmeyer, Mark, *Terror in the Mind of God: The Global Rise of Religious Violence*, Berkeley: University of California Press, 2000.

Karouny, Mariam, 'Apocalyptic prophecies drive both sides to Syrian battle for end of time', *Reuters*, 1 April 2014, available at http://www.reuters.com/article/us-syria-crisis-prophecy-insight-idUSBREA3013420140401 (last accessed 25 May 2017).

Kepel, Gilles, *The Revenge of God: The Resurgence of Islam, Christianity, and Judaism in the Modern World*, Cambridge: Polity, 1994.

Kovács, Attila, 'The "New Jihadists" and the Visual Turn from al-Qaᶜida to ISIL/ISIS/Daᵓish,' *Biztpol Affairs*, 2: 3 (2014), pp. 47–69.

Křížek, Daniel, 'Millennialism in Sufi Perspective: The Case of Naqshbandiyya Haqqaniyya', in Zdeněk Vojtíšek (ed.), *Millennialism: Expecting the End of the World in the Past and Present*, Prague: Dingir, 2013, pp. 183–94.

Landes, Richard (ed.), *Encyclopaedia of Millennialism and Millennial Movements*, London: Routledge, 2000.

Landes, Richard, 'Enraged Millennialism', in Richard Landes (ed.), *Heaven on Earth: The Varieties of the Millennial Experience*, Oxford: Oxford University Press, 2011, pp. 421–66.

Landes, Richard, 'Jihad, Apocalypse, and Anti-Semitism: An Interview with Richard Landes', int. Manfred Gerstenfeld (September 2, no. 24), Jerusalem: Jerusalem Center for Public Affairs, 2004, available at http://www.jcpa.org/phas/phas-24.htm (last accessed 25 November 2017).

Lane, William Edward, *An Arabic-English Lexicon*, vol. 6, Beirut: Librairie du Liban, 1968.

Lange, Christian, *Paradise and Hell in Islamic Traditions*, Cambridge: Cambridge University Press, 2016.

Larsson, Göran, *Muslims and the New Media: Historical and Contemporary Debates*, Farnham: Ashgate, 2011.

Laycock, Joseph, 'Cyclops Baby of the Apocalypse? Another Day in ISIS Fundamentalism', *Religion Dispatches*, 23 September 2014, available at http://religiondispatches.org/cyclops-baby-of-the-apocalypse-another-day-in-isis-fundamentalism/ (last accessed 20 December 2017).

Lia, Brynjar, *Architect of Global Jihad: The Life of Al Qaeda Strategist Abu Musᵓab al-Suri*, London: Hurst & Company, 2014.

Lincoln, Bruce, *Discourse and the Construction of Society: Comparative Studies of Myth, Ritual, and Classification*, Oxford: Oxford University Press, 2014.

Lister, Charles R., *The Islamic State: A Brief Introduction*, Washington, DC: Brookings Institution Press, 2015.

Lister, Charles, *Profiling the Islamic State*, Brookings Doha Center Analysis Paper No. 13, Doha: Brookings Doha Center, November 2014, available at https://www.brookings.edu/wp-content/uploads/2014/12/en_web_lister.pdf (last accessed 26 November 2017).

Maggioni, Monica, and Paolo Magri (eds), *Twitter and Jihad: The Communication Strategy of ISIS*, Milan: ISPI, 2015.

Mah-Rukh, Ali, *ISIS and Propaganda: How ISIS Exploits Women*, Oxford: Reuters Institute Fellowship Paper, 2015, available at http://reutersinstitute.politics.ox.ac.uk/sites/default/files/research/files/Isis%2520and%2520Propaganda-%2520How%2520Isis%2520Exploits%2520Women.pdf (last accessed 12 December 2017).

McCants, William, 'The Believer', *Brookings Institution*, 1 September 2015, available at http://csweb.brookings.edu/content/research/essays/2015/thebeliever.html (last accessed 25 November 2017).

McCants, William, *The ISIS Apocalypse: The History, Strategy, and Doomsday Vision of the Islamic State*, New York: Picador, 2016.

McCants, William, 'ISIS fantasies of an apocalyptic showdown in northern Syria', *Brookings Institution*, 3 December 2014, available at https://www.brookings.edu/blog/markaz/2014/10/03/isis-fantasies-of-an-apocalyptic-showdown-in-northern-syria/ (last accessed 3 November 2017).

McCants, William, 'Why ISIS Really Wants to Conquer Baghdad', *Brookings Institution*, 12 November 2014, available at https://www.brookings.edu/blog/markaz/2014/11/12/why-isis-really-wants-to-conquer-baghdad/ (last accessed 23 November 2017).

Melčák, Miroslav, and Ondřej Beránek, 'ISIS's Destruction of Mosul's Historical Monuments: Between Media Spectacle and Religious Doctrine', *International Journal of Islamic Architecture*, 6: 2 (2017), pp. 389–415.

Mirza, Younus, '"The Slave Girl Gives Birth to Her Master": Female Slavery from the Mamlūk Era (1250–1517) to the Islamic State (2014–)', *Journal of the American Academy of Religion*, February 2017, pp. 1–23.

Morrow, John A. (ed.), *Islamic Images and Ideas: Essays on Sacred Symbolism*, Jefferson: McFarland & Company, 2014.

al-Muqaddam, Muḥammad b. Ismāʿīl, *Fiqh ashrāṭ al-sāʿa*, Alexandria: Dār al-khulafāʾ al-rāshidūn, 2017.

Musselwhite, Matthew H., *ISIS & Eschatology: Apocalyptic Motivations Behind the Formation and Development of the Islamic State*, unpublished thesis,

Western Kentucky University, 2016, available at http://digitalcommons.wku.edu/cgi/viewcontent.cgi?article=2614&context=theses (last accessed 20 May 2017).

Necipoğlu, Gülru, 'The Dome of the Rock as Palimpsest: ᶜAbd al-Malik's Grand Narrative and Sultan Suleyman Glosses', *Muqarnas*, 25 (2008), pp. 17–105, available at https://archnet.org/system/publications/contents/6779/original/DPC3643.pdf?1384802697 (last accessed 25 May 2017).

Nomani, Asra, and Hala Arafa, 'Inside the symbols and psychology of the Islamic State', *MSNBC*, 2 November 2015, available at http://www.msnbc.com/msnbc/inside-the-symbols-and-psychology-the-islamic-state (last accessed 20 November 2017).

Olidort, Jacob, *Inside the Caliphate's Classroom: Textbooks, Guidance Literature, and Indoctrination Method of the Islamic State*, Washington, DC: The Washington Institute for Near East Policy, 2016, available at http://www.washingtoninstitute.org/uploads/Documents/pubs/PolicyFocus147-Olidort-5.pdf (last accessed 20 May 2017).

Olsson, Susanne, and Carool Kersten, *Alternative Islamic Discourses and Religious Authority*, London: Routledge, 2016.

Ostřanský, Bronislav, 'A Feeble Folk to Whom No Concern is Accorded: "Apocalyptic Responses" to ISIS and their Contextualization', *Central European Journal for Contemporary Religion*, 2: 1 (2018), pp. 57–76.

Ostřanský, Bronislav (ed.), *Konec tohoto světa: Milenialismus a jeho místo v judaismu, křesťanství a islámu* [*The End of This World: Millennialism and its Place in Judaism, Christianity and Islam*], Prague: Dingir, 2012.

Ostřanský, Bronislav, 'The Lesser Signs of the Hour: A Reconstruction of the Islamic Apocalyptic Overture', *Archiv Orientální*, 81: 2 (2013), pp. 1–50.

Ostřanský, Bronislav, 'The Sufi Journey to the Next World: Sepulchral Symbolism of Muslim Mystics, its Context and Interpretations', *Archiv Orientální*, 83: 3 (2015), pp. 475–500.

Petit, David N., 'Eschatology in the ISIS Narrative', The University of Texas, 2015, available at https://repositories.lib.utexas.edu/bitstream/handle/2152/39297/PETIT-MASTERSREPORT-2015.pdf?sequence=1 (last accessed 20 November 2017).

Pregill, Michael, 'ISIS, Eschatology, and Exegesis: The Propaganda of Dabiq and the Sectarian Rhetoric of Militant Shiᶜism', *Mizan: Journal of Interdisciplinary Approaches to Muslim Societies and Civilizations*, 1: 1

(2016), pp. 1–36, available at http://www.mizanproject.org/journal-post/eschatology-and-exegesis/ (last accessed 25 August 2017).

Rapoport, David C., 'The Islamic State Wants the West to Over-React and Hasten Apocalypse', *YaleGlobal Online*, Yale University, 8 December 2015, available at https://yaleglobal.yale.edu/content/islamic-state-wants-west-over-react-and-hasten-apocalypse (last accessed 28 November 2017).

Sachedina, Abdul Aziz, *Islamic Messianism: The Idea of the Mahdi in Twelver Shiᶜism*, Albany: State University of New York Press, 1981.

Said, Behnam, 'Jihadology Podcast: Nashids: History and Cultural Meaning', *Jihadology*, 29 February 2016, available at http://jihadology.net/2016/02/29/jihadology-podcast-nasheeds-history-and-cultural-meaning/ (last accessed 20 November 2017).

Schori Liang, Christina, *Cyber Jihad: Understanding and Countering Islamic State Propaganda*, GCSP Policy Paper 2015: 2, available at http://www.gcsp.ch/News-Knowledge/Publications/Cyber-Jihad-Understanding-and-Countering-Islamic-State-Propaganda (last accessed 15 April 2017).

Sells, Michael A., *Approaching the Qurᵓān: The Early Revelations*, Ashland: White Cloud Press, 1999.

Shandab, Māzin, *Munāẓara maᶜa ᶜaql dāᶜish: Ḥawla istrātījīya istiqṭāb al-nisāᵓ wa al-rijāl*, Beirut: al-Dār al-ᶜarabī li-l-ᶜulūm nāshirūn, 2016.

Smith, Jane I., and Yvonne Y. Haddad, *The Islamic Understanding of Death and Resurrection*, Oxford: Oxford University Press, 2002.

Solberg, Anne Ross, *The Mahdi Wears Armani: An Analysis of the Harun Yahya Enterprise*, Stockholm: Södertörn University, 2013, available at http://sh.diva-portal.org/smash/get/diva2:626688/FULLTEXT01.pdf (last accessed 25 August 2017).

Stern, Jessica, 'ISIS's Apocalyptic Vision', 2015, available at http://www.hoover.org/research/isiss-apocalyptic-vision (last accessed 9 July 2017).

Tabbaa, Yasser, 'The Mosque of Nūr al-Dīn in Mosul: 1170–1172', *Annales Islamologiques*, 36 (2002), pp. 339–60.

Velji, Jamel, *An Apocalyptic History of the Early Fatimid Empire*, Edinburgh: Edinburgh University Press, 2016.

Vergani, Matteo, and Ana-Maria Bliuc, 'The evolution of the ISIS' language: a quantitative analysis of the language of the first year of Dabiq magazine', *Sicurezza, Terrorismo e Società*, 2: 2 (2015), pp. 7–20.

Wagemakers, Joas, *Salafism in Jordan: Political Islam in a Quietist Community*, Cambridge: Cambridge University Press, 2016.

Warrick, Joby, *Black Flags: The Rise of ISIS*, New York: Anchor Books, 2016.

Weismann, Itzchak, 'The Myth of Perpetual Departure: Sufis in a New (Age) Global (Dis) Order', in Itzchak Weisman, Mark Sedgwick and Ulrika Martensson (eds), *Islamic Myths and Memories: Mediators of Globalizations*, Farnham: Ashgate, 2014, pp. 121–37, available at https://www.academia.edu/14098030/The_Myth_of_Perpetual_Departure_Sufis_in_a_New_Age_Global_Dis_Order (last accessed 25 May 2017).

Weiss, Michael, and Hassan Hassan, *ISIS: Inside the Army of Terror*, New York: Regan Arts, 2016.

Wessinger, Catherine (ed.), *Millennialism, Persecution, and Violence: Historical Cases*, New York: Syracuse University Press, 2000.

Winter, Charlie, *The Virtual 'Caliphate': Understanding Islamic State's Propaganda Strategy*, London: The Quilliam Foundation, 2015, available at http://www.stratcomcoe.org/charlie-winter-virtual-caliphate-understanding-islamic-states-propaganda-strategy (last accessed 25 November 2017).

Yücesoy, Hayrettin, *Messianic Beliefs and Imperial Politics in Medieval Islam: The Abbasid Caliphate in the Early Ninth Century*, Columbia: University of South Carolina Press, 2009.

Zackie, Masoud, 'An Analysis of Abu Musʾab al-Suri's "Call to Global Islamic Resistance"', *Journal of Strategic Security*, 6: 1 (2013), pp. 1–18, available at http://scholarcommons.usf.edu/cgi/viewcontent.cgi?article=1230&context=jss (last accessed 25 May 2017).

Zelin, Aaron Y., 'Abu Bakr al-Baghdadi: Islamic State's driving force', *BBC News*, 31 July 2014, available at http://www.bbc.com/news/world-middle-east-28560449 (last accessed 25 November 2017).

Zelin, Aaron Y., *The State of Global Jihad Online: A Qualitative, Quantitative, and Cross-Lingual Analysis*, Washington, DC: New America Foundation, 2013, pp. 1–24, available at http://www.washingtoninstitute.org/uploads/Documents/opeds/Zelin20130201-NewAmericaFoundation.pdf (last accessed 20 December 2017).

Index